MW01096879

GLENCOE FRENCH 1A

Bon voyage!

WITH FEATURES BY

NATIONAL
GEOGRAPHIC
SOCIETY

Conrad J. Schmitt • Katia Brillié Lutz

 **Glencoe
McGraw-Hill**

New York, New York   Columbus, Ohio   Woodland Hills, California   Peoria, Illinois

About the Authors

Conrad J. Schmitt

Conrad J. Schmitt received his B.A. degree magna cum laude from Montclair State University. He received his M.A. from Middlebury College. He did additional graduate work at New York University.

Mr. Schmitt has taught Spanish and French at all levels—from elementary school to university graduate courses. He served as Coordinator of Foreign Languages for the Hackensack, New Jersey Public Schools. He also taught Methods of Teaching a Foreign Language at the Graduate School of Education, Rutgers University. Mr. Schmitt was Editor-in-Chief of Foreign Languages and ESL/EFL materials for the School Division of McGraw-Hill and McGraw-Hill International Book Company.

Mr. Schmitt has authored or co-authored more than one hundred books, all published by Glencoe/McGraw-Hill or by McGraw-Hill. He has addressed teacher groups and given workshops in all states of the United States and has lectured and presented seminars throughout the Far East, Latin America, and Canada. In addition, Mr. Schmitt has traveled extensively throughout France, French-speaking Canada, North Africa, French-speaking West Africa, the French Antilles, and Haiti.

Katia Brillié Lutz

Ms. Lutz has her **Baccalauréat** in Mathematics and Science from the Lycée Molière in Paris and her **Licence ès Lettres** in languages from the Sorbonne. She was a Fulbright scholar at Mount Holyoke College.

Ms. Lutz has taught French language at Yale University and French language and literature at Southern Connecticut State College. She also taught French at the United Nations in New York City.

Ms. Lutz was Executive Editor of French at Macmillan Publishing Company. She also served as Senior Editor at Harcourt Brace Jovanovich and Holt Rinehart and Winston. She was a news translator and announcer for the BBC Overseas Language Services in London.

Ms. Lutz is the author of many language textbooks at all levels of instruction.

Glencoe/McGraw-Hill

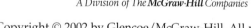

A Division of The **McGraw·Hill** Companies

The feature in this textbook entitled **Reflets** was designed and created by the National Geographic Society's School Publishing Division. Copyright 2002. National Geographic Society. All rights reserved.

The name "National Geographic" and the yellow border are registered trademarks of the National Geographic Society.

Printed in the United States of America.

Send all inquiries to:
Glencoe/McGraw-Hill
8787 Orion Place
Columbus, OH 43240-4027

ISBN 0-07-824265-7 (Student Edition)
ISBN 0-07-824267-3 (Teacher Wraparound Edition)

3 4 5 6 7 8 9   071   06 05 04 03 02

Teacher Reviewers

We wish to express our appreciation to the numerous individuals throughout the United States and the French-speaking world who have advised us in the development of these teaching materials. Special thanks are extended to the people whose names appear below.

Anne-Marie Baumis
Bayside, NY

Claude Benaiteau
Austin, TX

Sr. M. Elayne Bockey, SND
St. Wendelin High School
Fostoria, OH

Linda Burnette
Rockville Junior/Senior
High School
Rockville, IN

Linda Butt
Loyola Blakefield
Towson, MD

Betty Clough
Austin, TX

Yolande Helm
Ohio University
Athens, OH

Jan Hofts
Northwest High School
Indianapolis, IN

Kathleen A. Houchens
The Ohio State University
Columbus, OH

Dominique Keith
Lake Forest, CA

Raelene Noll
Delmar, NY

Nancy Price
Fort Atkinson High School
Fort Atkinson, WI

Sally Price
Marysville-Pilchuck
High School
Marysville, WA

Bonita Sanders
Eisenhower High School
New Berlin, WI

Deana Schiffer
Hewlett High School
Hewlett, NY

Julia Sheppard
Delaware City Schools
Delaware, OH

James Toolan
Tuxedo High School
Tuxedo, NY

Mary Webster
Romeo High School
Romeo, MI

Marian Welch
Austin ISD
Austin, TX

Richard Wixom
Miller Middle School
Lake Katrine, NY

Brian Zailian
Tamalpais High School
Mill Valley, CA

Table des matières

La francophonie

Le monde francophone xv
Le monde xvi
La francophonie xviii
La France xxiv
Paris xxv
Le Canada xxvi
L'Afrique xxvii

Why Learn French? xxviii

L'alphabet français xxx

Leçons préliminaires

Objectifs

In these preliminary lessons you will learn to:

✔ *greet people*

✔ *say good-bye to people*

✔ *ask people how they are*

✔ *ask and tell names*

✔ *express simple courtesies*

✔ *find out and tell the days of the week*

✔ *find out and tell the months of the year*

✔ *count from 1 to 30*

✔ *find out and tell the time*

A Bonjour! 2

B Au revoir! 4

C Les noms 6

D La politesse 8

E La date 10

F L'heure 12

CHAPITRE ① Une amie et un ami

Objectifs

In this chapter you will learn to:

✔ *ask or tell what someone is like*

✔ *ask or tell where someone is from*

✔ *ask or tell who someone is*

✔ *describe yourself or someone else*

✔ *talk about students from France and Martinique*

Vocabulaire

Mots 1 18
  Comment est la fille? 18
  Comment est le garçon? 19
Mots 2 22
  Une sœur et un frère 22
  Une école et un collège 22

Structure

  Les articles au singulier 26
  L'accord des adjectifs 28
  Le verbe **être** au singulier 30
  La négation 33

Conversation

  Il est d'où, Luc? 34

Prononciation

  L'accent tonique 35

Lectures culturelles

  Un garçon et une fille 36
  Le français en Afrique 38
  Un artiste français 39

Connexions

  La géographie 40

C'est à vous 42

Assessment 44

Technotour 47

CHAPITRE ② Les cours et les profs

Objectifs

In this chapter you will learn to:

✔ *describe people and things*

✔ *talk about more than one person or thing*

✔ *tell what subjects you take in school and express some opinions about them*

✔ *speak to people formally and informally*

✔ *talk about French-speaking people in the United States*

Vocabulaire

Mots 1 50
  Les élèves et les profs 50
  Comment sont les cours? 51
Mots 2 54
  Les matières 54
  En cours de français 55

Structure

  Le pluriel: articles, noms et adjectifs 58
  Le verbe **être** au pluriel 60
  Tu et **vous** 64

Conversation

  Quel prof? 66

Prononciation

  Les consonnes finales 67

Lectures culturelles

  Le français aux États-Unis 68
  La scolarité en France 70
  Un message 71

Connexions

  La biologie, la physique et la chimie 72

C'est à vous 74

Assessment 76

Technotour 79

CHAPITRE ③ Pendant et après les cours

Objectifs

In this chapter you will learn to:

- ✔ *talk about what you do in school*
- ✔ *talk about what you and your friends do after school*
- ✔ *identify and shop for school supplies*
- ✔ *talk about what you don't do*
- ✔ *tell what you and others like and don't like to do*
- ✔ *discuss schools in France*

Vocabulaire

Mots 1 82
   Une journée à l'école 82
Mots 2 86
   Des fournitures scolaires 86
   Après les cours 87

Structure

   Les verbes réguliers en **-er** au présent 90
   La négation des articles indéfinis 94
   Verbe + infinitif 95

Conversation

   Un élève français aux États-Unis 96

Prononciation

   Les sons /é/ et /è/. 97

Lectures culturelles

   Une journée avec Jacqueline 98
   Qui travaille? 100
   Un groupe de rap—Manau 101

Connexions

   L'ordinateur 102

C'est à vous 104

Assessment 106

Technotour 109

CHAPITRE ④ La famille et la maison

Objectifs

In this chapter you will learn to:

✔ talk about your family

✔ describe your home and neighborhood

✔ tell your age and find out someone else's age

✔ tell what belongs to you and others

✔ describe more people and things

✔ talk about families and homes in French-speaking countries

Vocabulaire

Mots 1 112
  La famille Morel 112
  L'anniversaire de Marie 113
Mots 2 116
  La maison 116
  L'immeuble 116
  Les pièces de la maison 117

Structure

Avoir au présent 120
Les adjectifs possessifs 123
D'autres adjectifs 126

Conversation
Ma nouvelle adresse 128

Prononciation
Le son /ã/ 129

Lectures culturelles
Où habitent les Français? 130
Le logement dans d'autres pays 132
Les noms de famille 133

Connexions
Art et histoire 134

C'est à vous 136

Assessment 138

Technotour 141

RÉVISION

Chapitres 1–4 142

☐ NATIONAL GEOGRAPHIC

Reflets de la France 148

LITTÉRATURE 1

La petite Fadette
George Sand **504**

CHAPITRE ⑤ Au café et au restaurant

Objectifs

In this chapter you will learn to:

✔ order food or a beverage at a café or restaurant

✔ tell where you and others go

✔ tell what you and others are going to do

✔ give locations

✔ tell what belongs to you and others

✔ describe more activities

✔ compare eating habits in the United States and in the French-speaking world

Vocabulaire

Mots 1 154
  À la terrasse d'un café 154
Mots 2 158
  Le couvert 158
  Au restaurant 158
  Les trois repas de la journée 159

Structure

  Le verbe **aller** au présent 162
  Aller + infinitif 165
  Les contractions avec **à** et **de** 166
  Le verbe **prendre** 168

Conversation 🔄

  Au restaurant 170

Prononciation

  Le son /r/ 171

Lectures culturelles 🔄

  Au restaurant? Vraiment? 172
  Les repas en France 174
  Les goûts changent 175

Connexions

  L'arithmétique 176

C'est à vous 🔄 178

Assessment 180

Technotour 183

CHAPITRE ⑥ La nourriture et les courses

Objectifs

In this chapter you will learn to:

✔ *identify more foods*

✔ *shop for food*

✔ *tell what you or others are doing*

✔ *ask for the quantity you want*

✔ *talk about what you or others don't have*

✔ *tell what you or others are able to do or want to do*

✔ *talk about French food-shopping customs*

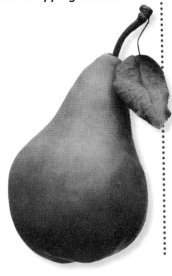

Vocabulaire

Mots 1 186
   À la boulangerie-pâtisserie 186
   À la crémerie. 186
   À la boucherie. 186
   À la poissonnerie 186
   À la charcuterie. 186
   À l'épicerie 186
Mots 2 190
   Au marché. 190

Structure

   Le verbe **faire** au présent. 194
   Le partitif et l'article défini 196
   Le partitif au négatif. 198
   Les verbes **pouvoir** et **vouloir**. 201

Conversation 🔄

   Au marché. 204

Prononciation

   Les sons /œ/ et /œ/. 205

Lectures culturelles 🔄

   Les courses 206
   Les grandes surfaces 208
   Les marchés. 209

Connexions

   Les conversions. 210

C'est à vous 🔄 212

Assessment. 214

Technotour 217

CHAPITRE 7 Les vêtements

Objectifs
In this chapter you will learn to:
- ✔ identify and describe articles of clothing
- ✔ state color and size preferences
- ✔ shop for clothing
- ✔ describe people's activities
- ✔ compare people and things
- ✔ express opinions and make observations
- ✔ discuss clothes and clothes shopping in the French-speaking world

RÉVISION

NATIONAL GEOGRAPHIC

LITTÉRATURE 2

Vocabulaire
Mots 1 220
  Les vêtements sport 220
  Les vêtements pour hommes. 221
  Les vêtents pour femmes 221
Mots 2 224
  On fait des courses. 224

Structure
Le verbe **mettre**. 228
Le comparatif des adjectifs 230
Les verbes **voir** et **croire**. 232

Conversation
Dans une petite boutique. 234

Prononciation
Les sons /**sh**/ et /**zh**/ 235

Lectures culturelles
On fait des courses où, à Paris?. . . . 236
Les vêtements 238
Les tailles. 239

Connexions
La poésie 240

C'est à vous 242

Assessment 244

Technotour 247

Chapitres 5–7 . . . . . **248**

Reflets de l'Afrique. **254**

«Dors mon enfant»
Elolongué Epanya Yondo **510**

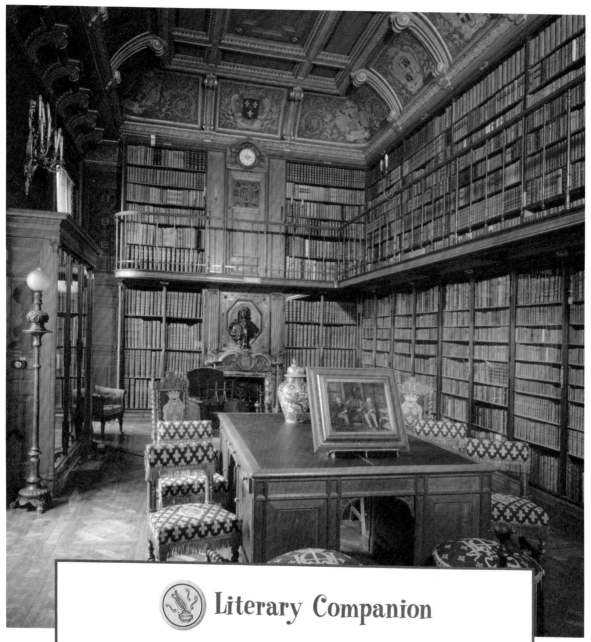

Literary Companion

La petite Fadette   **George Sand** 504

«Dors mon enfant»   **Elolongué Epanya Yondo** 510

Handbook

InfoGap Activities H2

Study Tips H51

Verb Charts H68

French-English Dictionary H72

English-French Dictionary H85

Index H98

Table des matières

Guide to Symbols

Throughout **Bon voyage!** you will see these symbols, or icons. They will tell you how to best use the particular part of the chapter or activity they accompany. Following is a key to help you understand these symbols.

 Audio Link This icon indicates material in the chapter that is recorded on compact disk format and/or audiocassette.

 Recycling This icon indicates sections that review previously introduced material.

 Paired Activity This icon indicates sections that you can practice orally with a partner.

 Group Activity This icon indicates sections that you can practice together in groups.

 Encore Plus This icon indicates additional practice activities that review knowledge from current chapters.

 Allez-y! This icon indicates the end of new material in each section and the beginning of the recombination section at the end of the chapter.

 Literary Companion This icon appears in the review lessons to let you know that you are prepared to read the literature selection indicated if you wish.

 Interactive CD-ROM This icon indicates that the material is also on an Interactive CD-ROM.

Le monde francophone

The French geographer Onésime Reclus first coined the word *francophonie* in 1880 to designate geographical entities where French was spoken. Today, *la francophonie* refers to the collective body of over one hundred million people all over the world who speak French, exclusively or in part, in their daily lives. The term *francophonie* refers to the diverse official organizations, governments, and countries that promote the use of French in economic, political, diplomatic, and cultural exchanges. Politically, French remains the second most important language in the world. In some Francophone nations, French is the official language (France), or the co-official language (Cameroon); in others, it is spoken by a minority who share a common cultural heritage (Andorra). The French language is present in Europe, Africa, the Americas, and Oceania.

Le monde

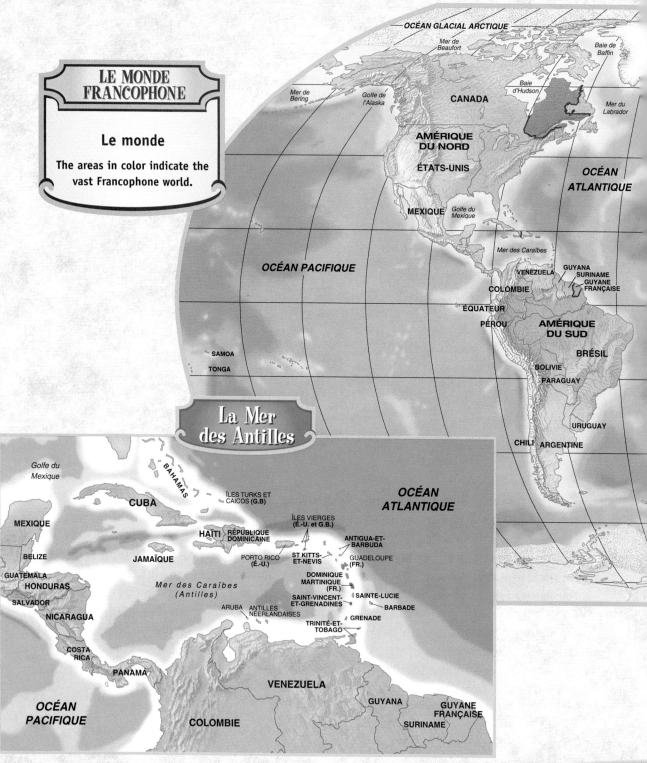

LE MONDE FRANCOPHONE

Le monde

The areas in color indicate the vast Francophone world.

La Mer des Antilles

OCÉAN GLACIAL ARCTIQUE

Mer de Beaufort

Baie de Baffin

Mer de Bering

Golfe de l'Alaska

CANADA

Baie d'Hudson

Mer du Labrador

AMÉRIQUE DU NORD

ÉTATS-UNIS

OCÉAN ATLANTIQUE

MEXIQUE

Golfe du Mexique

OCÉAN PACIFIQUE

Mer des Caraïbes

VENEZUELA

GUYANA
SURINAME
GUYANE FRANÇAISE

COLOMBIE

ÉQUATEUR

PÉROU

AMÉRIQUE DU SUD

BRÉSIL

SAMOA

TONGA

BOLIVIE

PARAGUAY

URUGUAY

CHILI ARGENTINE

Golfe du Mexique

BAHAMAS

ÎLES TURKS ET CAICOS (G.B)

OCÉAN ATLANTIQUE

CUBA

MEXIQUE

HAÏTI RÉPUBLIQUE DOMINICAINE

ÎLES VIERGES (É.-U. et G.B.)

ANTIGUA-ET-BARBUDA

JAMAÏQUE

PORTO RICO (É.-U.)

ST KITTS-ET-NEVIS

GUADELOUPE (FR.)

BELIZE

GUATEMALA
HONDURAS

SALVADOR

NICARAGUA

Mer des Caraïbes (Antilles)

DOMINIQUE
MARTINIQUE (FR.)

SAINT-VINCENT-ET-GRENADINES

SAINTE-LUCIE

BARBADE

ARUBA ANTILLES NÉERLANDAISES

GRENADE

TRINITÉ-ET-TOBAGO

COSTA RICA

PANAMA

OCÉAN PACIFIQUE

COLOMBIE

VENEZUELA

GUYANA

GUYANE FRANÇAISE

SURINAME

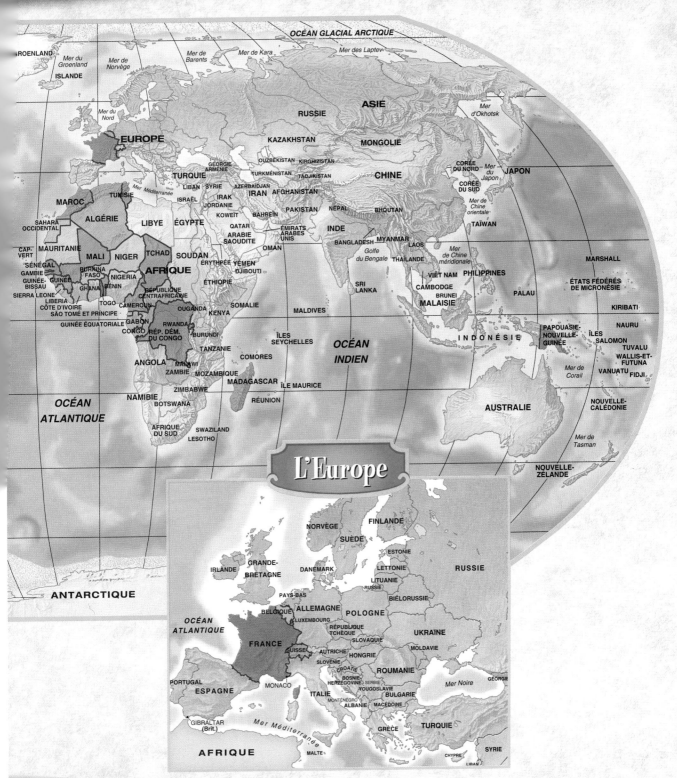

OCÉAN GLACIAL ARCTIQUE

GROENLAND
Mer du Groenland
Mer de Norvège
Mer de Barents
Mer de Kara
Mer des Laptev

ISLANDE

ASIE

Mer du Nord
RUSSIE
Mer d'Okhotsk

EUROPE
KAZAKHSTAN
MONGOLIE

GÉORGIE
ARMÉNIE
OUZBÉKISTAN KIRGHIZISTAN
CORÉE DU NORD
Mer du Japon
JAPON

TURQUIE
TURKMÉNISTAN
TADJIKISTAN
CHINE
CORÉE DU SUD

LIBAN SYRIE
AZERBAIDJAN
AFGHANISTAN

MAROC
TUNISIE
ISRAËL
IRAK
IRAN
Mer de Chine orientale

Mer Méditerranée
JORDANIE
PAKISTAN
NÉPAL
BHOUTAN

SAHARA OCCIDENTAL
ALGÉRIE
LIBYE
ÉGYPTE
KOWEIT
QATAR
TAÏWAN

CAP-VERT
MAURITANIE
ARABIE SAOUDITE
ÉMIRATS ARABES UNIS
INDE
BANGLADESH
MYANMAR
LAOS
Mer de Chine méridionale
MARSHALL

SÉNÉGAL
MALI
NIGER
TCHAD
SOUDAN
OMAN
YÉMEN
ÉRYTHRÉE
Golfe du Bengale
THAÏLANDE

GAMBIE
BURKINA FASO
AFRIQUE
DJIBOUTI
VIÊT NAM
PHILIPPINES
ÉTATS FÉDÉRÉS DE MICRONÉSIE

GUINÉE-BISSAU
GUINÉE
NIGERIA
ÉTHIOPIE
CAMBODGE
BRUNEI
PALAU

SIERRA LEONE
GHANA
BÉNIN
SRI LANKA
MALDIVES
MALAISIE
KIRIBATI

LIBERIA
CÔTE D'IVOIRE
TOGO
CAMEROUN
SOMALIE

SÃO TOMÉ ET PRINCIPE
OUGANDA
KENYA

GUINÉE ÉQUATORIALE
GABON
CONGO
RWANDA
RÉP. DÉM. DU CONGO
BURUNDI
ÎLES SEYCHELLES
OCÉAN INDIEN
INDONÉSIE
PAPOUASIE-NOUVELLE-GUINÉE
ÎLES SALOMON
NAURU
TUVALU

TANZANIE
COMORES
WALLIS-ET-FUTUNA

ANGOLA
MALAWI
ZAMBIE
MOZAMBIQUE
MADAGASCAR
ÎLE MAURICE
VANUATU
FIDJI

ZIMBABWE
Mer de Corail

NAMIBIE
BOTSWANA
RÉUNION
AUSTRALIE
NOUVELLE-CALÉDONIE

OCÉAN ATLANTIQUE
AFRIQUE DU SUD
SWAZILAND
LESOTHO
Mer de Tasman

NOUVELLE-ZÉLANDE

ANTARCTIQUE

L'Europe

NORVÈGE
FINLANDE
SUÈDE
ESTONIE

IRLANDE
GRANDE-BRETAGNE
DANEMARK
LETTONIE
RUSSIE

LITUANIE
RUSSIE
BIÉLORUSSIE

PAYS-BAS
ALLEMAGNE
POLOGNE

BELGIQUE
LUXEMBOURG
RÉPUBLIQUE TCHÈQUE
UKRAINE

OCÉAN ATLANTIQUE
SLOVAQUIE

FRANCE
SUISSE
AUTRICHE
HONGRIE
MOLDAVIE
SLOVÉNIE
CROATIE
ROUMANIE

PORTUGAL
MONACO
BOSNIE-HERZÉGOVINE
SERBIE
GÉORGIE
ESPAGNE
ITALIE
MONTÉNÉGRO
YOUGOSLAVIE
BULGARIE
Mer Noire

ALBANIE
MACÉDOINE

GIBRALTAR (Brit.)
Mer Méditerranée
GRÈCE
TURQUIE

SYRIE
AFRIQUE
MALTE
CHYPRE
LIBAN

La francophonie

L'Afrique

L'Algérie

CAPITAL
Algiers

POPULATION
30,774,000

FUN FACT
Algeria is called "the geographic giant" of the Maghreb. It is four times the size of France. Most of the country lies in the Sahara desert.

La République Centrafricaine

CAPITAL
Bangui

POPULATION
3,445,000

FUN FACT
The Central African Republic has two very expensive exports—gold and diamonds.

Le Burkina Faso

CAPITAL
Ouagadougou

POPULATION
11,576,000

FUN FACT
Burkina Faso is known for its friendly people. Villagers are fond of allowing foreigners to live in their homes and take part in village life.

Le Burundi

CAPITAL
Bujumbura

POPULATION
5,736,000

FUN FACT
Burundi was first under German control. It then became Ruanda-Urundi under Belgian control. It became independent in 1962.

Le Cameroun

CAPITAL
Yaoundé

POPULATION
15,456,000

FUN FACT
Cameroon is known for its fantastic landscapes: Saharan desert, equatorial rain forest, tree-laden savannah, grassy plains, volcanic mountains with crater lakes, the swampy basin of Lake Chad, and one of the highest mountains in Africa.

Le Bénin

CAPITAL
Porto-Novo

POPULATION
6,186,000

FUN FACT
Benin has one of the most popular tourist attractions in all of West Africa—the fishing village of Ganvié built on stilts in the middle of a lagoon not far from the capital, Porto Novo.

Les Comores

CAPITAL
Moroni

POPULATION
563,000

FUN FACT
The beautiful Comores Islands in the Indian Ocean are known for their lovely, isolated beaches. These islands are among the few areas in the world where natural beauty reigns.

La République du Congo

CAPITAL
Brazzaville

POPULATION
2,717,000

FUN FACT
Seventy percent of the population lives in the capital city or near the railroad between it and Pointe-Noire about 250 miles to the west.

La République Démocratique du Congo

Kinshasa

CAPITAL
Kinshasa

POPULATION
42,200,000

FUN FACT
The population of the Democratic Republic of the Congo is made up of six major ethnic groups which are divided into over 250 subgroups.

La Côte d'Ivoire

Yamoussoukro

CAPITAL
Yamoussoukro

POPULATION
15,818,000

FUN FACT
The Côte d'Ivoire's principal city, Abidjan, is West Africa's most cosmopolitan city and is often referred to as the "Paris of West Africa."

Djibouti

Djibouti

CAPITAL
Djibouti

POPULATION
629,000

FUN FACT
Djibouti is the name of both the republic and its capital. Its position at the entrance to the Red Sea makes it one of the most important seaports in Africa.

Le Gabon

Libreville

CAPITAL
Libreville

POPULATION
1,197,000

FUN FACT
More than three-quarters of the territory of Gabon is covered by forests. Its capital, Libreville (appropriately named), was founded by Catholic missionaries to house liberated slaves.

La Guinée

Conakry

CAPITAL
Conakry

POPULATION
7,539,000

FUN FACT
Guinea is a country known for its strong tradition of live music. Almost any evening, you can find a wonderful musical celebration in the streets of Conakry, its capital.

La Guinée Équatoriale

Malabo

CAPITAL
Malabo

POPULATION
442,000

FUN FACT
Equatorial Guinea is the only country in Africa where both Spanish and French are spoken even though French is considered the official language.

Madagascar

Antananarivo

CAPITAL
Antananarivo

POPULATION
14,417,000

FUN FACT
Madagascar is a beautiful and, in some areas, rocky volcanic island in the Indian Ocean.

Le Mali

Bamako

CAPITAL
Bamako

POPULATION
10,960,000

FUN FACT
Mali is the home of Timbuktu, which was and still is the terminus of a camel caravan route across the Sahara, linking Arabia with West Africa since ancient times.

Le Maroc

Rabat

CAPITAL
Rabat

POPULATION
28,248,000

FUN FACT
Morocco is a country of many beautiful, fascinating cities, such as Casablanca, Tangiers, Fez, and Marrakech.

L'île Maurice

CAPITAL
Port Louis

POPULATION
1,172,000

FUN FACT
Mauritius is a volcanic island in the Indian Ocean known for its natural beauty.

La Mauritanie

CAPITAL
Nouakchott

POPULATION
23,000,000

FUN FACT
Mauritania is a bridge between the Maghreb in the North and sub-Saharan Africa in the South.

Le Niger

CAPITAL
Niamey

POPULATION
9,962,000

FUN FACT
Niger is a starkly dramatic country with its desert terrain. The capital, Niamey, on the fringe of the Sahara, is a city of modern buildings and wide boulevards—where many times you will see camels walking.

La Réunion

PRÉFECTURE
Saint-Denis

POPULATION
705,000

FUN FACT
Réunion, a French overseas department, is a beautiful island in the Indian Ocean with many beaches. It has a very hot, tropical climate.

Le Rwanda

CAPITAL
Kigali

POPULATION
8,155,000

FUN FACT
Ruanda, located in Central Africa, is a country of many lakes. It has one of the densest populations in all of Africa.

Le Sénégal

CAPITAL
Dakar

POPULATION
9,240,000

FUN FACT
Senegal is a country that has a fabulous mix of Afro-French characteristics. More visitors go to Senegal than to any other Western African country.

Les Seychelles

CAPITAL
Victoria

POPULATION
80,000

FUN FACT
The Republic of the Seychelles is made up of more than one hundred islands and is a vacationer's paradise. The Seychelles attract people from all over the world.

Le Tchad

CAPITAL
N'Djamena

POPULATION
7,714,000

FUN FACT
Chad has a lake in the southwest of the country that doubles in size during the rainy season.

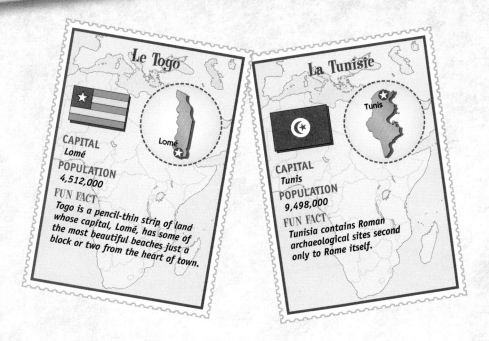

Le Togo

CAPITAL
Lomé

POPULATION
4,512,000

FUN FACT
Togo is a pencil-thin strip of land whose capital, Lomé, has some of the most beautiful beaches just a block or two from the heart of town.

La Tunisie

CAPITAL
Tunis

POPULATION
9,498,000

FUN FACT
Tunisia contains Roman archaeological sites second only to Rome itself.

L'Amérique du Nord et du Sud

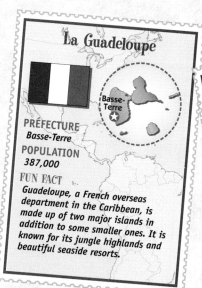

La Guadeloupe

PRÉFECTURE
Basse-Terre

POPULATION
387,000

FUN FACT
Guadeloupe, a French overseas department in the Caribbean, is made up of two major islands in addition to some smaller ones. It is known for its jungle highlands and beautiful seaside resorts.

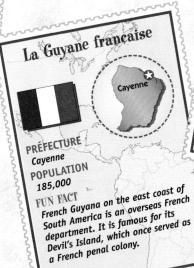

La Guyane française

PRÉFECTURE
Cayenne

POPULATION
185,000

FUN FACT
French Guyana on the east coast of South America is an overseas French department. It is famous for its Devil's Island, which once served as a French penal colony.

Haïti

CAPITAL
Port-au-Prince

POPULATION
7,751,000

FUN FACT
Haiti shares the island of Hispaniola with the Dominican Republic. Its friendly people are known for their musical and artistic talents. Haitian primitive art is sought after in art galleries around the world.

La Martinique

PRÉFECTURE
Fort-de-France

POPULATION
359,500

FUN FACT
Martinique, like Guadeloupe, is a French overseas department in the Caribbean Sea. It is a highly developed island famous for its beautiful, exotic flowers—orchids, hibiscus, and flamingo flowers.

La province de Québec

CAPITAL
Québec

POPULATION
7,040,000

FUN FACT
Quebec is the oldest and largest of Canada's provinces. About 90 percent of Quebec's inhabitants are French-speaking.

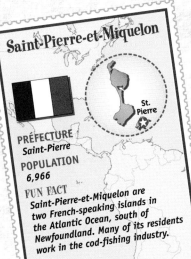

Saint-Pierre-et-Miquelon

PRÉFECTURE
Saint-Pierre

POPULATION
6,966

FUN FACT
Saint-Pierre-et-Miquelon are two French-speaking islands in the Atlantic Ocean, south of Newfoundland. Many of its residents work in the cod-fishing industry.

L'Europe

La principauté d'Andorre

CAPITAL
Andorre-la-Vieille

POPULATION
66,000

FUN FACT
Andorra is a co-principality governed by France's president and a Spanish bishop.

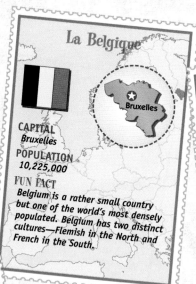

La Belgique

CAPITAL
Bruxelles

POPULATION
10,225,000

FUN FACT
Belgium is a rather small country but one of the world's most densely populated. Belgium has two distinct cultures—Flemish in the North and French in the South.

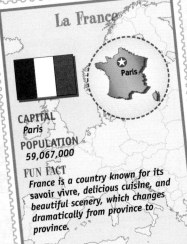

La France

CAPITAL
Paris

POPULATION
59,067,000

FUN FACT
France is a country known for its savoir vivre, delicious cuisine, and beautiful scenery, which changes dramatically from province to province.

Le grand-duché de Luxembourg

CAPITAL
Luxembourg
POPULATION
432,000

FUN FACT
Luxembourg is smaller than the state of Rhode Island. The native Luxembourgers all speak three languages fluently: Luxembourgish, German, and French.

La principauté de Monaco

CAPITAL
Monaco
POPULATION
33,000

FUN FACT
Monaco is one of the world's smallest sovereign states. It is located on a horseshoe-shaped strip of land bathed by the Mediterranean on one side and shielded by alpine peaks on the other.

La Suisse

CAPITAL
Berne
POPULATION
7,119,000

FUN FACT
The beautiful country of Switzerland is dominated by the Alps. Its population density is among the lowest in Europe. Thus, it has fabulous wide-open spaces.

Vanuatu

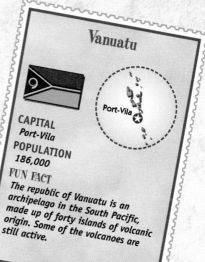

CAPITAL
Port-Vila
POPULATION
186,000

FUN FACT
The republic of Vanuatu is an archipelago in the South Pacific, made up of forty islands of volcanic origin. Some of the volcanoes are still active.

L'Océanie

La Nouvelle-Calédonie

CAPITAL
Nouméa
POPULATION
212,000

FUN FACT
New Caledonia is a French overseas territory in the South Pacific. It is made up of one large island and numerous small, beautiful coral islands.

La Polynésie française

CAPITAL
Papeete
POPULATION
234,000

FUN FACT
French Polynesia is a French overseas territory made up of approximately 130 islands. The islands are known for their volcanic mountains, tropical climate, and beautiful bays and coves.

Wallis-et-Futuna

CAPITAL
Mata Utu
POPULATION
14,000

FUN FACT
Wallis-et-Futuna is a French overseas territory in the South Pacific. The mountainous islands of the archipelago are surrounded by coral reefs.

La France

ANGLETERRE

Mer du Nord

PAYS-BAS

BELGIQUE

ALLEMAGNE

Manche

Calais

Lille

Nord-Pas-de-Calais

LUXEMBOURG

Le Havre
Caen
Rouen

Haute-Normandie

Amiens

Picardie

Brest

Basse-Normandie

Seine

Paris

Châlons-en-Champagne

Metz

Marne

Bretagne

Rennes

Île-de-France

Lorraine

Meuse

Rhine

Le Mans

Orléans

Champagne-Ardenne

Strasbourg

Pays de la Loire

Loire

Centre

Alsace

Nantes

Bourgogne

Besançon

Poitiers

Dijon

Franche-Comté

OCÉAN
ATLANTIQUE

Poitou-Charentes

Moulins

SUISSE

Limoges

Clermont-Ferrand

Saône

Limousin

Lyon

Bordeaux

Auvergne

Rhône-Alpes

Garonne

Grenoble

Aquitaine

ITALIE

Rhône

Midi-Pyrénées

Toulouse

Montpellier

Provence-Alpes-Côte d'Azur

Monaco
Nice

Languedoc-Roussillon

MONACO

Marseille

ESPAGNE

Corse

Mer Méditerranée

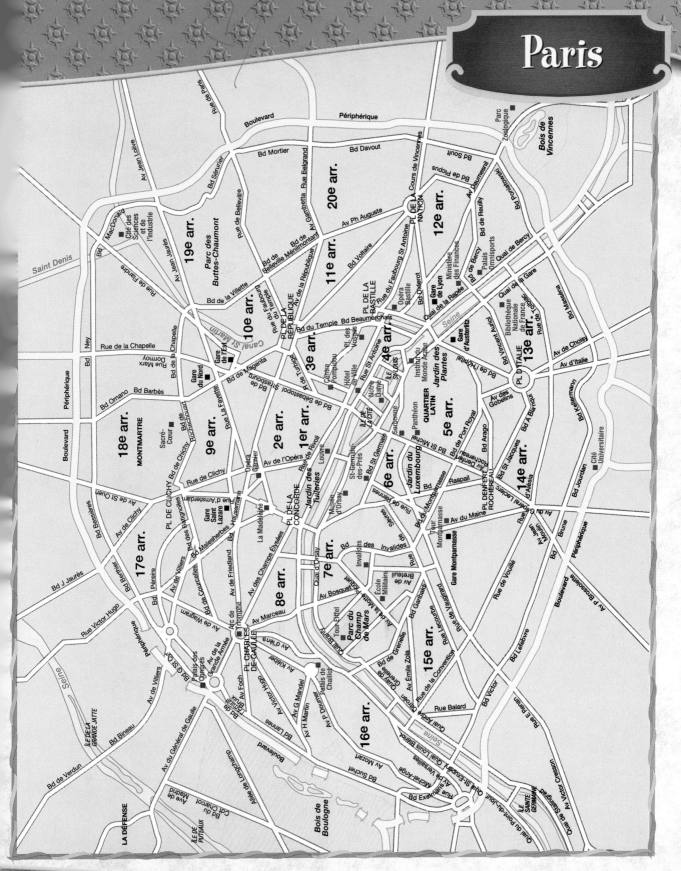

Paris

Le Canada

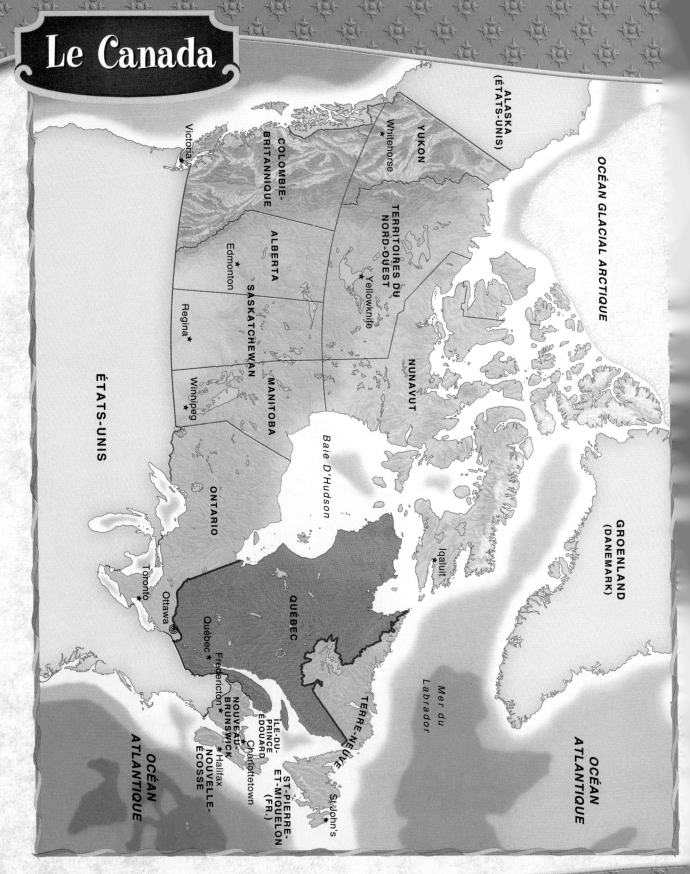

OCÉAN GLACIAL ARCTIQUE

ALASKA (ÉTATS-UNIS)

Victoria ★

COLOMBIE-BRITANNIQUE

YUKON

Whitehorse ★

TERRITOIRES DU NORD-OUEST

Yellowknife ★

ALBERTA

Edmonton ★

SASKATCHEWAN

Regina ★

MANITOBA

Winnipeg ★

NUNAVUT

ÉTATS-UNIS

Baie D'Hudson

Iqaluit ★

GROENLAND (DANEMARK)

ONTARIO

Toronto ★

Ottawa

QUÉBEC

Québec ★

Fredericton ★

NOUVEAU-BRUNSWICK

ÎLE-DU-PRINCE-ÉDOUARD

Charlottetown ★

Halifax ★

NOUVELLE-ÉCOSSE

TERRE-NEUVE

Mer du Labrador

ST-PIERRE-ET-MIQUELON (FR.)

St. John's ★

OCÉAN ATLANTIQUE

OCÉAN ATLANTIQUE

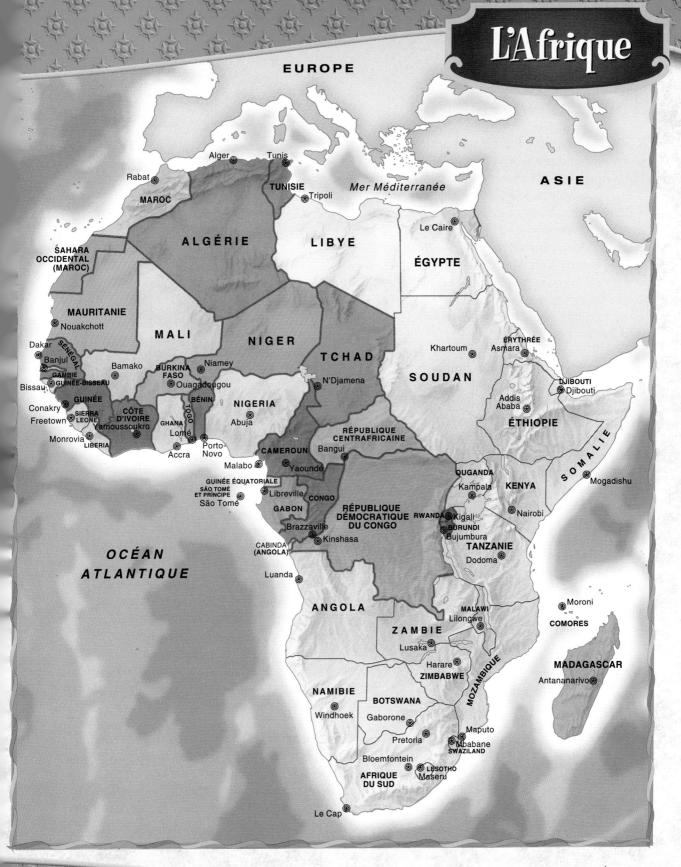

L'Afrique

EUROPE

ASIE

Mer Méditerranée

Alger
Tunis
Rabat
TUNISIE
Tripoli
MAROC
Le Caire
ALGÉRIE
LIBYE
ÉGYPTE
SAHARA
OCCIDENTAL
(MAROC)
MAURITANIE
Nouakchott
MALI
NIGER
Khartoum
ÉRYTHRÉE
Asmara
Dakar
SÉNÉGAL
Banjul
Bamako
Niamey
TCHAD
SOUDAN
DJIBOUTI
Djibouti
GAMBIE
BURKINA
FASO
N'Djamena
Bissau
GUINÉE-BISSEAU
Ouagadougou
Addis
Ababa
GUINÉE
BÉNIN
Conakry
Freetown
SIERRA
LEONE
CÔTE
D'IVOIRE
NIGERIA
Abuja
ÉTHIOPIE
Yamoussoukro
GHANA
TOGO
SOMALIE
Monrovia
LIBERIA
Lomé
Accra
Porto-
Novo
RÉPUBLIQUE
CENTRAFRICAINE
CAMEROUN
Bangui
OUGANDA
Malabo
Yaoundé
Kampala
KENYA
Mogadishu
GUINÉE ÉQUATORIALE
SÃO TOMÉ
ET PRÍNCIPE
Libreville
CONGO
Nairobi
São Tomé
GABON
RÉPUBLIQUE
DÉMOCRATIQUE
DU CONGO
RWANDA
Kigali
Brazzaville
BURUNDI
Bujumbura
CABINDA
(ANGOLA)
Kinshasa
TANZANIE
OCÉAN
ATLANTIQUE
Luanda
Dodoma
Moroni
COMORES
ANGOLA
MALAWI
Lilongwe
MADAGASCAR
ZAMBIE
Lusaka
Antananarivo
Harare
ZIMBABWE
MOZAMBIQUE
NAMIBIE
BOTSWANA
Windhoek
Gaborone
Maputo
Pretoria
Mbabane
SWAZILAND
Bloemfontein
LESOTHO
Maseru
AFRIQUE
DU SUD
Le Cap

Why Learn French?

The Francophone World

Culture Knowing French will open doors to you around the world. As you study the language, you will also come to understand and appreciate the way of life, customs, values, and cultures of people from many different countries. Look at the map on page xxii to see the areas of the world in which French is spoken, either as a first or second language. You might be surprised to see that people speak French in places as close to home as Haiti, Martinique, Quebec, and Louisiana.

Learning French can be fun and will bring you a sense of accomplishment. You'll be really pleased when you are able to carry on a conversation with a French-speaking person in French. You will also be able to read French literature, keep up with current events in French magazines and newspapers, and understand French films without relying on subtitles. The French language will be a source of enrichment for the rest of your life.

Career Opportunities

Business Your knowledge of French will also be an asset to you in a variety of careers. Many French companies are multinational and have branches around the world, including the United States. Some of the fields in which French companies excel are: clothing and fashion, cosmetics, tourism, agriculture, the automotive and aerospace industries, and technology.

Research France is also a world leader in high-energy physics research and medical genetics. Did you know that French and English are the two major languages of the Internet? French can help you in almost any career path you choose.

Language Link

Another benefit to learning French is that it will improve your English. Once you know another language, you can make comparisons between the two and gain a greater understanding of how languages function. As a result, your use of English will be more effective. You'll also come across many French words that are used in English. Just a few examples are: **rouge, chaise longue, chic, crêpe, à la mode, omelette, chargé d'affaires, déjà vu, détente,** and **laisser faire.** French will also be helpful if you decide to learn yet another language. Once you learn a second language, the learning process for acquiring other languages becomes much easier.

French is a beautiful, rich language that is spoken on many continents. Many people use French on a daily basis as their second language. Whatever your motivation is for choosing to study it, French will expand your horizons and increase your job opportunities. **Vive la langue française! Et bon voyage!**

L'alphabet français

a *a*mis

b *b*ébé

c *c*irque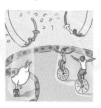

d *d*eux

e *l*eçon

f *f*enêtre

g *g*iraffe

h *h*uit

i *i*gloo

j *j*eu

k *k*ilo

l *l*ivre

m *m*aison

n *n*ez

o *o*live

p *p*ain

q *q*uatre

r *r*eine

s *s*oupe

t *t*able

u *u*nivers

v *v*iolette

w *w*agon

x e*x*tra

y *y*eux

z *z*èbre

Leçons préliminaires

Bienvenue

Objectifs

In these preliminary lessons you will learn to:

- ✔ greet people
- ✔ say good-bye to people
- ✔ ask people how they are
- ✔ ask and tell names
- ✔ express simple courtesies
- ✔ find out and tell the days of the week
- ✔ find out and tell the months of the year
- ✔ count from 1 to 30
- ✔ find out and tell the time

3.

2.

4.

1.

AIR MAIL
PAR AVION

Miss Melisse Kingston
7 Elm Street
Ardsley-on-Hudson, NY 10533
Etats-Unis d'Amérique

PRIORITAIRE
PRIORITY
PAR AVION / AIR MAIL

1. Karim Ashour, Tunis, Tunisie
2. Yvonne Senghor, Abidjan, Côte d'Ivoire
3. Jacques Ferrand, Montréal, Canada
4. Thérèse Nguyen, Lyon, France
5. Yves Clémenceau, **Fort-de-France**, Martinique
6. **Ahmed Rashid**, Paris, France
7. Vincent Daudet, Rouen, France
8. Élodie Lutz, Strasbourg, France
9. Marie Robert, Marseille, France

5.

6.

7.

8.

9.

Greeting people 🎧

When someone wants to know how you are doing and asks **Ça va?**, there are several different answers you can give.

> **Ça va.**
> **Bien, merci.**
> **Ça va très bien.**
> **Pas mal, merci.**

1 Salut!

Get up from your desk. Walk around the classroom. Say hello to each classmate you meet.

2 Ça va?

Work with a classmate. Greet one another and find out how things are going.

More greetings 🎧

1. **Salut!** is an informal greeting that you can use with people your own age. When you greet an older person, you may use the following expressions.

Bonjour, monsieur.

Bonjour, madame.

Bonjour, mademoiselle.

2. Note that the titles **monsieur, madame,** and **mademoiselle** are almost always used without the last name of the person.

3 Bonjour!

Draw some figures on the board. Some will represent friends your own age and others will represent older people. Greet each of the figures on the board properly.

4 Salutations

Look at these photographs of young people in France and Martinique. As they greet one another they do some things that are different from what we do when we greet each other. What do you notice in the photographs?

Préliminaire B

Saying good-bye 🎧

Au revoir, madame.

Au revoir, Christine.

Ciao, Thomas. À tout à l'heure.

Ciao, Charlotte.

1. A very common expression to use when saying good-bye to someone is **Au revoir.**

2. If you plan to see the person again soon, you can say **À bientôt!** If you plan to see the person very soon, you can say **À tout à l'heure.** If you plan to see the person the next day, you can say **À demain.**

3. An informal expression you often hear is **Ciao.** It comes from Italian and is used in many parts of Europe.

1 Ciao!

Go over to a classmate and say good-bye to him or her.

2 À bientôt!

Work with a classmate. Say **Ciao** to each other and let one another know when you will be getting together again.

3 Au revoir!

Say good-bye to your French teacher. Use **monsieur, madame,** or **mademoiselle,** as appropriate. Then say good-bye to a friend. Use a different expression with each person.

Conversation

4 ## Salut!

Work with a classmate. Have a conversation in French. Say as much as you can to each other.

5 ## Bonjour!

Work with a classmate. One of you will pretend to be an older person. Have a conversation. Say as much as you can to each other.

Préliminaire C Les noms

Finding out a person's name 🎧

When you want to find out the name of a person who is about the same age as you, you can ask **Tu t'appelles comment?** However, you would not use this expression with an older person. You will learn the more formal forms at a later time.

1 Tu t'appelles comment?

Get up from your desk. Walk around the room. Find out several of your classmates' names. Let them know your name, too.

Conversation

2 Salut!

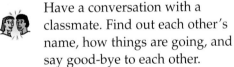

Have a conversation with a classmate. Find out each other's name, how things are going, and say good-bye to each other.

3 Je m'appelle...

Look at this photograph of young French people introducing each other. Are they doing something that you probably would not do? What is it?

Préliminaire D

Ordering food politely

Bonjour, mademoiselle.

Une limonade, s'il vous plaît.

Merci.

Je vous en prie.

Expressions of politeness are always appreciated. The following are the French expressions for "please," "thank you," and "you're welcome."

Formal	Informal
S'il vous plaît.	S'il te plaît.
Merci (madame).	Merci.
Je vous en prie.	Je t'en prie.

1 La politesse

With a classmate, practice reading the preceding conversation aloud.
Be as animated and as polite as you can.

2 Une limonade, s'il vous plaît.

You are at a café in Canada. Order the following things. Your partner will be
the server. Be polite when you order.

1.

un sandwich

2.

un coca

3.

une limonade

4.

un café

5.

une pizza

6.

une saucisse de Francfort,
un hot-dog

7.

une crêpe

LA POLITESSE

Préliminaire E

Telling the days of the week 🎧

To find out and give the day of the week, you say:

C'est quel jour aujourd'hui?
(Aujourd'hui), c'est lundi.
Demain, c'est mardi.

LUNDI	MARDI	MERCREDI	JEUDI	VENDREDI	SAMEDI	DIMANCHE
1	2	3	4	5	6	7
8	9	10	11	12	13	14

1 ## C'est quel jour?

Answer the following questions in French.

1. C'est quel jour aujourd'hui?
2. Et demain? C'est quel jour?

Telling the months 🎧

janvier	mai	septembre
février	juin	octobre
mars	juillet	novembre
avril	août	décembre

Les nombres de 1 à 30

1 un	7 sept	13 treize	19 dix-neuf	25 vingt-cinq
2 deux	8 huit	14 quatorze	20 vingt	26 vingt-six
3 trois	9 neuf	15 quinze	21 vingt et un	27 vingt-sept
4 quatre	10 dix	16 seize	22 vingt-deux	28 vingt-huit
5 cinq	11 onze	17 dix-sept	23 vingt-trois	29 vingt-neuf
6 six	12 douze	18 dix-huit	24 vingt-quatre	30 trente

Finding out and giving the date 🎧

Quelle est la date aujourd'hui?

(C'est) le trente et un août.

	A O Û T					
LUNDI	MARDI	MERCREDI	JEUDI	VENDREDI	SAMEDI	DIMANCHE
1	2	3	4	5	6	7
8	9	10	11	12	13	14
15	16	17	18	19	20	21
22	23	24	25	26	27	28
29	30	㉛				

Premier is used for the first day of the month. For other days you use **deux, trois, quatre,** etc.

> **le premier août**
> **le deux septembre**

2 La date, s'il vous plaît.

Answer the following questions in French.

1. Quelle est la date aujourd'hui?
2. Et demain?

le 6 janvier

le 14 juillet à Paris

3 En quel mois?

Each of you will stand up in class and give the date of your birthday in French. Listen carefully and keep a record of how many of you were born in the same month. Then tell in French in which month the greatest number of students were born. In which month were the fewest born?

Préliminaire F

Telling time 🎧

1. To find out the time, you ask:

Il est quelle heure?

2. To give the time on the hour, you say:

1 h
Il est une heure.

2 h
Il est deux heures.

10 h
Il est dix heures.

12 h
Il est midi.

12 h
Il est minuit.

3. To give the time after the hour, you say:

1 h 05
Il est une heure cinq.

3 h 10
Il est trois heures dix.

4 h 25
**Il est quatre heures
vingt-cinq.**

4. To give the time before the hour, you say:

4 h 50
**Il est cinq heures
moins dix.**

5 h 40
**Il est six heures moins
vingt.**

9 h 35
**Il est dix heures moins
vingt-cinq.**

5. To express time on the quarter hour and half hour, you say:

2 h 15	6 h 45	6 h 30
Il est deux heures et quart.	**Il est sept heures moins le quart.**	**Il est six heures et demie.**

6. If you need to specify whether it is A.M. or P.M., you can use the following expressions.

Il est six heures du matin.	**Il est quatre heures de l'après-midi.**	**Il est onze heures du soir.**

1 Il est quelle heure?

Look at each clock and give the time.

1.

4.

2.

5.

3.

6.

Conversation

> Salut, Julie. Il est quelle heure, s'il te plaît?

> Il est trois heures vingt.

> Trois heures vingt! Déjà? Zut! Au revoir!

> Au revoir, Vincent. À bientôt!

2 Ciao!

Work with a classmate. Greet each other. Find out the time and react as if you have to get going.

3 Il est quelle heure, s'il te plaît?

Get up from your desk and walk around the room. Go up to a classmate. Greet the person quickly and ask the time. Show your classmate a piece of paper with a time on it. He or she will give you the time.

Leçons préliminaires

Greeting people

Salut!	Ça va?	Bien.
Bonjour!	Pas mal.	Très bien.

Giving titles

Monsieur	Madame	Mademoiselle

Saying good-bye

Au revoir.	À bientôt.
Ciao!	À demain.
À tout à l'heure.	

Finding out a person's name

Tu t'appelles comment?
Je m'appelle…

Being courteous

S'il te plaît.	Je t'en prie.
S'il vous plaît.	Je vous en prie.
Merci.	

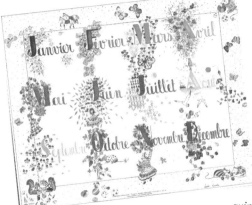

How well do you know your vocabulary?

- Choose an expression from the list to begin a conversation.
- Have a classmate respond.
- Take turns.

Telling the days of the week

lundi	jeudi	samedi	C'est quel jour?
mardi	vendredi	dimanche	aujourd'hui
mercredi			demain

Telling the months of the year

Quelle est la date?	avril	août	novembre
janvier	mai	septembre	décembre
février	juin	octobre	
mars	juillet		

Telling time

Il est quelle heure?	Il est midi.
Il est ____ heure(s).	Il est minuit.
du matin	
de l'après-midi	
du soir	

Une amie et un ami

Objectifs

In this chapter you will learn to:

✔ *ask or tell what someone is like*

✔ *ask or tell where someone is from*

✔ *ask or tell who someone is*

✔ *describe yourself or someone else*

✔ *talk about students from France and Martinique*

Victor Gabriel Gilbert *Enfants jouant au cerceau*

Vocabulaire

Comment est la fille?

brune

petite

amusante

grande

C'est qui?
C'est Julie Lacroix.
Julie est française.

Elle est d'où, Julie?
Julie est de Paris.

Comment est le garçon?

brun

petit

amusant

grand

C'est qui?
C'est Olivier Charpentier.
Olivier est français aussi.

Il est d'où, Olivier?
Il est de Nice.

Note

Many words in French and English look alike even though they are pronounced differently. These words are called "cognates." You can use the following cognates to describe people.

américain   intelligent
blond   intéressant
patient

Here are some words used to express degree.

Il est amusant.
Il est assez amusant.
Il est très amusant.
Il est vraiment amusant.

Commençons
Let's use our new words

1 **Historiette** Une fille française
Inventez une histoire. *(Make up a story.)*

1. Sophie est française ou américaine?
2. Elle est de Paris ou de New York?
3. Elle est brune ou blonde?
4. Elle est amusante?
5. Elle est grande ou petite?

Sophie Legrand

2 **Historiette** Un garçon français
Inventez une histoire. *(Make up a story.)*

1. Christophe est américain ou français?
2. Il est de Lyon ou de Houston?
3. Il est brun ou blond?
4. Il est amusant?
5. Il est très intelligent?
6. Il est assez patient?

Christophe Gaudin

Bill

Henri

3 **Un Français ou un Américain?**
Répondez d'après les photos.
(Answer according to the photos.)

1. Qui est américain?
2. Qui est français?
3. Qui est de Paris?
4. Qui est de Los Angeles?
5. Qui est blond?
6. Qui est brun?

4 **Il est... ? Elle est... ?** Look at the following people and say two things about each of them. Then, find out who they are. They are all famous.

5 **C'est qui?** Think of a student in the class. A classmate will ask you questions about the person and try to guess who it is. Take turns.

*For more practice using words from **Mots 1**, do Activity 1 on page H2 at the end of this book.*

Vocabulaire

Une sœur et un frère

le frère

la sœur

une amie

un ami

Voilà Nathalie et Luc Simonet.
Nathalie est la sœur de Luc.
Luc est le frère de Nathalie.

Voilà Philippe.
Philippe n'est pas le frère de Nathalie.
Philippe est un ami de Nathalie.

Une école et un collège

une école
américaine

WESTERVILLE NORTH

OPEN HOUSE
SEPT 14
7 PM

une élève

un collège français

un élève

Carol est élève dans une école américaine.

Bruno est élève dans un collège français.
Un collège est une école secondaire en France.

Bonjour, tout le monde!
Je m'appelle Mark.
Je suis américain.
Je suis de Californie.
Je suis un ami de Mae.

Mae est une amie de Mark.
Mae est très sympathique.
Mark est très sympa aussi.

Note 🎧

You can also use the following cognates to describe people.

dynamique   égoïste
énergique   enthousiaste
populaire   sociable
timide

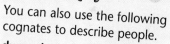

Les nombres de 30 à 60

30 trente	35 trente-cinq	40 quarante
31 trente et un	36 trente-six	50 cinquante
32 trente-deux	37 trente-sept	60 soixante
33 trente-trois	38 trente-huit	
34 trente-quatre	39 trente-neuf	

Commençons
Let's use our new words

6 **Historiette** **Une élève française** Choisissez la bonne réponse.
(Choose the right answer.)

1. _____ est française.
   a. Céline Dupont   **b.** Thomas Duhamel
2. Céline est élève dans _____.
   a. une école américaine   **b.** un collège français
3. Elle est _____.
   a. de Paris   **b.** de Miami
4. Céline est _____ de Karim.
   a. un ami   **b.** une amie
5. Karim est _____ de Céline.
   a. un ami   **b.** un élève
6. David est _____ de Céline.
   a. la sœur   **b.** le frère
7. Céline est _____ de David.
   a. le frère   **b.** la sœur

7 **Qui est d'où?** Répondez d'après la carte.
(Answer according to the map.)

1. Qui est de Bordeaux?
2. D'où est Maïa?
3. Et Olivia, elle est d'où?
4. Et Ahmed, il est d'où?

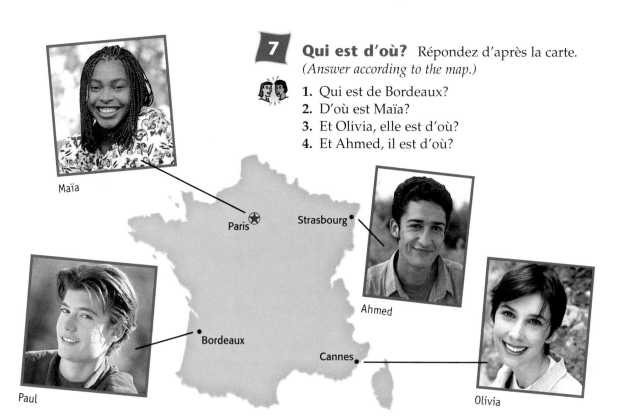

Maïa

Paris

Strasbourg

Ahmed

Bordeaux

Cannes

Paul

Olivia

Historiette David Williams, un garçon américain

Inventez une histoire. *(Make up a story.)*

1. Qui est américain, David Williams ou Serge Legrand?
2. D'où est David Williams? Il est de New York ou de Paris?
3. Il est de quelle nationalité? Il est français ou américain?
4. David est élève dans un collège français ou dans une école américaine?
5. Comment est David? Il est timide ou sociable?

 Historiette Sophie est vraiment amusante. Complétez. *(Complete.)*

Sophie Bellecour est de Lyon. Elle est __1__. Elle n'est pas américaine. Sophie est blonde. Elle n'est pas __2__. Elle n'est pas timide. Pas du tout! Elle est très __3__. Elle est très sympa aussi. Elle est __4__ dans un collège à Lyon.

Lyon, France

Pascal Denjean

 Pascal Denjean Here is a photo of Pascal Denjean. He is a student from Bordeaux. Say a few things about Pascal.

 Élodie Denjean The blonde girl in the photo is Élodie Denjean. She is Pascal's sister. She is also a student in Bordeaux. Say a few things about Élodie.

Élodie Denjean

 Jeu **Un nombre secret** Think of a number between 1 and 60. Your partner tries to guess the number you have in mind. Use a hand gesture to indicate whether the number you are thinking of is higher or lower. Continue until your partner guesses the correct number. Take turns.

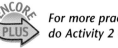 *For more practice using words from **Mots 2**, do Activity 2 on page H3 at the end of this book.*

Structure

Talking about a person or a thing
Les articles au singulier

1. A noun is the name of a person, place, or thing. In French, every noun has a gender, either masculine or feminine. Except for people, you cannot tell what the gender of a noun is by just looking at it. You need other clues.

2. Many words that accompany nouns can indicate gender. They are called "gender markers." **Une** and **un** are gender markers. They are indefinite articles and correspond to *a (an)* in English. **Une** accompanies a feminine noun and **un** accompanies a masculine noun.

LES ARTICLES INDÉFINIS

Féminin	Masculin
une amie	un ami
une sœur	un frère
une école	un collège

3. **Le, la,** and **l'** are definite articles and often correspond to *the* in English.

LES ARTICLES DÉFINIS

Féminin	Masculin
la fille	le garçon
la sœur	le frère
l'amie	l'ami

Attention!

Note that the definite articles **le** and **la** are shortened to **l'** when they accompany a noun that begins with a vowel. When pronounced, the vowel sound is dropped. This is called "elision."

la amie → **l'amie**
le ami → **l'ami**

The **n** of the indefinite article **un** is pronounced when it accompanies a noun beginning with a vowel. This is called "liaison."

un‿ami **un‿élève**

Une sœur et un frère

Continuons
Let's put our words together

13 Historiette Olivier et Marie Complétez avec **un** ou **une.**
(Complete with un *or* une.*)*

Olivier est __1__ garçon très sympa. Olivier est __2__ ami de Christophe.
Christophe est __3__ élève très intelligent. Il est élève dans __4__ école
secondaire à New York.

Marie est __5__ amie de Christophe. Marie est __6__ élève intelligente aussi.
Marie est __7__ fille vraiment amusante.

14 Historiette Brendan Jones et Sabine Morel
Complétez avec **le, la** ou **l'.** *(Complete with* le, la, *or* l'.*)*

__1__ garçon, Brendan Jones, est américain, mais __2__ fille, Sabine Morel,
n'est pas américaine. Elle est française. Sabine est __3__ amie de Ludovic Girard
et __4__ sœur de Luc Morel. Brendan n'est pas __5__ ami de Sabine; il est de
Miami et Sabine est de Strasbourg. Brendan est __6__ ami de Karen Miller et
__7__ frère de Melissa Jones. Brendan est élève et Sabine est élève aussi.
__8__ école de Brendan est à Miami. __9__ collège de Sabine est à Strasbourg.

Strasbourg, France

Describing a person or a thing
L'accord des adjectifs

1. An adjective is a word that describes a noun. The highlighted words in the following sentences are adjectives.

> **La fille est blonde. Le garçon est blond aussi.**
> **Jeanne est française. Vincent aussi est français.**

2. In French, an adjective must agree with the noun it describes or modifies. Adjectives that end in a consonant such as **blond** and **français** have two forms in the singular. Study the following.

Féminin	Masculin
La fille est blonde.	Le garçon est blond.
La fille est française.	Le garçon est français.
La fille est brune.	Le garçon est brun.
La fille est intelligente.	Le garçon est intelligent.
L'école est grande.	Le collège est grand.

3. Adjectives that end in **e,** such as **énergique** and **sympathique,** are both feminine and masculine.

Féminin	Masculin
Charlotte est très énergique.	Nicolas est très énergique.
Elle est sympathique.	Il est sympathique.

Le garçon est très amusant.

Attention!

When a final consonant is followed by an e, you pronounce the consonant. When a word ends in a consonant, you don't pronounce it.

petite	petit
française	français
intéressante	intéressant

Continuons
Let's put our words together

15 **Historiette** **Chloé et Adrien Chancel** Répondez
d'après le dessin. (*Answer according to the illustration.*)

1. Chloé est française ou américaine?
2. Elle est blonde ou brune?
3. Elle est grande ou petite?
4. Elle est amusante?
5. Adrien est le frère de Chloé?
6. Adrien est blond ou brun?
7. Il est grand ou petit?
8. Il est amusant?
9. Chloé est élève dans un collège français ou
   dans une école américaine?
10. Et le frère de Chloé, il est élève dans un collège
    français ou dans une école américaine?

16 **Historiette** **Maïa, Emmanuel et moi** Complétez. (*Complete.*)

1. Maïa est une amie _____ et _____. (amusant, sympathique)
2. Emmanuel est le frère de Maïa. Il est _____ aussi. Il est _____ et très
   _____! (sympathique, amusant, sociable)
3. Maïa est _____. (français)
4. Et moi, je m'appelle _____ (*your name*). Je suis _____. Je ne suis pas
   _____. (américain, français)
5. Je suis élève dans une école _____ _____. (secondaire, américain)
6. Je ne suis pas élève dans un collège _____. (français)

17 **Jeu** **Devinez.** You often hear French teenagers
talk about their friends' younger siblings and say
something like: «**Oh, la petite sœur de Corinne, elle est
vraiment casse-pieds!**» (literally, *a foot-breaker*). Can you
guess what expression we use in English?

18 **Un ami idéal ou une amie
idéale**

What are some qualities an ideal
friend would have? With a
classmate, discuss what you think
an ideal friend is like.

19 **C'est qui?** Work with a classmate. Say three things that describe someone in the class. First your partner will tell you whether you're describing a boy or a girl. Then, he or she will guess who it is. Take turns.

—brun, grand, amusant
—C'est un garçon. C'est Marc.

Identifying people and things
Le verbe **être** au singulier

1. The verb *to be* in French is **être.** Study the following forms.

ÊTRE
je suis
tu es
il est
elle est

2. You use **je** to talk about yourself.   You use **tu** to address a friend.

Je suis française.

Tu es américain?

You use **il** to talk about a boy or a man.   You use **elle** to talk about a girl or a woman.

Il est blond.

Elle est brune.

3. You also use **il/elle** when referring to things.

Le collège? Il est grand.
L'école? Elle est petite.

Continuons
Let's put our words together

20 **Historiette** **Sylvie Latour** Voici une photo de Sylvie Latour. Décrivez Sylvie d'après les indications. *(Here is a photo of Sylvie Latour. Describe Sylvie using the cues.)*

1. canadienne
2. blonde
3. amusante et intelligente
4. sociable
5. de Montréal

21 **En France** Répétez la conversation. *(Repeat the conversation.)*

Salut! Tu es l'ami américain de Sandrine Valois, n'est-ce pas?

Oui, je m'appelle Matt, Matt Porter.

Tu es de New York?

Oui, je suis de New York.

22 **Historiette** **Matt Porter** Parlez de Matt. *(Say all you can about Matt.)*

23 **Pardon!** Répondez d'après le modèle. *(Answer according to the model.)*

Je suis de Paris.

Pardon, tu es d'où?

1. Je suis de Nice.
2. Je suis d'Antibes.
3. Je suis de Lille.
4. Je suis de Strasbourg.

24 **Je suis...** Donnez des réponses personnelles. *(Give your own answers.)*

Je m'appelle __1__ *(name)*. Je suis de __2__ *(place)*. Je suis __3__ *(nationality)*. Je suis __4__ *(occupation)*.

25 **Une interview** Posez des questions à un(e) ami(e). *(Ask a friend the following questions.)*

1. Tu es français(e) ou américain(e)?
2. Tu es d'où?
3. Tu es élève dans une école secondaire?
4. Tu es sociable ou timide?

26 **Rémi** Voici une photo de Rémi Tonon. Il est de Nîmes. Posez des questions à Rémi d'après le modèle. *(Ask Rémi questions according to the model. Your partner will answer as if he were Rémi.)*

français
—**Rémi, tu es français?**
—**Oui, je suis français.**

1. de Nîmes
2. élève dans un collège de Nîmes
3. sociable
4. intelligent

Rémi Tonon

27 **Historiette** **Antoine Delcourt** Complétez. *(Complete.)*

Voici Antoine Delcourt. Il __1__ français. Il est de Marseille. Moi aussi, je __2__ de Marseille. Marseille __3__ un port important en France. Antoine __4__ élève dans un collège à Marseille. Le collège est assez grand. Et toi, tu __5__ français(e) ou américain(e)? Tu __6__ d'où? Tu __7__ élève dans une école secondaire? L'école __8__ petite?

Marseille, France

Making a sentence negative
La négation

To make a sentence negative in French, you put **ne… pas** around the verb. Note that **ne** becomes **n'** before a vowel.

Affirmatif	Négatif
Je suis américain.	Je ne suis pas français.
Tu es amusant.	Tu n'es pas timide.
Il est sociable.	Il n'est pas égoïste.
Elle est de Lyon.	Elle n'est pas de Paris.

Continuons
Let's put our words together

Lycée Henri IV, Paris

28 **Non, Justine n'est pas américaine.**
Mettez à la forme négative. *(Change to the negative.)*

1. Justine est américaine.
2. Elle est de San Francisco.
3. Et moi, je suis français(e).
4. Je suis de Paris.
5. Je suis élève dans un collège à Paris.

29 **Tu es français(e)?** Donnez des réponses personnelles. *(Give your own answers.)*

1. Tu es français(e)?
2. Tu es de Lyon?
3. Tu es timide?
4. Tu es l'ami(e) de Justine?

30 **Un petit ami ou une petite amie** A classmate will pretend that he or she has a new boyfriend or girlfriend. Ask as many questions as you can to find out who it is.

ENCORE PLUS *For more practice using the verb **être**, do Activity 3 on page H4 at the end of this book.*

Vous êtes sur le bon chemin. Allez-y!

Conversation

Il est d'où, Luc?

Sophie: Luc, tu es de Paris, non?

Luc: Non. Je ne suis pas de Paris.

Sophie: Tu es d'où, alors?

Luc: Je suis de Cannes.

Sophie: Tu es de Cannes… sur la Côte d'Azur?

Luc: Oui.

Sophie: C'est super, la Côte d'Azur!

Après la conversation

Répondez. *(Answer.)*

1. Luc est de Paris?
2. Il est d'où?
3. Où est Cannes?
4. Comment est la Côte d'Azur?

Parlons un peu plus
Let's talk some more

 A **Au café** You've just met a student your own age at a café in Antibes, near Cannes. Have a conversation to get to know each other better.

Antibes, France

 B **Jeu** **Tu es... !** Play a guessing game. Think of someone in the class. Pretend you are this person and describe yourself. Your classmates have to guess who you are.

Prononciation

L'accent tonique

1. In English, you stress certain syllables more than others. In French, you pronounce each syllable evenly. Compare the following pairs of English and French words.

timid / **timide**   *patient* / **patient**
popular / **populaire**   *American* / **américain**
sociable / **sociable**

2. Repeat the following sentences. Notice how each word is linked to the next so that the sentence sounds like one long word.

Élisabeth est l'amie de Nathalie.
Paul est le frère de Nathalie.
Il est très sympathique.

Lectures culturelles

Un garçon et une fille

Un Parisien

Nicolas Martin est français. Il est de Paris, la capitale de la France. Nicolas est un garçon sympa. Il est très intelligent aussi. Nicolas est élève dans un lycée à Paris, le lycée Henri IV. Un lycée est aussi une école secondaire en France, mais après[1] le collège. Le lycée Henri IV à Paris est une école excellente.

[1] après *after*

Lycée Henri IV, Paris

La Polynésie française

Tahiti

Haïti

La France

BELGIQUE·BELGIE   La Suisse

BELGIE

La Belgique

La Tunisie

Le Maroc

Le Mali

Une Martiniquaise

Valérie Boucher est française aussi. Elle est de Fort-de-France, la ville[2] principale de la Martinique. La Martinique est une île[3] française dans la mer des Caraïbes (la mer des Antilles). Valérie est élève dans un lycée à Fort-de-France—le lycée Bellevue. Le lycée Bellevue est une école excellente.

[2] ville *city*   [3] île *island*

Fort-de-France, Martinique

Après la lecture

A Un Parisien Répondez. *(Answer.)*

1. Nicolas Martin est de quelle nationalité?
2. Il est d'où?
3. Quelle est la capitale de la France?
4. Comment est Nicolas?
5. Il est élève où?

B Une Martiniquaise Vrai ou faux? *(True or false?)*

1. Valérie Boucher est espagnole.
2. Elle est de Pointe-à-Pitre.
3. La Martinique est une île portugaise.
4. Valérie est élève dans une école américaine.

Lecture supplémentaire 1

Le français en Afrique

Bonjour! Je m'appelle Diane Koffi. Je suis d'Abidjan. Abidjan est la ville principale de la Côte d'Ivoire. La Côte d'Ivoire est un pays[1] d'Afrique Occidentale[2]. C'est un pays francophone[3].

Moi, je m'appelle Karim Ashour. Je suis tunisien. Je suis de Tunis, la capitale de la Tunisie. La Tunisie est un pays nord-africain sur la mer Méditerranée. La langue officielle de la Tunisie est l'arabe. Le français est la deuxième[4] langue.

[1] pays *country*
[2] Occidentale *Western*
[3] francophone *French-speaking*
[4] deuxième *second*

Abidjan, Côte d'Ivoire

Tunis, Tunisie

Après la lecture

A **Diane** Complétez. *(Complete.)*
1. Diane Koffi est d'_____.
2. Abidjan est la ville principale de la _____.
3. La Côte d'Ivoire est un pays d'_____ Occidentale.

B **Karim** Vrai ou faux? *(True or false?)*
1. Karim Ashour est une fille.
2. Karim est algérien.
3. Karim est de Tunis.
4. Tunis est la capitale de la Tunisie.
5. La Tunisie est en Europe.
6. La langue officielle de la Tunisie est le français.

Un artiste français

Henri de Toulouse-Lautrec est un peintre français. Il est d'Albi, une petite ville dans le sud de la France. La famille d'Henri est noble et assez riche.

Le jeune Henri est très petit. Il est boiteux[1]. Le petit garçon souffre de beaucoup de[2] fractures. Mais le jeune Henri possède un grand talent. Il adore la peinture[3].

Un sujet favori de Toulouse-Lautrec est la vie[4] parisienne.

Un autre sujet favori de Toulouse-Lautrec est le cirque. Le clown est très amusant, n'est-ce pas?

[1] boiteux *lame*
[2] beaucoup de *many*
[3] peinture *painting*
[4] vie *life*

Albi, France

Après la lecture

A **Un peintre français** Répondez.
(Answer.)
1. Qui est Toulouse-Lautrec?
2. Il est d'où?
3. Comment est la famille Toulouse-Lautrec?
4. Comment est le jeune Henri?
5. Il souffre de beaucoup de fractures?
6. Il adore la peinture?
7. Il adore le cirque?

B **Stratégie de lecture** Trouvez les mots apparentés dans la lecture.
(Find the following cognates in the reading.)
1. family
2. talent
3. rich
4. subject
5. possess
6. favorite
7. circus
8. painter

La Belgique

La Tunisie

Le Mali

CONNEXIONS

Les sciences sociales

La géographie

Geography is the study of the earth. It deals with all the earth's features, such as mountains, rivers, and seas. It is also the study of where people live and how the earth's features affect their lives. It is a subject that has interested human beings since the earliest of times.

Look at the map of France. Notice how many geographical terms you are able to recognize in French. See how easy it is to read about geography in French.

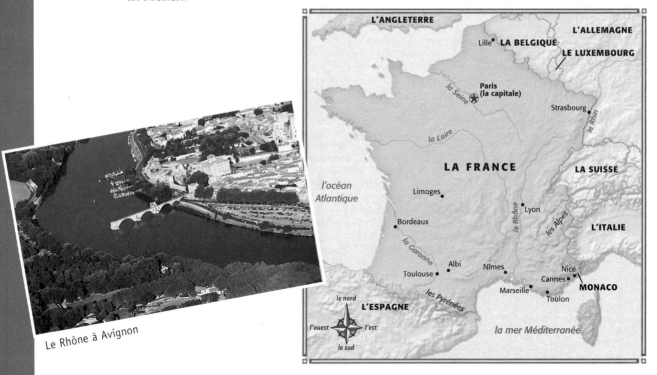

Le Rhône à Avignon

La Seine à Paris

La France

Villes

La France est en Europe. La France est un pays important dans le monde[1]. La capitale, Paris, est une ville culturelle. Lille, dans le nord, est une ville industrielle. Marseille, dans le sud, est un port important sur la mer Méditerranée.

Fleuves

Il y a[2] cinq fleuves[3] en France. La Seine passe à Paris. La Seine est un fleuve très calme. La Loire est un fleuve très long. Le Rhin forme une frontière naturelle entre la France et l'Allemagne. Le Rhône est un fleuve important: c'est une grande source d'énergie électrique. La Garonne est un fleuve assez violent.

[1] monde *world* [2] Il y a *There are* [3] fleuves *rivers*

Musée du Louvre, Paris

La Loire à Orléans

Après la lecture

Un peu de géographie
Vrai ou faux? *(True or false?)*

1. La France est un continent.
2. Paris est une ville industrielle.
3. Lille est dans le sud de la France.
4. Marseille est un port.
5. La Seine est un fleuve violent.
6. La Loire est un fleuve très long.
7. Un fleuve forme une frontière naturelle entre la France et l'Allemagne.

C'est à vous

Use what you have learned

PARLER

1 Un ami

✔ *Describe a male friend and answer questions about him*

Work with a classmate. Here's a picture of Vincent Terrier, a friend of yours from Paris, France. Say as much as you can about him. Answer any questions your partner may have about Vincent.

PARLER

2 Une élève

✔ *Ask a female friend questions and tell her about yourself*

Jeanne Marin (a classmate) is a new girl in your school. She is from Montreal, Canada. You want to get to know her better and help her feel at home. Find out as much as you can about her. Tell Jeanne about yourself, too.

Jeanne Marin

Saint-Tropez, France

PARLER

3 Dis donc, c'est qui?

✔ *Ask someone questions about another person*

You and a friend (a classmate) are at a sidewalk café in Saint-Tropez, on the French Riviera. You see an attractive girl or boy sitting a few tables away. It just so happens that your friend knows the person. Ask your friend as many questions as you can to find out about the boy or girl you're interested in.

ÉCRIRE
4 **Un ami français**
✔ *Write a postcard to a friend about yourself*

Here's a postcard you just received from a new pen pal. First read his message. Then answer it. Give Christophe similar information about yourself.

Notre-Dame

PARIS

> *Salut!*
>
> *Je m'appelle Christophe Legrand. Je suis de Paris, la capitale de la France. Je suis français. Je suis élève dans un collège à Paris – le collège Eugène Delacroix. C'est un collège excellent.*
>
> *Je suis brun et assez grand. Je suis très sociable. Je ne suis pas timide. Pas du tout!*
>
> *À bientôt,*
>
> *Christophe*

Writing Strategy

Freewriting One of the easiest ways to begin any kind of personal writing is simply to begin—to let your thoughts flow and write the first thing that comes to mind. Sometimes as you think of one word, another word you know will come to mind. If you get stuck, take several minutes to think of another word or phrase you have already learned. Brainstorming and freewriting are often methods for generating ideas when writing about yourself.

ÉCRIRE
5 **Moi**

On a piece of paper, write down as much as you can about yourself in French. Your teacher will collect the descriptions and choose students to read them to the class. You'll all try to guess who's being described.

Assessment

Vocabulaire

1 **Répondez d'après la photo.**
(Answer according to the photo.)

To review Mots 1, turn to pages 18–19.

1. Jeanne est française ou américaine?
2. Elle est de Paris ou de Boston?
3. Elle est blonde ou brune?

2 **Choisissez.** *(Choose.)*

4. Guillaume est _____ dans un collège français.
   a. ami **b.** élève

5. Guillaume est _____ de Françoise.
   a. le frère **b.** la sœur

Paris, France

To review Mots 2, turn to pages 22–23.

Structure

3 **Complétez avec «un» ou «une».**
(Complete with un or une.)

6. Sylvie est élève dans _____ collège français.
7. Sylvie est _____ fille très sympa.
8. Paul est _____ ami de Sylvie.
9. Paul est _____ garçon sympa aussi.

To review these gender markers, turn to page 26.

4 **Complétez avec «le», «la» ou «l'».**
(Complete with le, la, or l'.)

10. _____ fille, Sylvie, est de Lyon.
11. Jean-Pierre est _____ frère de Sylvie.
12. _____ école de Sylvie est grande.

5 **Complétez.** *(Complete.)*

To review agreement of adjectives, turn to page 28.

13. C'est une école assez _____. (petit)
14. Martine est une fille très _____. (dynamique)
15. Le garçon _____ est amusant. (américain)
16. Robert est un élève _____. (intelligent)

6 **Complétez avec «être».** *(Complete with être.)*

17. Dominique, tu ____ français?
18. Oui, je ____ de Bordeaux.
19. La fille blonde, elle ____ américaine?
20. Non, elle ____ canadienne.

To review the verb **être**, turn to page 30.

7 **Répondez au négatif.** *(Answer in the negative.)*

21. Alain Gérard est américain?
22. Il est timide?
23. Alain est le frère de Julie?

To review making a sentence negative, turn to page 33.

Culture

8 **Choisissez.** *(Choose.)*

24. Un lycée est ____ secondaire en France.
    a. un collège **b.** un élève **c.** une école
25. La ville principale de la Martinique est ____.
    a. Bellevue **b.** Fort-de-France **c.** Paris

To review this cultural information, turn to pages 36–37.

Grand-Rivière, Martinique

Vocabulaire

Identifying a person or thing

un garçon	un frère
une fille	une sœur
un ami	une école
une amie	un collège
un(e) élève	être

Describing a person

petit(e)	sympa(thique)
grand(e)	timide
brun(e)	énergique
blond(e)	égoïste
amusant(e)	dynamique
patient(e)	populaire
intelligent(e)	sociable
intéressant(e)	enthousiaste

Stating nationality

français(e)
américain(e)

Finding out information

Qui?	C'est qui?
D'où?	De quelle nationalité?
Comment?	

How well do you know your vocabulary?

- Choose five words that describe a good friend.
- Use these words to write several sentences about him or her.

Expressing degrees

assez
très
vraiment

Other useful words

voilà
aussi
secondaire

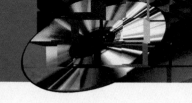

Technotour
BON VOYAGE!

VIDÉO • Épisode 1

Avant de visionner

In this video episode, Vincent and Chloé, each hoping to get a great shot of le Sacré-Cœur, bump into each other on the steps below the church.

Vincent et Chloé à Montmartre

Une vue splendide de Paris

FRENCH ONLINE

À découvrir

Learn more about le Sacré-Cœur and la place du Tertre—the heart of Montmartre—online.

La basilique du Sacré-Cœur

FRENCH Online

In the Chapter 1 Internet activity, you will have a chance to learn more about the geography of the Francophone world. To begin your virtual adventure, go to the Glencoe French Web site: **french.glencoe.com**

Les cours et les profs

Objectifs

In this chapter you will learn to:

✓ *describe people and things*

✓ *talk about more than one person or thing*

✓ *tell what subjects you take in school and express some opinions about them*

✓ *speak to people formally and informally*

✓ *talk about French-speaking people in the United States*

Pierre Bonnard *Écriture de fille*

Vocabulaire

Les élèves et les profs

les professeurs (les profs)

la prof

le prof

les amis, les copains

les amies, les copines

Karine et Stéphanie sont françaises.
Pierre et Alexandre sont français aussi.

Les quatre copains sont de Rouen.
Ils sont élèves dans le même lycée.
Ils sont tous très sympathiques.

Comment sont les cours? 🎧

la salle de classe

la classe

les élèves

Le cours de français est facile.
La prof n'est pas trop stricte. Juste un peu.

Mais les cours de sciences sont vraiment difficiles. Toi, tu es d'accord ou pas?

Non, je ne suis pas d'accord. Pour moi, les cours de sciences sont très faciles.

Commençons
Let's use our new words

Rennes, France

Des lycéens de Rennes

1 ## Historiette
Deux copines françaises
Inventez une histoire. *(Make up a story.)*

1. Léa et Touria sont françaises ou américaines?
2. Elles sont copines?
3. Elles sont de Rennes?
4. Elles sont élèves dans le même lycée?
5. Le lycée est à Rennes?
6. Elles sont dans la salle de classe?

2 ## Historiette
Deux copains français
Inventez une histoire. *(Make up a story.)*

1. Paul et Jamal sont français ou américains?
2. Ils sont copains?
3. Ils sont amusants?
4. Ils sont sympathiques?
5. Ils sont de Rennes?
6. Ils sont élèves dans le même lycée?

FRENCH Online

For more information about Rennes and other cities in France, go to the Glencoe French Web site: french.glencoe.com

3 **Le cours de français** Donnez des réponses personnelles. *(Give your own answers.)*

1. Qui est le/la prof de français?
2. Il/Elle est sympa?
3. Il/Elle est strict(e)?
4. Il/Elle est de quelle nationalité?
5. Le cours de français est facile ou difficile?
6. Pour toi, les cours de sciences sont faciles ou difficiles?

4 **Le prof idéal ou la prof idéale** Work with a classmate. Share ideas as to what you look for in an ideal teacher. Let your classmate know whether you agree with him or her. You may want to use some of the following words.

Un cours de français aux États-Unis

For more practice using words from ***Mots 1,*** *do Activity 4 on page H5 at the end of this book.*

Vocabulaire

Les matières

Les sciences naturelles

la biologie
la chimie
la physique

Les mathématiques (Les maths)

l'algèbre
la géométrie
la trigonométrie
le calcul

Les langues

le français
l'italien
l'espagnol
l'allemand
l'anglais
le latin

Les sciences sociales

l'histoire
la géographie
l'économie

D'autres matières

la littérature
l'informatique
la gymnastique
la musique
le dessin

En cours de français 🎧

Salut les copains!
Nous sommes américains.
Nous sommes de New York.
Et vous, vous êtes américains
aussi, n'est-ce pas?

Nous sommes tous très
forts en français!

C'est pas vrai!
Vous êtes très mauvais!

M. Boursier est le prof de français.
Maintenant, nous sommes en
cours de français.

Les nombres de 70 à 100

70 soixante-dix	80 quatre-vingts	90 quatre-vingt-dix
71 soixante et onze	81 quatre-vingt-un	91 quatre-vingt-onze
72 soixante-douze	82 quatre-vingt-deux	92 quatre-vingt-douze
73 soixante-treize	83 quatre-vingt-trois	93 quatre-vingt-treize
74 soixante-quatorze	84 quatre-vingt-quatre	94 quatre-vingt-quatorze
75 soixante-quinze	85 quatre-vingt-cinq	95 quatre-vingt-quinze
76 soixante-seize	86 quatre-vingt-six	96 quatre-vingt-seize
77 soixante-dix-sept	87 quatre-vingt-sept	97 quatre-vingt-dix-sept
78 soixante-dix-huit	88 quatre-vingt-huit	98 quatre-vingt-dix-huit
79 soixante-dix-neuf	89 quatre-vingt-neuf	99 quatre-vingt-dix-neuf
		100 cent

Commençons
Let's use our new words

Un cours de chimie à Paris

5 **Sciences ou langues?** Vrai ou faux? *(True or false?)*

1. La chimie est une science.
2. L'histoire et la géographie sont des mathématiques.
3. Le calcul est une langue.
4. Le latin et l'espagnol sont des langues.
5. Pour vous, le français est un cours obligatoire.

6 **Des cours faciles et difficiles** Donnez des réponses personnelles. *(Give your own answers.)*

1. Le cours de français est facile ou difficile?
2. Pour toi, quels sont les cours faciles?
3. Quels sont les cours difficiles?
4. Tu es fort(e) en français?
5. Tu es fort(e) en sciences?
6. Tu es très fort(e) en quelle matière?
7. Tu es assez mauvais(e) en quelle matière?

7 **Historiette** **Des élèves américains** Inventez une histoire. *(Make up a story.)*

1. Les élèves sont de quelle nationalité?
2. Ils sont élèves dans une école secondaire américaine?
3. Ils sont en cours de français?
4. Le cours de français est facile ou difficile?
5. Les élèves sont forts en français?

8 **C'est quel cours?** Identifiez le cours. *(Identify the course.)*

1. la littérature, la grammaire anglaise
2. la conversation, la culture française
3. un poème, une pièce de théâtre, une fable
4. un microbe, un animal, une plante, un microscope
5. un cercle, un rectangle, un triangle, un parallélogramme
6. un piano, un violon, un concert, un opéra
7. les montagnes, les villes, les villages, les capitales, les océans
8. la peinture, la sculpture, les statues, les artistes
9. une disquette, un moniteur, un microprocesseur, un bit

9 **Comment est la classe?** With a classmate, look at the illustration. Take turns asking each other questions about it. Use the following question words: **qui, où, quel cours, à quelle heure, comment.**

LUGAGNE-DELPON Olivier
257 r Lecourbe 15ᵉ..................01 45 58 96 30
LUGAGNE DELPON Paul
4 r Chevert 7ᵉ......................01 44 05 55 31
LUGAGNE-DELPONT Véronique
15 r Marie et Louise 10ᵉ...........01 43 41 37 85
LUGAN Benoît
34 pl Marché St-Honoré 1ᵉ........01 42 97 55 05
  » **Bernard et Gabrielle**
5 bd Grenelle 15ᵉ.................01 45 75 47 83
  » **Bruno et Stéphanie** Bat A2
64 r Compans 19ᵉ.................01 40 18 13 57
  » **Hermann**
11 r Vasco de Gama 15ᵉ.........01 45 55 44 35
  » **Jacques** 75 av Ledru Rollin 12ᵉ......01 43 47 84 57

10 **Le numéro de téléphone** Look at this page from the Paris phone book with a classmate. Give a telephone number. Your classmate will tell whose number it is. Then reverse roles.

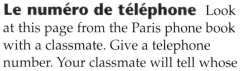

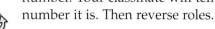

11 **Jeu** **Quelle matière?**
Work with a classmate. Think of a school subject and use whatever means necessary (voice, hands, drawings) to help your partner guess which subject it is.

Un cours de dessin à Paris

For more practice using words from **Mots 2**, *do Activity 5 on page H6 at the end of this book.*

Structure

Talking about more than one person or thing
Le pluriel: articles, noms et adjectifs

1. The articles you know (**un/une, le/la/l'**) are singular markers. The plural forms of these articles are plural markers. Study the following.

LES ARTICLES INDÉFINIS

Masculin		Féminin	
Singulier	Pluriel	Singulier	Pluriel
un garçon	des garçons	une fille	des filles
un‿ami	des‿amis	une amie	des‿amies
un collège	des collèges	une école	des‿écoles

LES ARTICLES DÉFINIS

Masculin		Féminin	
Singulier	Pluriel	Singulier	Pluriel
le garçon	les garçons	la fille	les filles
l'ami	les‿amis	l'amie	les‿amies
le collège	les collèges	l'école	les‿écoles

2. In French, you form the plural of most nouns by adding an **s**. This **s**, however, is not pronounced. It is the article **les** or **des** that lets you know the noun is plural: **un prof ➝ des prof$**; **la prof ➝ les prof$.**

3. When a noun is plural, any adjective that describes or modifies it must also be in the plural. You form the plural of most adjectives in French by adding an **s**. The **s** is not pronounced.

Singulier	Pluriel
La classe est petite.	Les classes sont petites.
La prof est patiente.	Les profs sont patientes.
Le lycée est grand.	Les lycées sont grands.
Le prof est intéressant.	Les profs sont intéressants.

Note: You do not add an **s** if the word already ends in **s**.

    un cours   **des cours**

Continuons
Let's put our words together

12 **Ils sont comment?** Mettez au pluriel.
(Put in the plural.)

—Le garçon est blond.
—Les garçons sont blonds.
1. La fille est blonde.
2. Le garçon est brun.
3. La sœur de Valentin est amusante.
4. Le frère de Stéphane est égoïste.
5. Le prof est intéressant.
6. Le cours est assez difficile.
7. La salle de classe est petite.
8. L'ami de Paul est vraiment sympathique.
9. L'élève est très intelligent.
10. L'ami de Valérie est amusant.

Deux lycéennes de Yerres, France

13 **Pour toi...** Citez... *(Name . . .)*

Pour moi, deux matières très intéressantes sont _____ et _____.
1. deux matières très intéressantes
2. deux cours très intéressants
3. deux écoles excellentes
4. deux élèves populaires
5. deux professeurs stricts
6. deux filles très intelligentes
7. deux garçons très sympas
8. deux élèves fort(e)s en géographie
9. deux élèves assez mauvais(es) en musique

Structure

14 **En commun** Inventez des points communs.
(Make up what these people have in common.)

Caroline et Marie
Elles sont amusantes, fortes en algèbre…

1. Laurent et Christian
2. Isabelle et Sandrine
3. Romain et Christophe
4. Marine et Nathalie
5. Loïc et Mathias

15   **Comme moi** Work with a classmate. Tell your partner what you and your friends have in common. Your partner will agree or disagree.

> Sue et Jennifer sont sociables… comme moi.

> Moi, je ne suis pas d'accord. Elles ne sont pas sociables du tout!

Les vrais amis sont amis pour la vie

 Talking about more than one
Le verbe **être** au pluriel

1. You have already learned the singular forms of the verb **être.** Now study the plural forms.

ÊTRE

Singulier	Pluriel
je suis	nous sommes
tu es	vous ₂ êtes
il/elle est	ils/elles sont

2.

You use **nous** when referring to yourself and another person or other people.

You use **vous** when talking to several people.

You use **ils** when referring to two or more males or to a group of males and females.

You use **elles** when referring to two or more females.

Savez-vous que... ?

You also use **ils/elles** when referring to things.

Les cours? Ils sont très faciles.

Les salles? Elles sont petites.

Continuons
Let's put our words together

16   **Vous êtes d'où?** Répétez la conversation. *(Repeat the conversation.)*

17 **Historiette** **Ils sont américains.** Complétez d'après la conversation. *(Complete according to the conversation.)*

Les deux garçons __1__ américains. Ils ne __2__ pas de New York. Ils __3__ de Boston. Boston __4__ une grande ville américaine.

Les deux filles ne __5__ pas américaines. Elles __6__ françaises. Elles __7__ de Toulouse. Toulouse __8__ une grande ville française.

18 **À vous** Répondez en utilisant **nous**. *(Choose a partner and answer for both of you using* nous.*)*

1. Vous êtes américain(e)s?
2. Vous êtes d'où?
3. Vous êtes élèves dans une école secondaire?
4. Vous êtes dans la classe de quel professeur?
5. Vous êtes fort(e)s en français?

 *For more practice using the verb **être**, do Activity 6 on page H7 at the end of this book.*

19 **Des questions** Posez des questions et répondez d'après le modèle. (*Ask and answer questions according to the model.*)

américaine / française
—**Vous êtes américaines ou françaises?**
—**Nous sommes françaises.**

1. martiniquaise / américaine
2. petit / grand
3. sociable / timide
4. brune / blonde

20 **Historiette** **L'ami de Christophe**
Complétez en utilisant **être**. (*Complete with* être.)

Je __1__ un ami de Christophe. Christophe __2__ très sympa et très amusant. Nous __3__ français, Christophe et moi. Nous __4__ de Cancale, un petit village breton (en Bretagne). Cancale __5__ vraiment très pittoresque.

Nous __6__ élèves dans un collège. Où __7__ le collège? À Dinard. Tous les deux, nous __8__ forts en anglais. La prof d'anglais, Mlle Fielding, __9__ anglaise. Elle __10__ de Liverpool. Elle __11__ assez stricte et le cours d'anglais n'__12__ pas facile. Mais les élèves de Mlle Fielding __13__ très intelligents!

21 **Vous êtes américains?** Complétez la conversation. (*Complete the conversation.*)

—Vous _____ américains, n'est-ce pas?

—Oui, nous _____ américains. Nous _____ de _____.

—Vous _____ élèves dans une école secondaire?

—Oui, et nous _____ très forts en français.

—Vraiment? Qui _____ le/la prof de français?

—C'est _____.

—Il/Elle _____ comment?

—Il/Elle _____ _____.

22 **Tous les deux** Work with a classmate. Discuss things you have in common.

—**Nous sommes sympathiques, intelligent(e)s, fort(e)s en...**

Dinard, Bretagne

Talking to people formally or informally
Tu et vous

1. As you already know, there are two ways to say *you* in French: **tu** and **vous.** You use **tu** when talking to a friend, a person your own age, or to a family member.

Éric, tu es trop timide!

Maman, tu es d'accord?

2. You use **vous** when talking to several people.

Vous deux, vous êtes d'accord?

3. You also use **vous** when talking to an older person, a person whom you do not know very well, or anyone to whom you wish to show respect.

Monsieur, s'il vous plaît! Vous êtes le professeur de musique?

Continuons
Let's put our words together

23 **Vous êtes français?** Regardez les photos et posez la question.
(Ask the people in the photographs if they are French.)

1.

2.

3.

4.

5.

6.

24 **D'autres questions** Ask the same people other questions.
You may want to use some of the following words or expressions:
d'où, de quelle nationalité, d'accord, patient, fort en.

Vous êtes sur le bon chemin. Allez-y!

Conversation

Quel prof?

Paul: Vous êtes dans la classe de Mme Martin?

Anne: Non, nous sommes dans la classe de M. Lepic.

Paul: M. Lepic?

Anne: Ben oui, le prof de maths.

Paul: Ah oui. Comment il est?

Anne: Un peu strict, mais sympa.

Paul: Oui, mais toi et Samuel, vous êtes forts en maths.

Anne: Ben, toi aussi.

Paul: Moi? Je suis très mauvais en maths. Je suis complètement nul!

Après la conversation

Répondez. (*Answer.*)

1. Anne et Samuel sont dans la classe de Mme Martin?
2. Ils sont dans la classe de quel professeur?
3. Qui est M. Lepic?
4. Il est comment?
5. Samuel et Anne sont forts en maths?
6. Et Paul, il est fort en maths?

Parlons un peu plus
Let's talk some more

 A **D'accord ou pas?** Make a chart like the one below. List all your classes and rate them. Then compare your chart with that of a classmate.

—Pour moi, le cours de français n'est pas difficile. Tu es d'accord?

—Oui, je suis d'accord. / Non, je ne suis pas d'accord. Pour moi, le cours de français est très difficile.

Cours	Pas difficile	Assez difficile	Très difficile
le français	✓		
l'algèbre			✓

 B **Jeu** **Quel cours?** Work with a classmate. He or she gives you one word about a class. Guess what class it is. If you're wrong, your partner will give you another hint until you can guess the class. Take turns.

Prononciation

Les consonnes finales

1. In French, you do not usually pronounce the final consonant you see at the end of a word. Repeat the following.

petit grand intéressant français
amusant intelligent patient blond

2. You also do not pronounce the final **s** you add to a word to make it plural. This is why a singular noun and its plural sound alike. Repeat the following pairs of words and then the sentences.

un copain → des copains une copine → des copines
le garçon → les garçons la fille → les filles

Tous les copains de Vincent sont sympathiques.
Les cours de maths sont très difficiles.

intelligent

Lectures culturelles

Deux copains haïtiens

Une plage près de Port-au-Prince, Haïti

Le français aux États-Unis

L'influence haïtienne

Bonjour! Nous sommes Abélard Jean-Baptiste et Nicole Jolicœur. Nous sommes élèves dans une école secondaire à Miami. Et pour nous, le cours de français est vraiment très facile! Pour nous, le français n'est pas une langue étrangère[1]. Nous sommes haïtiens. Nous sommes de Port-au-Prince, la capitale d'Haïti. En Haïti, il y a[2] deux langues—le français et le créole. Le créole est une langue à base de français, d'espagnol et de divers dialectes africains.

Deux amis de Montpelier

L'influence canadienne

Et nous? Nous sommes Antonine Gagnon et Donald Maillet. Nous sommes de Montpelier dans le Vermont. Comme beaucoup de personnes de la Nouvelle-Angleterre[3], nous sommes d'origine canadienne. Et pour nous, le français n'est pas une langue étrangère. Le français est la langue maternelle des Canadiens français.

[1] étrangère *foreign*
[2] il y a *there are*
[3] Nouvelle-Angleterre *New England*

L'influence «cajun»

Bonjour! Ici Alice Richard et Pierre Doucet. Nous sommes de Louisiane. Nous sommes cajuns. Nous les Cajuns, nous sommes des descendants des Acadiens. Les Acadiens sont les Français expulsés[4] de l'est du Canada par les Anglais.

L'influence cajun est assez forte en Louisiane. Il y a même[5] deux langues officielles en Louisiane—l'anglais et le français.

[4] expulsés *expelled*   [5] même *even*

Deux élèves de Louisiane

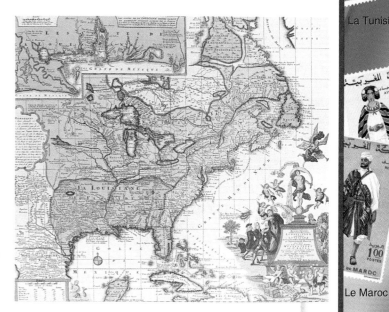

Après la lecture

A Les Haïtiens
Répondez. *(Answer.)*
1. Abélard Jean-Baptiste et Nicole Jolicœur sont d'où?
2. Pour Abélard et Nicole, le français est facile?
3. Ils sont de quelle nationalité?
4. Le créole est à base de quelles langues?

B Les descendants des Canadiens français Répondez. *(Answer.)*
1. D'où sont Antonine et Donald?
2. Montpelier est dans quel état?
3. Il y a beaucoup de personnes d'origine canadienne en Nouvelle-Angleterre?
4. Quelle est la langue maternelle des Canadiens français?

C Les Cajuns Répondez. *(Answer.)*
1. Qui sont les Cajuns?
2. Quelles sont les deux langues officielles en Louisiane?

La scolarité en France

Le collège en France est une école secondaire. Les élèves sont des collégiens. Le collège est obligatoire pour quatre ans.

Après[1] le collège, le lycée est aussi une école secondaire, mais pour trois ans. Les élèves sont des lycéens. Il y a[2] deux diplômes d'études secondaires—un diplôme professionnel après deux ans et le baccalauréat après trois ans. Le baccalauréat ou «le bac» est nécessaire pour entrer à l'université.

Voici l'emploi du temps de Louise Belleroche. Elle est en troisième, l'équivalent de *ninth grade*. Il y a combien de[3] cours en troisième en France?

[1] Après *After*   [2] Il y a *There are*   [3] combien de *how many*

Lycée Pasteur,
Neuilly, France

A La scolarité Vrai ou faux?
(True or false?)

1. En France un collège est une petite université.
2. Le collège n'est pas obligatoire.
3. Le lycée est une école secondaire.
4. Le «bac» est un diplôme universitaire.
5. Le «bac» est nécessaire pour entrer à l'université.

B L'emploi du temps de Louise Répondez. *(Answer.)*

1. Il y a combien de cours?
2. Le cours de maths est quels jours? À quelle heure?
3. Et le cours d'anglais?
4. Et le cours de français?
5. Et le cours de biologie?
6. Et le cours d'histoire/géographie?
7. Et le cours de dessin?

Lecture supplémentaire 2

Un message

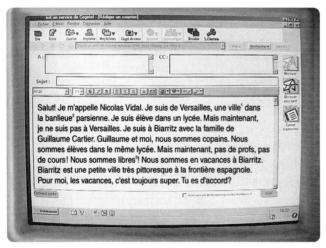

Salut! Je m'appelle Nicolas Vidal. Je suis de Versailles, une ville[1] dans la banlieue[2] parisienne. Je suis élève dans un lycée. Mais maintenant, je ne suis pas à Versailles. Je suis à Biarritz avec la famille de Guillaume Cartier. Guillaume et moi, nous sommes copains. Nous sommes élèves dans le même lycée. Mais maintenant, pas de profs, pas de cours! Nous sommes libres[3]! Nous sommes en vacances à Biarritz. Biarritz est une petite ville très pittoresque à la frontière espagnole. Pour moi, les vacances, c'est toujours super. Tu es d'accord?

[1] ville *town*   [2] banlieue *suburbs*   [3] libres *free*

Biarritz, France

Versailles, France

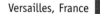

Après la lecture

A Deux copains Répondez. *(Answer.)*
1. D'où est Nicolas?
2. Où est Versailles?
3. Où est Nicolas maintenant?
4. Il est à Biarritz avec qui?
5. Les deux garçons sont copains?
6. Les deux copains sont en vacances? Où?

B Un peu de géographie
Vrai ou faux? *(True or false?)*
1. Versailles est sur la Côte d'Azur.
2. Versailles est dans la banlieue parisienne.
3. Biarritz est aussi dans la banlieue parisienne.
4. Biarritz est à la frontière espagnole.
5. Biarritz est en Espagne.
6. Biarritz est en France.

La Belgique

La Tunisie

Maroc

Le Mali

CONNEXIONS

Les sciences naturelles

La biologie, la physique et la chimie

Sciences are an important part of the school curriculum. If you like science, it would be fun to be able to read some scientific material in French. You will see how easy it is. It's easy because you already have some background in science from your science courses. In addition, many scientific terms are cognates.

La biologie

La biologie est l'étude des organismes vivants. En biologie, il y a trois catégories importantes: l'anatomie, la zoologie et la botanique. L'anatomie est l'étude du corps humain. La zoologie est l'étude des animaux et la botanique est l'étude des plantes.

La botanique est l'étude des plantes.

La zoologie est l'étude des animaux.

La physique et la chimie

La physique est l'étude de la matière et de l'énergie. La chimie est l'étude des caractéristiques des éléments.

Les savants

Dans un laboratoire, le savant (le biologiste, le chimiste ou le physicien) observe et analyse des phénomènes scientifiques. Le biologiste, par exemple, observe et analyse des microbes[1], des cellules, des bactéries et des virus à l'aide d'un microscope.

[1] microbes *germs*

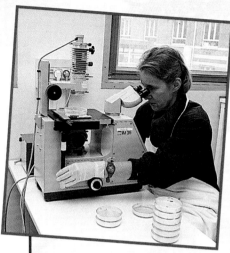
Une biologiste

Des élèves dans un laboratoire à Paris

Après la lecture

A Des termes scientifiques
Préparez une liste. *(Make a list of scientific terms you recognize in the reading.)*

B C'est quelle science? Répondez. *(Answer.)*

1. l'étude des animaux
2. l'étude des plantes
3. l'étude de la matière et de l'énergie
4. l'étude du corps humain

C Stratégie de lecture Note that the words in each of the following groups are all related to one another. If you know the meaning of one word, you can guess the meanings of the others. Can you figure them all out?

1. la biologie, un(e) biologiste, biologique
2. analyser, une analyse, analytique
3. un microbe, microbien
4. une bactérie, bactérien
5. un virus, viral

C'est à vous

Use what you have learned

L'école internationale de Paris

1 **Nous**

✔ *Describe yourself and someone else*

Work with a classmate. You are at an international student gathering in France. You and your partner introduce yourselves to the other students. Try to get to know one another better. You may use the following as a guide:

- say who you are
- give your nationality
- tell where you're from
- give the name of your school
- describe some of your qualities or faults

2 **L'école idéale**

✔ *Talk about school*

Work with a classmate. Describe what for each of you is an ideal school. Say as much as you can about the teachers, classes, and students. Determine whether or not you share the same opinions.

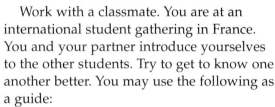

Lycée Janson de Sailly, Paris

3 Un message
✔ *Write about your classes and friends*

You answer an e-mail message from a student in France who wants to know about your life in the United States. Give him or her as many details as possible about your classes and your friends.

Collège de Montois, Noyen-sur-Seine

Writing Strategy

Keeping a journal There are many kinds of journals you can keep, each having a different purpose. One type of journal is the kind in which you write about daily events and record your thoughts and impressions about these events. It's almost like "thinking aloud." By keeping such a journal, you may find that you discover something new that you were not aware of.

4 Les cours et les professeurs

You've been in school for about a month. You've had a chance to get to know what your courses are like and to become familiar with your teachers. Create a journal entry about school. Try to write about your classes, the days and times of each, what the class is like, who the teacher is, and what he or she is like. When you have finished, reread your journal entry. Did you discover anything about your courses or your teachers that you hadn't thought of before?

Assessment

Vocabulaire

1 Choisissez. *(Choose.)*

To review **Mots 1,** turn to pages 50–51.

1. Christophe et Julien sont amis. Ils sont _____.
   a. frères   b. sœurs   c. copains
2. Les deux garçons sont _____ dans un lycée français.
   a. élèves   b. profs   c. cours
3. Le cours de français n'est pas difficile. Le cours de français est _____.
   a. strict   b. facile   c. comique
4. La prof n'est pas très stricte. Juste _____.
   a. difficile   b. d'accord   c. un peu

2 Vrai ou faux? *(True or false?)*

To review **Mots 2,** turn to pages 54–55.

5. L'algèbre et la musique sont des sciences naturelles.
6. L'économie est une langue.
7. Pour les élèves américains, l'anglais est un cours obligatoire.
8. L'allemand est une science sociale.

Structure

3 Mettez au pluriel. *(Put in the plural.)*

To review plural articles, nouns, and adjectives, turn to page 58.

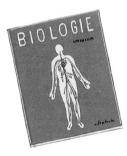

9. Le copain de Lucie est amusant.
   _____ copain_____ de Lucie sont amusant_____.
10. La sœur de Monique est intelligente.
    _____ sœur_____ de Monique sont intelligente_____.
11. L'ami de Frédéric est français.
    _____ ami_____ de Frédéric sont français_____.
12. Le prof de biologie est strict.
    _____ prof_____ de biologie sont strict_____.
13. La fille brune est américaine.
    _____ fille_____ brune_____ sont américaine_____.

4 **Complétez avec «être».**
(Complete with être.)

To review the verb **être**, turn to page 60.

14. Nous ____ élèves dans une école secondaire américaine.
15. Ils ____ élèves dans un lycée français.
16. Vous ____ élèves où?
17. Les élèves de Madame Fauvet ____ intelligents.
18. Qui ____ le prof de géométrie?

Culture

To review this cultural information, turn to pages 68–69.

5 **Choisissez.** *(Choose.)*

19. En Haïti, il y a deux langues—le français et ____.
   a. l'anglais   **b.** le créole   **c.** l'espagnol
20. Il y a beaucoup d'influence «cajun» en ____.
   a. Nouvelle-Angleterre   **b.** Haïti   **c.** Louisiane

La Nouvelle-Orléans, Louisiane

Vocabulaire

Identifying a person or thing

un professeur	une copine	un cours
un(e) prof	un lycée	une classe
un copain	une salle de classe	une matière

Identifying school subjects

les sciences naturelles	les langues *(f. pl.)*	les sciences sociales	d'autres matières
la biologie	le français	l'histoire *(f.)*	la littérature
la chimie	l'espagnol *(m.)*	la géographie	l'informatique *(f.)*
la physique	l'italien *(m.)*	l'économie *(f.)*	la gymnastique
les mathématiques,	l'allemand *(m.)*		la musique
les maths *(f. pl.)*	l'anglais *(m.)*		le dessin
l'algèbre *(f.)*	le latin		
la géométrie			
la trigonométrie			
le calcul			

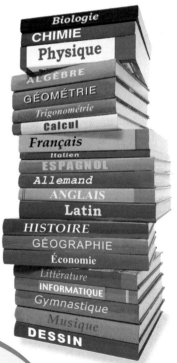

Describing teachers, students, and courses

facile	strict(e)	fort(e)
difficile	intéressant(e)	mauvais(e)

Agreeing and disagreeing

Tu es d'accord?
Oui, je suis d'accord.
Non, je ne suis pas d'accord.
C'est vrai.
Ce n'est pas vrai. C'est pas vrai.

Other useful words and expressions

en cours de (français, maths, etc.)
même
tous
trop
juste un peu

How well do you know your vocabulary?

- Choose your favorite school subject. Choose words to describe this subject.
- Use these words to describe the subject and your teacher.

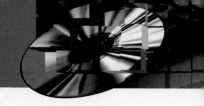

Technotour
BON VOYAGE!

Avant de visionner

In this video episode, Vincent is at the lycée Louis-le-Grand, interviewing students there about their teachers and courses.

Vincent et une amie, Élodie,
au lycée Louis-le-Grand

Manu et Vincent en cours de chimie

FRENCH ONLINE

À découvrir

The lycée Louis-le-Grand is situated in the heart of Paris. Learn more about Paris online.

L'île de la Cité, le centre historique de Paris

FRENCH
Online

In the Chapter 2 Internet Activity, you will have a chance to learn more about schools in the Francophone world. To begin your virtual adventure, go to the Glencoe French Web site: **french.glencoe.com**

FÊTE DU TIMBRE

LA POSTE 2000

3,00F 0,46€

RF

Pendant et après les cours

Objectifs

In this chapter you will learn to:

✔ *talk about what you do in school*

✔ *talk about what you and your friends do after school*

✔ *identify and shop for school supplies*

✔ *talk about what you don't do*

✔ *tell what you and others like and don't like to do*

✔ *discuss schools in France*

Pierre Auguste Renoir *La lecture*

PRIORITAIRE
PRIOR

PAR AVION / AIR MAIL

Miss M
7 Elm
Arsdsl
États

Vocabulaire

Une journée à l'école

une maison
une rue **quitter**

arriver

Patrick habite près de Paris.
Il habite rue Saint-Paul.
Patrick quitte la maison.

Le matin, Patrick arrive à l'école.
À quelle heure?
Il arrive à l'école à huit heures.
Il passe la journée à l'école.

parler
un CD
écouter

Le prof parle.
Les élèves écoutent bien.
Les élèves étudient.

Les élèves regardent une vidéo.
Deux élèves écoutent des cassettes.

la main

Moi, je n'aime pas du tout les examens. Je déteste les examens.

Note

The expression **passer un examen** is an example of a false cognate (**un faux ami**). It means "to take an exam," not "to pass an exam."

Vincent passe un examen.
Il n'aime pas les examens.

Sophie lève la main.
Elle pose une question.

la cantine

Les élèves déjeunent à la cantine.
Ils déjeunent à midi (12 h).

jouér

la cour

Note

The popular word **rigoler** means "to joke around."
Tu rigoles! means "You don't mean it!" or "You're joking!"

Pendant la récré(ation) les élèves
    jouent dans la cour.
Il y a beaucoup d'élèves dans la cour.
Ils rigolent.
Ils parlent entre les cours.

VOCABULAIRE

quatre-vingt-trois ⚜ **83**

Commençons
Let's use our new words

1 **Historiette** **Un élève parisien**
Inventez une histoire. *(Make up a story.)*

1. Fabien est de Paris?
2. Il habite rue Jacob?
3. Il quitte la maison à quelle heure?
4. Il passe la journée où?
5. Il déjeune à la cantine?

2 **Toujours des questions**
Répondez. *(Answer.)*

Le matin, les élèves arrivent à l'école à huit heures.

1. Qui arrive à l'école?
2. Ils arrivent où?
3. Ils arrivent à quelle heure?
4. Ils arrivent à l'école le matin ou à midi?

Les élèves déjeunent à la cantine à midi.

5. Qui déjeune?
6. Les élèves déjeunent où?
7. Ils déjeunent à la cantine à quelle heure?

Un lycéen français

3 **Historiette** **En classe** Complétez. *(Complete.)*

En classe la prof __1__ et les élèves __2__. Anne est une élève excellente. Elle __3__ beaucoup. Sophie est dans la même classe. Elle __4__ la main et __5__ une question.

Vincent __6__ un examen. Les examens sont difficiles. Vincent n'__7__ pas les examens. Il __8__ les examens.

4 Pardon! Préparez une petite conversation d'après le modèle.
(Prepare a short conversation according to the model.)

Sandrine écoute une cassette.

Pardon? Qu'est-ce qu'elle écoute?

1. Sandrine écoute un CD.
2. Sandrine regarde une vidéo.
3. Sandrine lève la main.
4. Sandrine pose une question.
5. Sandrine passe un examen.
6. Sandrine adore les vidéos.

5 Historiette Dans la cour Répondez. *(Answer.)*

1. Les élèves sont dans la cour?
2. Ils sont dans la cour pendant la récréation?
3. Ils parlent entre les cours?
4. Ils jouent où?
5. Ils rigolent avec les copains?
6. Ils déjeunent dans la cour?

6 En classe With a classmate, look at the illustration. Take turns saying as much as you can about it.

For more practice using words from **Mots 1**, *do Activity 7 on page H8 at the end of this book.*

Vocabulaire

Des fournitures scolaires

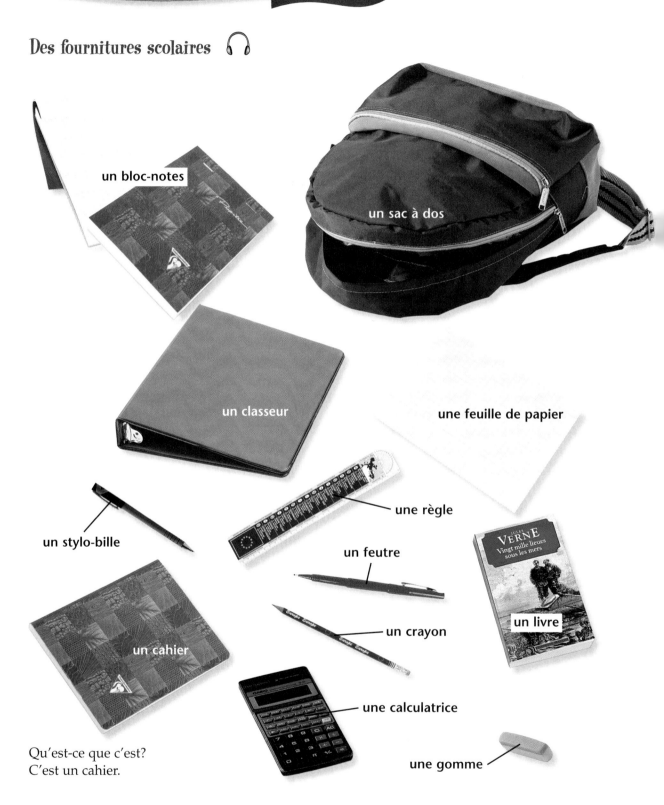

un bloc-notes

un sac à dos

un classeur

une feuille de papier

une règle

un stylo-bille

un feutre

un livre

un crayon

un cahier

une calculatrice

une gomme

Qu'est-ce que c'est?
C'est un cahier.

Après les cours 🎧

"Le sac à dos, c'est combien, s'il vous plaît?"

"Vingt dollars cinquante."

la caisse

payer

un magasin

Lucette travaille après les cours.
Elle travaille dans une papeterie.
Combien d'heures par semaine?
Dix heures.

Sylvain regarde un sac à dos.
Il demande combien coûte le sac à dos.
Il achète le sac à dos.
Il paie à la caisse.

Les nombres de 100 à 1 000

100 cent	400 quatre cents
101 cent un	500 cinq cents
102 cent deux	600 six cents
200 deux cents	700 sept cents
220 deux cent vingt	800 huit cents
300 trois cents	900 neuf cents
350 trois cent cinquante	1000 mille

Après les cours, Patrick ne travaille pas.
Il rentre à la maison l'après-midi.
Il rentre chez lui.

Il écoute la radio.
Il parle un peu au téléphone.

VOCABULAIRE

Commençons
Let's use our new words

7 **Des fournitures scolaires** Préparez une liste de fournitures scolaires. (*Make a list of important school supplies.*)

8 **Historiette** **Loïc est français.**
Répondez d'après l'indication.
(*Answer according to the cues.*)

1. Loïc est français ou américain? (français)
2. Il habite où? (près de Paris)
3. Il travaille après les cours? (non)
4. Il rentre chez lui après les cours? (oui)
5. Qu'est-ce qu'il écoute? (la radio)
6. Qu'est-ce qu'il regarde? (une vidéo)
7. Il parle au téléphone? (oui)
8. Avec qui? (les copains)

Une papeterie,
Montréal, Canada

9 **Historiette** **Dans une papeterie** Inventez une histoire.
(*Make up a story.*)

1. Catherine est canadienne?
2. Elle travaille après les cours?
3. Elle travaille combien d'heures par semaine?
4. Elle travaille dans une papeterie?
5. Où est la papeterie?
6. Qu'est-ce qu'il y a dans une papeterie?
7. Il y a beaucoup d'élèves dans la papeterie?
8. Un garçon paie à la caisse?
9. Un cahier coûte combien?

10 **Historiette** **À la papeterie** Choisissez la bonne réponse. *(Choose the correct completion.)*

1. Sandrine ____ dans une papeterie.
   a. étudie   **b.** habite   **c.** travaille
2. Elle ____ à un client au téléphone.
   a. écoute   **b.** parle   **c.** paie
3. Les élèves ____ des fournitures scolaires dans la papeterie.
   a. travaillent   **b.** rentrent   **c.** regardent
4. Un garçon ____ un cahier.
   a. regarde   **b.** joue   **c.** rentre
5. Il ____ une calculatrice pour le cours de maths.
   a. passe   **b.** quitte   **c.** achète
6. La calculatrice ____ six dollars canadiens.
   a. paie   **b.** habite   **c.** coûte
7. Le garçon ____ à la caisse.
   a. quitte   **b.** coûte   **c.** paie

11 **Pour la rentrée des classes** Work with a classmate. It's back-to-school time and you're buying the school supplies below. Take turns being the customer and the salesperson.

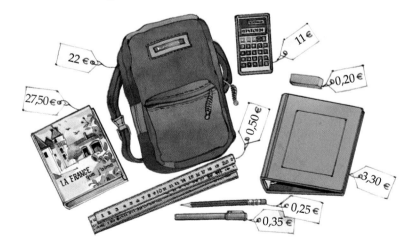

12 **Jeu** **Qu'est-ce que c'est?** Work with a classmate. Have your partner close his or her eyes. Hand your partner a school supply. Have your partner guess what it is. Take turns.

For more practice using words from Mots 2, do Activity 8 on page H9 at the end of this book.

Structure

Talking about people's activities
Les verbes réguliers en **-er** au présent

1. A word that expresses an action or a state is a verb. **Parler** (*to speak*), **écouter** (*to listen to*), and **aimer** (*to like*) are verbs in the infinitive form. They are called regular verbs because they all follow a regular pattern. Their infinitives end in **-er.**

2. French verbs change endings with each subject. To form the stem to which the endings are added, you drop the **-er** from the infinitive.

Infinitive	Stem
parler	parl-
écouter	écout-
aimer	aim-

3. You add the ending for each subject to the stem. Note that, although the endings for the **je, tu, il,** and **ils** forms are spelled differently, they are pronounced the same.

		PARLER	AIMER
je	parl -e	je parle	j' aime
tu	parl -es	tu parles	tu aimes
il/elle	parl -e	il/elle parle	il/elle aime
nous	parl -ons	nous parlons	nous ᵤaimons
vous	parl -ez	vous parlez	vous ᵤaimez
ils/elles	parl -ent	ils/elles parlent	ils ᵤ/elles ᵤaiment

4. You will see and hear the word **on** a great deal. **On** has several meanings, such as "we," "they," and "people." **On** always takes the **il/elle** form of the verb. In spoken French, people use **on** more often than **nous.**

> On parle français en France.
> On travaille beaucoup.
> On arrive à l'école le matin.

Attention!

There is elision when **je** or **ne** is followed by a verb that begins with a vowel or silent **h.**
J'habite à Paris.   **Je n'habite pas à Lyon.**
J'aime les maths.   **Je n'aime pas les sciences.**

There is a liaison with all plural subject pronouns and a verb that begins with a vowel or silent **h.** The **s** on the pronoun is pronounced as a **z.**
nous ᵤétudions   vous ᵤaimez   ils ᵤhabitent

Continuons
Let's put our words together

Un cours de français aux États-Unis

13 **Historiette** **Un Américain**
Inventez une histoire. *(Make up a story.)*

1. Kevin est français ou américain?
2. Il habite à Paris ou à Chicago?
3. Il parle anglais ou français?
4. Il étudie quelle langue?
5. Il parle beaucoup en classe?
6. Il travaille bien à l'école?

14 **Historiette** **Les élèves ou les profs?** Suivez le modèle. *(Follow the model.)*

—**Qui arrive à l'école le matin?**
—**Les élèves et les profs arrivent à l'école.**

1. Qui parle en classe?
2. Qui écoute quand le prof parle?
3. Qui écoute des cassettes?
4. Qui passe des examens?
5. Qui étudie beaucoup?
6. Qui lève la main?
7. Qui pose des questions?
8. Qui rigole dans la cour?

15 **Aux États-Unis** Un(e) élève français(e) pose des questions à un(e) élève américain(e). *(You are a French student. Ask a classmate about life in the United States.)*

On arrive à l'école à quelle heure?

On arrive à l'école à huit heures.

1. On arrive à l'école à quelle heure?
2. On quitte l'école à quelle heure?
3. On travaille beaucoup à l'école?
4. On aime beaucoup les examens?
5. On travaille après les cours?
6. On écoute des CD?
7. On regarde la télé?
8. On parle au téléphone?

16 **Tu parles français?** Répétez la conversation.
(Repeat the conversation.)

Bruxelles, Belgique

Sue: Tu n'es pas français, toi?

Luc: Non, je ne suis pas français.

Sue: Mais tu parles français!

Luc: Bien sûr que je parle français.

Sue: Et comment ça, si tu n'es pas français?

Luc: Mais je suis belge.

Sue: Ah, c'est vrai. On parle français en Belgique.

17 **Historiette** **À votre tour!** Donnez des réponses personnelles. *(Give your own answers.)*

1. Tu habites dans quelle ville?
2. Tu quittes la maison à quelle heure le matin?
3. Tu arrives à l'école à quelle heure?
4. Est-ce que tu parles français avec les copains?
5. Tu aimes quelles matières?
6. Tu aimes quels profs?
7. Tu détestes quelles matières?
8. Tu travailles après les cours?
9. Tu parles beaucoup avec les copains au téléphone?
10. Tu regardes la télé?

18 **Pardon?** Posez des questions d'après le modèle. *(Ask questions according to the model.)*

Nous écoutons des CD.

Pardon? Qu'est-ce que vous écoutez?

1. Nous détestons les examens.
2. Nous regardons la télé.
3. Nous regardons des magazines.
4. Nous écoutons la radio.
5. Nous aimons l'école.
6. Nous étudions l'espagnol.

19 **Nous tous** Donnez des réponses personnelles en utilisant **nous.** (*Give answers about you and your classmates. Use nous.*)

1. Vous arrivez à l'école à quelle heure le matin?
2. Vous quittez l'école à quelle heure l'après-midi?
3. Vous passez combien d'heures à l'école?
4. Vous aimez les cours?
5. Vous écoutez bien quand le professeur parle en classe?
6. Vous aimez ou vous détestez les examens?

20 **Historiette** **À l'école** Complétez. (*Complete.*)

Nous __1__ (arriver) à l'école à sept heures et demie. Et vous, vous __2__ (arriver) à quelle heure? Avant les cours, j'__3__ (aimer) parler un peu avec les copains. On __4__ (rigoler). Mais en classe, non! On __5__ (travailler) beaucoup. Moi, j'__6__ (écouter) bien quand les profs __7__ (parler). Et toi, tu __8__ (travailler) beaucoup aussi? Tu __9__ (passer) des examens? Tu __10__ (aimer) les examens ou pas?

21 **Une journée typique** Work with a classmate. Tell each other about a typical school day. Find out what activities you have in common.

22 **Tu travailles ou pas?** Get together in small groups and find out who works after school in your group. Find out where, how many hours a week, etc. Here are some words you may want to use.

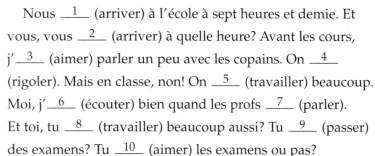

 *For more practice using -**er** verbs in the present, do Activity 9 on page H10 at the end of this book.*

Structure

Talking about what you don't do
La négation des articles indéfinis

In the negative, the indefinite articles **un, une,** and **des** change to **de** (or **d'**).

Affirmatif	Négatif
Julie regarde un CD.	Éric ne regarde pas de CD.
Julie regarde une vidéo.	Éric ne regarde pas de vidéo.
Julie regarde des photos.	Éric ne regarde pas de photos.

Attention!

Note the elision with **de.**
Je suis content: pas
d'examen aujourd'hui!

Continuons
Let's put our words together

23 **En classe** Répondez que non. *(Answer with* non.*)*

1. Tu écoutes un CD?
2. Tu regardes une vidéo?
3. Tu poses des questions?
4. Tu écoutes des cassettes?
5. Tu passes un examen aujourd'hui?

24 **Historiette** **Dans une papeterie**
Répondez d'après les indications. *(Answer according to the cues.)*

1. René est dans une papeterie? (oui)
2. Il regarde un feutre et un cahier? (oui)
3. Il achète un stylo-bille? (non)
4. Il achète un feutre? (oui)
5. Il achète une cassette? (non)
6. Il achète une vidéo? (oui)

25 **J'achète ou je n'achète pas.** Work with a classmate. Take turns telling what you buy or don't buy.

Discussing likes and dislikes
Verbe + infinitif

1. In French when the verbs **aimer, adorer,** and **détester** are followed by another verb, the second verb is in the infinitive form.

> **Il aime rigoler.**
> **J'adore écouter la radio.**
> **On déteste travailler.**

2. In a negative sentence, the **ne… pas** goes around the first verb.

> **Vous n'aimez pas travailler?**

Continuons
Let's put our words together

26 **Tu aimes travailler?** Posez les questions suivantes à un copain ou une copine. (*Ask a classmate the following questions.*)

—**Tu aimes travailler?**

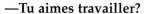

—**Bien sûr. J'aime beaucoup travailler./**
  Non, pas du tout. Je déteste travailler.

1. Tu aimes regarder la télé?
2. Tu aimes écouter la radio?
3. Tu aimes étudier?
4. Tu aimes rigoler?
5. Tu aimes parler au téléphone?

27 **On aime ou on n'aime pas!**
Work with a classmate. Tell some things you like and don't like to do.

N° 16

5
La Cinquième
LE MENSUEL DES PROGRAMMES

Semaine spéciale **orientation**

À l'occasion du Salon du lycéen et de l'étudiant, La Cinquième organise une semaine exceptionnelle destinée à informer les futurs étudiants sur le fonctionnement de l'université.

SÉRIE
Flipper, l'ami des enfants

PATRIMOINE
Raconte-moi la France

CANNES
50 jours pour 50 Palmes

Vous êtes sur le bon chemin. Allez-y!

Conversation

Un élève français aux États-Unis

Carol: En France, tu arrives à quelle heure à l'école le matin?

Cédric: Moi, j'arrive à l'école vers sept heures et demie.

Carol: Et les cours commencent à quelle heure?

Cédric: À huit heures. J'aime parler un peu avec les copains avant la classe.

Carol: Et tu quittes l'école à trois heures?

Cédric: À trois heures! Tu rigoles! En France on quitte l'école à cinq heures.

Carol: À cinq heures! C'est pas vrai!

Cédric: Si, c'est vrai.

Après la conversation

Répondez. (*Answer.*)

1. En France, Cédric arrive à l'école à quelle heure?
2. Cédric parle avec une amie américaine ou française?
3. Les cours de Cédric commencent à quelle heure?
4. Cédric quitte l'école à quelle heure?
5. Et Carol, elle quitte l'école à quelle heure?

Parlons un peu plus
Let's talk some more

A **Comparaisons** With a classmate, look at the illustrations. Then compare your own daily school habits with those of the students in the illustrations.

B **Jeu** **Les nombres** Give some numbers in a mathematical pattern but leave one out. Your partner will guess what the missing number is. Take turns. Use the model as a guide.

—**deux cents, quatre cents, _____, huit cents**
—**six cents**

Prononciation

Les sons /**é**/ et /**è**/ 🎧

élève

1. There is an important difference in the way French and English vowels are pronounced. When you say the French word **des,** your mouth is tense, in one position. You can repeat the sound /**é**/ many times without moving your mouth at all. But when you pronounce the English word *day*, your mouth is relaxed and you actually say two vowel sounds.

2. Listen to the word **élève.** It has two distinct vowel sounds. The sound /**é**/ is "closed" and the sound /**è**/ is "open." This describes the positions of the mouth for each sound. Repeat the following.

Le son /é/: **la télé   l'école   la journée   parler   écoutez**
Le son /è/: **après   la cassette   vous êtes   le collège**

Après l'école, les élèves aiment écouter des cassettes.
Elles aiment regarder la télé.

CONVERSATION

quatre-vingt-dix-sept ⚜ **97**

Lectures culturelles

Une journée avec Jacqueline

Jacqueline est une élève française. Elle habite rue Jacob à Paris. La rue Jacob est dans le Quartier latin, tout près de[1] la Sorbonne. La Sorbonne est une université célèbre[2] à Paris. Le Quartier latin est un quartier très fréquenté par les étudiants d'université et les lycéens.

[1] tout près de *very near*
[2] célèbre *famous*

Reading Strategy

Using pictures and photographs

Before you begin to read, look at the pictures, photographs, or any other visuals that accompany a reading. By doing this, you can often tell what the reading selection is about before you actually read it.

Une librairie, boulevard Saint-Michel, Paris

La Sorbonne, Paris

La Polynésie française

Tahiti

Haïti

Jacqueline est élève au lycée Louis-le-Grand. Le matin, elle quitte la maison à sept heures et demie. Les cours commencent à huit heures. Jacqueline passe la journée au lycée. Comme tous[3] les lycéens, Jacqueline travaille beaucoup, à Louis-le-Grand et à la maison. À la récréation, Jacqueline retrouve[4] des copains dans la cour. Ils parlent et ils rigolent un peu. À midi, ils déjeunent à la cantine. Ils ne rentrent pas à la maison pour déjeuner.

Jacqueline quitte le lycée à cinq heures de l'après-midi. Et vous, vous quittez l'école à quelle heure?

[3] Comme tous *Like all*
[4] retrouve *meets, gets together with*

Lycée Louis-le-Grand, Paris

Après la lecture

A Une élève française Répondez. *(Answer.)*
1. Qui est Jacqueline?
2. Elle habite où?
3. Jacqueline quitte la maison à quelle heure?
4. Les cours commencent à quelle heure?
5. Elle retrouve des copains où?
6. À midi, elle rentre chez elle pour déjeuner?
7. Elle déjeune avec qui?
8. Elle quitte le lycée à quelle heure?

B Paris Trouvez les informations dans la lecture.
(Find the information in the reading.)
1. la rue où Jacqueline habite
2. le nom d'une université célèbre à Paris
3. un quartier de Paris fréquenté par les étudiants et les lycéens
4. le nom du lycée de Jacqueline

Qui travaille?

Le centre commercial «Place de la Cathédrale»

   Antoine est canadien. Il est québécois. Il est de Montréal, la deuxième ville francophone du monde après Paris. Après les cours, il travaille dans une papeterie pour gagner un peu d'argent[1]. Il travaille dix heures par semaine. La papeterie où il travaille est dans le centre commercial[2] «Place de la Cathédrale». C'est un très grand centre commercial souterrain[3].

Un restaurant fast-food, Montréal

   Aux États-Unis et au Québec aussi, un grand nombre d'élèves travaillent après les cours. Ils travaillent dans un magasin, dans un supermarché ou dans un restaurant fast-food (de restauration rapide). Ils gagnent de l'argent pour acheter des CD, des cassettes, un blue jean. En France, non. Très peu de collégiens ou de lycéens travaillent après les cours. C'est assez rare. Certains travaillent, mais seulement pendant les vacances. Mais… ils sont à l'école jusqu'à cinq heures de l'après-midi!

[1] gagner un peu d'argent *to earn a little money*
[2] centre commercial *mall*
[3] souterrain *underground*

Après la lecture

Au Québec Exprimez d'une autre façon.
(Express another way.)
1. Antoine est *du Canada.*
2. Montréal est la *seconde* ville francophone du monde.
3. Antoine travaille après *l'école.*
4. C'est un *immense* centre commercial.
5. Aux États-Unis, *beaucoup* d'élèves travaillent.
6. *Pas beaucoup* de lycéens français travaillent après les cours.

Lecture supplémentaire 2

Un groupe de rap-Manau

Quand les collégiens ou les lycéens français rentrent à la maison l'après-midi, qu'est-ce qu'ils écoutent? Eh bien, ils écoutent la même musique que les élèves américains. Ils écoutent du rap, par exemple.

Manau, c'est un groupe de rap très populaire chez les collégiens français. Et Manau n'est pas un groupe de rap ordinaire. C'est un groupe de rap «celtique». Les instruments de musique sont la cornemuse[1], le violon, la harpe… Les chansons[2] de Manau parlent de mythes et légendes celtes avec des druides et des dolmens.

Les deux garçons du groupe, Cédric et Martial, sont copains. Le musicien, c'est Cédric: Cédric est le compositeur de la musique. Et le texte, c'est Martial: Martial est l'auteur des paroles[3].

Les deux garçons sont de la région parisienne. Mais les mères[4] de Cédric et Martial sont de Bretagne. Comme beaucoup de Bretons, elles sont d'origine celtique. Le nom du premier[5] album de Manau? *Panique Celtique!*

[1] cornemuse *bagpipes*
[2] chansons *songs*
[3] paroles *words*
[4] mères *mothers*
[5] premier *first*

FRENCH Online
For more information about music in the Francophone world, go to the Glencoe French Web site: french.glencoe.com

Un dolmen près de Carnac, Bretagne

Après la lecture

Un groupe de rap Vrai ou faux? *(True or false?)*
1. Les collégiens français n'écoutent pas la même musique que les élèves américains.
2. Manau, c'est un groupe de rap ordinaire.
3. Les chansons de Manau parlent de l'école.
4. Cédric et Martial sont de Bretagne.

La Belgique

Tunisie

Le Maroc

Le Mali

CONNEXIONS

La technologie

L'ordinateur

Some years ago computers began to revolutionize the way people conduct their lives. They have changed the way we view the world. Computers have a place in our homes, in our schools, and in the world of business.

If you are interested in computers, you may want to familiarize yourself with some basic computer vocabulary in French. Then read the information about computers on the next page.

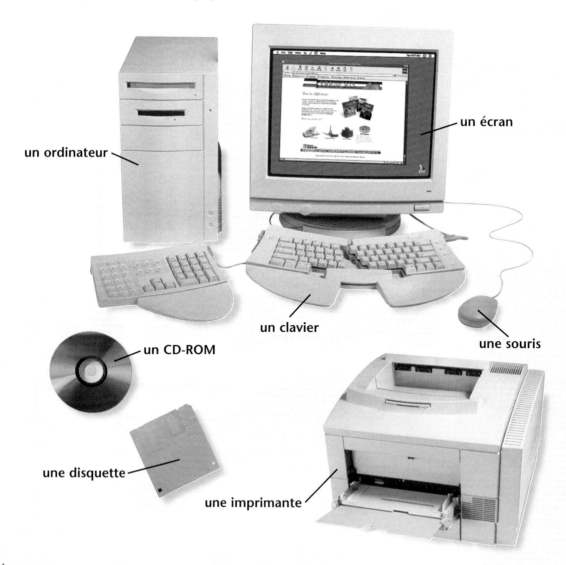

un ordinateur

un écran

un clavier

une souris

un CD-ROM

une disquette

une imprimante

L'ordinateur travaille!

Le hardware et le software

Un ordinateur exécute très rapidement les instructions d'un programme. Le hardware, c'est la partie électronique de l'ordinateur. Le software, c'est la partie programmation de l'ordinateur. Les logiciels sont des programmes. Un programme ou un logiciel est un groupe d'instructions. Un document est un fichier. L'ordinateur stocke des données[1]. On sauvegarde les documents importants sur une disquette. On utilise un modem pour connecter l'ordinateur à une ligne téléphonique. Grâce au[2] modem, un ordinateur est en liaison avec Internet et échange des informations dans le monde[3] entier.

Internet

Grâce à Internet, le monde entier est accessible. Le nombre des sites est infini. On télécharge[4] des informations sur l'histoire, l'économie, l'art, la musique et toutes sortes de domaines intéressants. Quand on navigue sur Internet, on est capable d'envoyer[5] un e-mail, parler avec des amis sur d'autres continents… Il n'y a pas de limites!

[1] données *data*
[2] Grâce au *Thanks to*
[3] monde *world*
[4] télécharge *download*
[5] envoyer *to send*

Après la lecture

A En français, s'il vous plaît.

Trouvez les mots suivants dans la lecture.
(Find the following words in the reading.)

1. hardware
2. software
3. program
4. file
5. modem
6. surf the net
7. e-mail
8. telephone line
9. site
10. save

B Une page Web Look at the monitor
on page 102. If you have access to the
Internet either at home or at school, go to
french.glencoe.com

C'est à vous

Use what you have learned

PARLER 1

Dans une papeterie

✔ *Identify and shop for school supplies*

With a classmate, take turns playing the parts of a student and a salesperson in a stationery store. Here are a few exchanges you may want to use.

—Où sont les _____, s'il vous plaît?

—Là-bas.

—Merci.

—_____, c'est combien?

—_____ euros.

—On paie à la caisse?

—Non, ici.

Une papeterie, Évry, France

2 Au café
✔ *Talk about school life in the United States*

You're seated at a café in Provins. You're chatting with a French student (your partner). He or she has some questions about school life in the United States. Have a conversation. Be sure to answer his or her questions.

3 Une journée typique
✔ *Write about a typical school day*

You can now go back to the e-mail you sent your new friend on page 75 and add more details about what a typical school day is like in the United States.

Un café, Provins, France

Writing Strategy

Preparing for an interview An interview is one way to gather information for a story or a report. A good interviewer should think about what he or she hopes to learn from the interview and prepare the questions ahead of time. The interview questions should be open-ended. Open-ended questions cannot be answered by "yes" or "no." They give the person being interviewed more opportunity to "open up" and speak freely.

4 Interview avec Charles Bauchart

Your first assignment for the school newspaper is to write an article about a new exchange student, Charles Bauchart, from Fort-de-France in Martinique. To prepare for your interview with him, write down as many questions as you can. Ask him about himself, his school, and his friends in Martinique. After you have prepared your questions, conduct the interview with a partner who plays the role of Charles. Write down your partner's answers. Then organize your notes and write your article.

Assessment

Vocabulaire

1 Choisissez. *(Choose.)*

To review **Mots 1,** turn to pages 82–83.

1. Sandrine _____ la maison à sept heures et demie.
   - **a.** quitte
   - **b.** arrive
   - **c.** habite

2. Les élèves passent _____ à l'école.
   - **a.** la cantine
   - **b.** la prof
   - **c.** la journée

3. Leïla pose une _____.
   - **a.** rue
   - **b.** question
   - **c.** maison

4. Vincent _____ des cassettes.
   - **a.** écoute
   - **b.** quitte
   - **c.** passe

5. Le prof _____ et les élèves écoutent bien.
   - **a.** travaille
   - **b.** regarde
   - **c.** parle

2 Identifiez. *(Identify.)*

To review **Mots 2,** turn to pages 86–87.

6.

7.

8.

9.

10.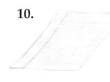

Structure

3 Complétez. *(Complete.)*

To review **-er** verbs in the present tense, turn to page 90.

11. Les élèves _____ à l'école le matin. (arriver)
12. Nous _____ entre les cours. (parler)
13. Je _____ à la cantine avec les copains. (déjeuner)
14. Luc _____ la télé après les cours. (regarder)
15. Tu _____ beaucoup à la maison? (travailler)
16. On _____ français en France. (parler)

4 Mettez à la forme négative. *(Make each sentence negative.)*

17. Sandrine achète un crayon à la papeterie.
18. Elle regarde une calculatrice.
19. Ils achètent des livres.
20. Les élèves passent un examen aujourd'hui.

To review indefinite articles in the negative, turn to page 94.

5 Choisissez. *(Choose.)*

21. On aime _____ la télé.
     a. regardent   **b.** regarder   **c.** regarde
22. Je déteste _____.
     a. travailler   **b.** travaille   **c.** travaillons

To review the use of verbs with infinitives, turn to page 95.

Culture

6 Vrai ou faux? *(True or false?)*

Une rue du Quartier latin, Paris

To review this cultural information, turn to pages 98–99.

23. La Sorbonne est une université célèbre à Paris.
24. La Sorbonne est dans le Quartier latin.
25. En France, les élèves quittent le lycée à trois heures de l'après-midi.

Vocabulaire

Getting to school

une maison	habiter
une rue	arriver
quitter	

Discussing classroom activities

passer la journée	étudier
parler	lever la main
écouter	poser une question
regarder	passer un examen

How well do you know your vocabulary?

- Identify the words and expressions that describe what you do at school and after school. Make two lists.

- Use as many words as you can from one of your lists to write a story about either your school activities or what you do after school.

Discussing recess and lunch activities

la récré(ation)	jouer
la cour	rigoler
la cantine	déjeuner

Discussing afterschool activities

rentrer à la maison	parler au téléphone
écouter la radio	travailler

Identifying school supplies

Qu'est-ce que c'est?	un stylo-bille	une calculatrice
des fournitures (f. pl.) scolaires	un feutre	une feuille de papier
un cahier	une gomme	un sac à dos
un bloc-notes	une règle	une cassette
un crayon	un livre	une vidéo
	un classeur	un CD

Shopping for school supplies

un magasin	acheter	coûter
une papeterie	payer	C'est combien?
la caisse	demander	Ça coûte combien?

Other useful words and expressions

aimer	pendant	le matin	combien de (d')
détester	entre	l'après-midi	beaucoup de (d')
après	chez	À quelle heure?	

Technotour
BON VOYAGE!

VIDÉO • Épisode 3

Avant de visionner

In this video episode, Amadou and Christine shop for school supplies before Christine's dance class at the École de Danse in the Marais.

Amadou et Christine dans la rue après les cours

Amadou et Christine dans la papeterie

FRENCH ONLINE

À découvrir

Learn more about the Marais area of Paris online.

La place des Vosges est dans le quartier du Marais, tout près de l'école de danse de Christine.

FRENCH Online

In the Chapter 3 Internet activity, you will have a chance to learn more about schools in the Francophone world. To begin your virtual adventure, go to the Glencoe French Web site:
french.glencoe.com

CHAPITRE

4

La famille et la maison

Objectifs

In this chapter you will learn to:

✔ talk about your family

✔ describe your home and neighborhood

✔ tell your age and find out someone else's age

✔ tell what belongs to you and others

✔ describe more people and things

✔ talk about families and homes in French-speaking countries

Pierre Auguste Renoir *Madame Charpentier et ses enfants*

Vocabulaire

La famille Morel 🎧

le mari — la femme

Marc — Anne

les parents

le père — la mère

le fils — la fille

les enfants

le frère — la sœur

Luc — Juliette

les petits-enfants — les grands-parents

le petit-fils — la grand-mère

la petite-fille — le grand-père

Luc — Juliette — Thérèse — André

Médor

Voici la famille Morel.
M. et Mme Morel ont deux enfants—un fils et une fille.
Les Morel ont un chien.
Leur chien est adorable.
le chien   La famille Morel n'a pas de chat.

le chat

L'anniversaire de Marie

C'est quand, l'anniversaire de Marie?
C'est le deux août.
Tout le monde a un cadeau pour Marie.
Il y a beaucoup de cadeaux.

Marie donne une fête pour son anniversaire.
Elle invite ses amis et ses cousins.

Note

In French, some of the words for family members are cognates. Can you guess who these family members are?

une tante	un oncle
une cousine	un cousin
une nièce	un neveu

Here are some words for other family members.

une belle-mère *stepmother*
un beau-père *stepfather*
une demi-sœur *half sister*
un demi-frère *half brother*

Commençons
Let's use our new words

1 **Historiette** **La famille Senghor**
Inventez une histoire. *(Make up a story.)*

1. Madame Senghor est la femme de Monsieur Senghor?
2. Monsieur Senghor est le mari de Madame Senghor?
3. La famille Senghor est française?
4. M. et Mme Senghor ont deux enfants? Ils ont un fils et une fille?
5. Les enfants ont quel âge?
6. Quelle est la date de l'anniversaire de la fille?
7. Il y a combien de personnes dans la famille Senghor?
8. Les Senghor ont un chien ou un chat?

Marie et Blaise Senghor habitent à Paris.

2 **Historiette** **L'anniversaire de Francine** Répondez d'après les indications. *(Answer according to the cues.)*

1. Elle a quel âge, Francine? (quinze ans)
2. C'est quand, son anniversaire? (aujourd'hui)
3. Quelle est la date aujourd'hui? (le deux août)
4. Qu'est-ce que Francine donne pour son anniversaire? (une fête)
5. Elle invite qui à la fête? (ses amis et ses cousins)
6. Qu'est-ce que tout le monde a pour Francine? (beaucoup de cadeaux)
7. Il y a un gâteau pour Francine? (oui)
8. Le gâteau a des bougies? (oui, quinze)

3 **La famille** Complétez. *(Complete.)*

1. Le frère de mon père est mon _____.
2. La sœur de mon père est ma _____.
3. Le frère de ma mère est mon _____.
4. La sœur de ma mère est ma _____.
5. Le fils de mon oncle et de ma tante est mon _____.
6. La fille de mon oncle et de ma tante est ma _____.
7. Le père de ma mère est mon _____.
8. Et la mère de mon père est ma _____.

4 **Moi** Choisissez la bonne réponse.
(Choose the correct answer.)

1. Moi, je suis ____ de mes grands-parents.
   a. le petit-fils   **b.** la petite-fille
2. Je suis ____ de mes parents.
   a. le fils   **b.** la fille
3. Je suis ____ de mon oncle.
   a. le neveu   **b.** la nièce
4. Je suis ____ de mes cousins.
   a. le cousin   **b.** la cousine

5 **Une famille** This country wedding, *Une noce à la campagne,* was painted by le Douanier Rousseau in 1905. Give the people names and decide who they are in relation to one another.

Une noce à la campagne

6 **Une fête d'anniversaire**
  With a classmate describe some things that take place at a typical birthday party. You may want to use some of the following words.

arriver

écouter

donner

préparer

danser

inviter

regarder

ENCORE PLUS

For more practice using words from ***Mots 1****, do Activity 10 on page H11 at the end of this book.*

Vocabulaire

La maison 🎧

une vieille maison

une fleur

un arbre

un garage

une voiture

un jardin

une terrasse

La vieille maison est très belle.
Il y a un jardin autour de la maison.
De la terrasse on a une vue du jardin.

L'immeuble 🎧

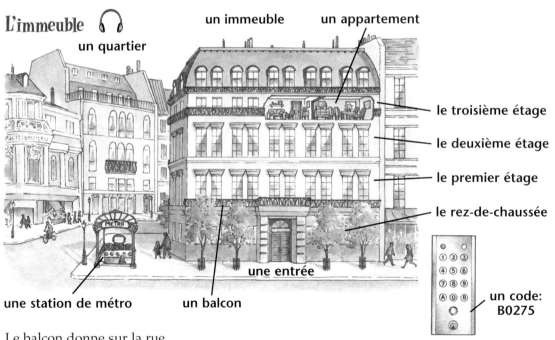

un immeuble

un appartement

un quartier

le troisième étage

le deuxième étage

le premier étage

le rez-de-chaussée

une entrée

une station de métro

un balcon

un code:
B0275

Le balcon donne sur la rue.
Les Briand ont un très joli appartement.
Il est dans un très beau quartier de Paris.
Leur immeuble est (tout) près d'une station de métro.
L'immeuble n'est pas loin d'une station de métro.

Attention! Il y a
un nouveau code!

Belle journée, hein!

une voisine

un voisin

la cour

Les voisins sont dans la cour.

un ascenseur

C'est pas rigolo!

monter à pied

un escalier

Les Briand montent toujours en ascenseur. Ils montent au troisième étage.

Les pièces de la maison 🎧

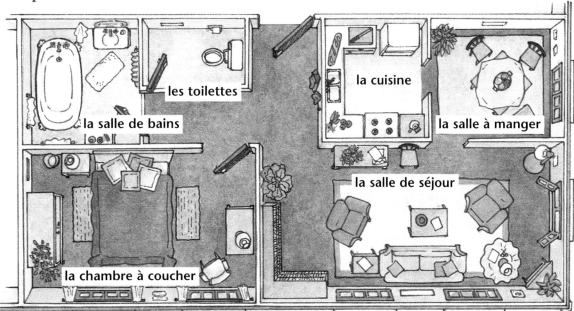

les toilettes

la salle de bains

la cuisine

la salle à manger

la salle de séjour

la chambre à coucher

Commençons
Let's use our new words

La maison de Claude Monet, Giverny

7 **Historiette** **La maison de Monet** Répondez que **oui.** (*Answer* oui.)

1. Monet est un artiste célèbre?
2. Il a une jolie maison?
3. Sa maison est grande?
4. Il y a un jardin autour de sa maison?
5. C'est un très beau jardin?
6. Il y a des arbres et des fleurs dans le jardin?

8 **Historiette** **L'appartement des Lapeyre**
Inventez une histoire. (*Make up a story.*)

1. La famille Lapeyre a un appartement dans un vieil immeuble à Paris?
2. Leur appartement est dans un beau quartier de Paris?
3. L'appartement est au rez-de-chaussée ou au troisième étage?
4. Leur balcon donne sur la rue ou sur la cour?
5. Il y a six pièces dans l'appartement de la famille Lapeyre?
6. Quelles pièces?
7. Les Lapeyre montent toujours à pied ou en ascenseur?
8. L'immeuble est près d'une station de métro ou loin d'une station de métro?
9. Il y a un code pour entrer dans l'immeuble?

FRENCH Online

For more information about French painters, go to the Glencoe French Web site:
french.glencoe.com

9 **Quelle pièce?** Choisissez la bonne réponse. (*Choose the correct answer.*)

1. On regarde la télé dans ____.
   a. la salle de bains   **b.** la salle à manger   **c.** la salle de séjour
2. On prépare le dîner dans ____.
   a. la salle à manger   **b.** la cuisine   **c.** la chambre à coucher
3. On parle avec ses voisins dans ____.
   a. la salle de bains   **b.** la cour   **c.** la chambre à coucher
4. On dîne dans ____.
   a. la salle à manger   **b.** la salle de séjour   **c.** la chambre à coucher
5. On a une belle vue ____.
   a. du balcon   **b.** de l'étage   **c.** de l'ascenseur

10 Historiette Chez moi Donnez des réponses personnelles.
(Give your own answers.)

1. Tu habites quelle rue?
2. Tu habites dans un appartement ou dans une maison privée?
3. Il y a combien de pièces dans l'appartement ou la maison?
4. Il y a combien de chambres à coucher?
5. Il y a un jardin ou un balcon?
6. La maison ou l'immeuble a un garage?
7. Il y a une voiture dans le garage?

11 Quelle maison pour nous? Work with a classmate. Your families plan to spend a month in France. Read the following real estate ads and discuss which house or apartment is good for your family.

Appartement

dans un bel immeuble, cinq pièces, deux chambres à coucher, une grande cuisine moderne, bien situé au centre-ville, près d'une station de métro

Très jolie villa

avec jardin et terrasse, vue sur l'océan, huit pièces, quatre chambres à coucher, garage pour deux voitures, située dans une rue très calme, loin de la ville

Petit bungalow

dans un vieux quartier, beaucoup de charme, trois pièces, une chambre à coucher, vingt minutes de la ville de Strasbourg

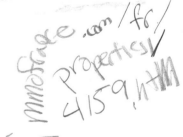

For more practice using words from **Mots 2**, *do Activity 11 on page H12 at the end of this book.*

Structure

Telling what you and others have
Avoir au présent

1. Study the following forms of the irregular verb **avoir** *(to have)*.

AVOIR	
j' ai	nous_z avons
tu as	vous_z avez
il/elle/on_n a	ils_z/elles_z ont

2. You also use the verb **avoir** to express age.

> **Tu as quel âge?**
> **Moi? J'ai quatorze ans.**

3. The expression **il y a** means "there is" or "there are."

> **Il y a un jardin autour de la maison.**
> **Il n'y a pas de fleurs dans le jardin.**

Rappelez-vous que...

Un, une, and **des** become **de (d')** after a negative. **J'ai une sœur mais Marc n'a pas de sœur.**

Continuons
Let's put our words together

12 **Historiette** **Les Binand**

Inventez une histoire.
(Make up a story.)

1. Suzanne Binand a un frère?
2. Guillaume a une sœur?
3. Monsieur et Madame Binand ont deux enfants?
4. La famille Binand a un appartement à Paris?
5. Ils ont un chat?

Deux amis, Narbonne, France

13 **Tu as un frère?** Répétez la conversation. *(Repeat the conversation.)*

Flore: Tu as un frère?
Rémi: Non, je n'ai pas de frère, mais j'ai une sœur.
Flore: Tu as une sœur? Elle a quel âge?
Rémi: Elle a quatorze ans.
Flore: Et toi, tu as quel âge?
Rémi: Moi, j'ai seize ans.
Flore: Et… vous avez un chien?
Rémi: Non, on n'a pas de chien. Mais on a un petit chat.

14 **Rémi** Complétez d'après la conversation. *(Complete according to the conversation.)*

1. Rémi n'____ pas ____ frère.
2. Il ____ une sœur.
3. Sa sœur ____ quatorze ans.
4. Rémi ____ seize ans.
5. Rémi et sa sœur n'____ pas ____ chien.
6. Mais ils ____ un petit chat adorable.

15 **Historiette** **Ma famille** Donnez des réponses personnelles. *(Give your own answers.)*

1. Tu as des frères? Tu as combien de frères?
2. Tu as des sœurs? Tu as combien de sœurs?
3. Tu as un chien ou un chat?
4. Tu as des amis?
5. Tu as des cousins?
6. Tu as combien de cousins?
7. Tu as une grande famille ou une petite famille?
8. Tu as quel âge?

Un père et son fils

16 **Dans mon sac à dos** Préparez une conversation d'après le modèle. (*Make up a conversation according to the model.*)

—Tu as des livres dans ton sac à dos?

—Oui, j'ai des livres dans mon sac à dos./
Non, je n'ai pas de livres dans mon sac à dos.

17 **Qu'est-ce que vous avez?** Préparez une conversation d'après le modèle. (*Make up a conversation according to the model.*)

une maison ou un appartement

—Vous avez une maison ou un appartement?

—Nous avons _____.

1. une grande famille ou une petite famille
2. une grande voiture ou une petite voiture
3. un chien ou un chat
4. un PC ou un Mac

18 **Historiette** **La famille Ghez** Complétez avec **avoir**.
(*Complete with avoir.*)

La famille Ghez __1__ un bel appartement à Nice. Leur appartement __2__
six pièces. Leur appartement __3__ un balcon. Le balcon donne sur la mer
Méditerranée. Du balcon les Ghez __4__ une très belle vue sur la mer.

Il y a quatre personnes dans la famille Ghez. Halima a dix-sept ans et son
frère, Ahmed, __5__ quinze ans. Halima et Ahmed __6__ un petit chat adorable.

Et toi, tu __7__ un chien ou un chat? Tu __8__ une petite ou une grande
famille? Vous __9__ un appartement ou une maison?

Moi, j'__10__ quinze ans et j'__11__ un chien adorable. J'adore mon petit chien.

Telling what belongs to you and others
Les adjectifs possessifs

1. You use a possessive adjective to show possession or ownership. Like other adjectives, a possessive adjective must agree with the noun it modifies.

2. The adjectives **mon** (*my*), **ton** (*your*), and **son** (*his/her*) each have three forms. The adjectives **notre** (*our*), **votre** (*your*), and **leur** (*their*) each have two forms.

SINGULIER		PLURIEL	
Masculin	**Féminin**	**Masculin**	**Féminin**
mon frère	ma sœur	mes frères	mes sœurs
ton frère	ta sœur	tes frères	tes sœurs
son frère	sa sœur	ses frères	ses sœurs
notre frère	notre sœur	nos frères	nos sœurs
votre frère	votre sœur	vos frères	vos sœurs
leur frère	leur sœur	leurs frères	leurs sœurs

3. **Son, sa,** and **ses** can mean "his" or "her." The adjective agrees with the item owned, not the owner.

   C'est le chien de Paul.   **C'est son chien.**
   C'est le chien de Marie.   **C'est son chien.**

4. You use **mon, ton,** or **son** before a feminine singular noun that begins with a vowel or silent **h.**

   son‿amie et mon‿amie

Une famille d'origine marocaine, Saint-André, France

> ## Attention!
>
> Liaison occurs with **mon, ton,** and **son,** as well as with all plural possessive adjectives.
>
> mon‿oncle   nos‿amis
> ton‿ami   vos‿amis
> son‿école   leurs‿amis

Continuons
Let's put our words together

19 **Historiette** **Ta famille et chez toi** Donnez des réponses personnelles. *(Give your own answers.)*

1. Où est ta maison ou ton appartement?
2. Ta maison ou ton appartement a combien de pièces?
3. Ta maison est grande ou petite? Ton appartement est grand ou petit?
4. C'est quand, ton anniversaire? Tu as quel âge?
5. Quel âge a ton frère, si tu as un frère?
6. Quel âge a ta sœur, si tu as une sœur?

Un beau chalet, Suisse

20 **J'ai une question pour toi.**
Suivez le modèle. *(Follow the model.)*

—Où est <u>ta</u> maison?
—Ma maison est dans la rue Jacob.

1. Qui est _____ amie?
2. Qui est _____ ami?
3. Où habitent _____ grands-parents?
4. _____ frère a quel âge?
5. _____ sœur a quel âge?
6. Où est _____ maison ou _____ appartement?
7. Tu aimes _____ cours de français?
8. _____ prof est sympa?

21 **Oui!** Suivez le modèle. *(Follow the model.)*

—Le frère de Marine est dans sa chambre?
—Oui, son frère est dans sa chambre.

1. Le père de Marine est dans la cuisine?
2. La sœur de Marine est blonde?
3. La sœur de Thomas est à Paris?
4. La maison de Thomas est jolie?
5. L'appartement de Marine est beau?
6. Les cousins de Thomas sont élèves?
7. Les grands-parents de Thomas ont un chien?

22 Historiette Notre école

Donnez des réponses personnelles.
(*Give your own answers.*)

1. Votre école est grande ou petite?
2. Votre école est près ou loin de votre maison?
3. Votre école a combien d'élèves?
4. Vos cours sont faciles ou difficiles?
5. Vos profs sont intéressants ou pas?
6. Vos classes sont grandes ou petites?

La Techno Parade, Paris

23 Historiette Leur maison

Complétez. (*Complete.*)

Fabien et Christophe sont frères. Ils sont dans __1__ chambre. Ils écoutent __2__ disques. __3__ collection de CD est surtout de la techno. __4__ amies, Catherine et Émilie, aiment aussi la techno. Fabien et Christophe, __5__ deux amies et __6__ copains écoutent souvent de la techno. Mais __7__ parents n'aiment pas du tout la techno.

24 Votre famille

 Draw your own family tree and say as many things as you can about your family to your classmates.

 *For more practice using **avoir** and possessive adjectives, do Activity 12 on page H13 at the end of this book.*

Describing more people and things
D'autres adjectifs

1. Most French adjectives follow the noun. Some common ones, such as **petit** and **grand,** come before the noun. The adjectives **beau** *(beautiful),* **nouveau** *(new),* and **vieux** *(old)* also come before the noun. These adjectives have several forms. Pay careful attention to both the spelling and the pronunciation of these adjectives.

SINGULIER

Féminin	Masculin (Voyelle)	Masculin (Consonne)
une belle maison	un bel appartement	un beau quartier
une nouvelle maison	un nouvel appartement	un nouveau quartier
une vieille maison	un vieil appartement	un vieux quartier

PLURIEL

Féminin	Masculin (Voyelle)	Masculin (Consonne)
de belles maisons	de beaux‿appartements	de beaux quartiers
de nouvelles maisons	de nouveaux‿appartements	de nouveaux quartiers
de vieilles maisons	de vieux‿appartements	de vieux quartiers

2. In formal French, **de** is used instead of **des** with a plural adjective that precedes the noun. In informal French, people use **des.**

Attention!

Liaison occurs with **beaux, nouveaux,** and **vieux** when they come before a word beginning with a vowel or silent **h.** The **x** is pronounced as a **z.**

mes nouveaux‿amis

les vieux‿appartements

De belles maisons,
Montréal, Canada

Continuons
Let's put our words together

25 **H**istoriette **Le bel appartement des Texier** Complétez. *(Complete.)*

1. Les Texier ont un ____ appartement dans un ____ immeuble dans un ____ quartier de la ville. (beau, vieux, beau)
2. Il y a de ____ et de ____ quartiers à Montréal. (nouveau, vieux)
3. L'appartement des Texier a de très ____ pièces. (beau)
4. Il a de ____ pièces et un très ____ balcon. (grand, beau)
5. De l'appartement il y a une très ____ vue sur la ville. (beau)
6. Les Texier ont une ____ voiture. (nouveau)
7. Leur ____ voiture est ____. (nouveau, beau)

Attention!

You have just learned that the plural of **beau** and **nouveau** is spelled with an **x**. Almost all words in French that end in **(e)au** or **eu** are spelled with **x**, not **s**, in the plural.

un cadeau	des cadeaux
un beau château	de beaux châteaux
mon neveu	mes neveux

Mettez au pluriel. *(Write in the plural.)*

1. Il a un très beau cadeau pour son neveu.
   Il a de très ____ ____ pour ses ____.
2. Le beau gâteau est aussi pour son neveu.
   Les ____ ____ sont aussi pour ses ____.
3. Il visite un beau château avec son neveu.
   Il visite de ____ ____ avec ses ____.

26 **Comme qui?** Work with a classmate. Take turns saying whom you and your family members take after. You may wish to use the following words.

Je suis intelligent(e) comme ma mère.
Mon frère est enthousiaste comme notre père.

petit

amusant blond sympa

grand beau brun

Vous êtes sur le bon chemin. Allez-y!

Conversation

Ma nouvelle adresse

Vincent:	Tu as ma nouvelle adresse?
Charlotte:	Ta nouvelle adresse? Non! Tu habites où maintenant?
Vincent:	21, avenue de la Bourdonnais.
Charlotte:	Ah, avenue de la Bourdonnais. C'est dans le 7e tout près de la tour Eiffel, non?
Vincent:	Oui. De notre balcon on a une très belle vue sur la tour Eiffel.
Charlotte:	Génial!

Après la conversation

Répondez. (*Answer.*)

1. Vincent parle à qui?
2. Charlotte a la nouvelle adresse de Vincent?
3. Quelle est sa nouvelle adresse?
4. Où est l'avenue de la Bourdonnais?
5. Est-ce que l'appartement de Vincent a un balcon?
6. De son balcon il a une vue sur la tour Eiffel?

Parlons un peu plus
Let's talk some more

A **Appartement ou maison?** Work with a classmate. Pretend you live in Rouen. One of you lives in a house, the other lives in an apartment. Decide who lives where. Then describe your house or apartment.

B **Jeu** **Qui est qui?** Work with a classmate. Write down the first names of some of your family members. Exchange lists and then ask each other who's who.

C'est qui, Paul?

C'est mon oncle. C'est le frère de ma mère.

Prononciation

Le son /ã/

1. There are three nasal vowel sounds in French: **/ã/** as in **cent, /õ/** as in **sont,** and **/ẽ/** as in **cinq.** They are called "nasal" because some air passes through the nose when they are pronounced. In this chapter, you will practice only the sound **/ã/** as in **cent.**

2. Repeat the following. Notice that there is no **/n/** sound after the nasal vowel.

Jean	cent	grand	amusant
français	parent	fantastique	

Voilà les grands-parents, les parents et les enfants.
Jean-François est fantastique. Il est français, grand, amusant.

les parents et les enfants

Lectures culturelles

Où habitent les Français?

Maisons et appartements

Beaucoup de Français qui habitent en ville, habitent dans un appartement. Il y a des appartements de toutes sortes: des studios, des petits appartements, des grands appartements. Pour les gens qui n'ont pas beaucoup d'argent il y a des H.L.M.[1] (Habitations à Loyer Modéré). Les H.L.M. sont généralement à l'extérieur des villes, à la périphérie ou en banlieue[2]. En banlieue, il y a aussi des petites maisons individuelles—des pavillons.

[1] H.L.M. *low-income housing*
[2] en banlieue *in the suburbs*

Une H.L.M.

Des pavillons de la banlieue parisienne

La famille Duval

Les Duval habitent à Paris. Leur appartement est dans un vieil immeuble dans le premier arrondissement. Les Duval habitent dans un très beau quartier.

L'immeuble où habitent les Duval a six étages. Les Duval habitent au cinquième. Ils ont un appartement de quatre pièces: une salle de séjour, une salle à manger et deux chambres à coucher. Il y a aussi, bien sûr, une cuisine, une salle de bains, des toilettes et même une petite entrée. La salle de séjour et la salle à manger donnent sur la rue. La cuisine et les chambres à coucher donnent sur la cour. De leur balcon, les Duval ont une très belle vue sur le musée du Louvre.

Un bel appartement à Paris

Après la lecture

A Le logement Vrai ou faux? (True or false?)

1. Beaucoup de Français habitent dans des appartements.
2. Il y a beaucoup de maisons individuelles dans les villes françaises.
3. Les H.L.M. sont pour les gens qui n'ont pas beaucoup d'argent, qui ne sont pas très riches.
4. Les H.L.M. sont toujours au centre-ville.
5. Le Louvre est dans le deuxième arrondissement.

B La famille Duval Répondez. (Answer.)

1. Où habitent les Duval?
2. Où est leur appartement?
3. Il y a combien d'étages dans l'immeuble?
4. Ils habitent au cinquième?
5. Quelles pièces donnent sur la rue?
6. Quelles pièces donnent sur la cour?
7. Du balcon de l'appartement, il y a une vue sur quel musée parisien?

Le logement dans d'autres pays

Une maison avec un toit de chaume, Sénégal

Dakar, Sénégal

En Afrique

Dans les grandes villes modernes de l'Afrique Occidentale comme Abidjan ou Dakar il y a beaucoup de grands immeubles où les Ivoiriens et les Sénégalais habitent dans de très beaux appartements de grand standing. Mais dans les petits villages de la brousse[1], les gens habitent dans des petites maisons avec un toit de chaume. Voilà une maison typique de la brousse.

À la Martinique

La Martinique est une belle île francophone dans la mer des Antilles (la mer des Caraïbes). La Martinique est un département français d'outre-mer[2]. Beaucoup de Martiniquais habitent dans des maisons en bois[3]. Les couleurs des maisons martiniquaises sont très belles.

[1] brousse *bush*
[2] d'outre-mer *overseas*
[3] en bois *wooden*

Après la lecture

Le monde francophone Donnez les informations suivantes. (*Give the following information.*)
1. deux grandes villes africaines
2. une région rurale dans beaucoup de pays africains
3. un département français d'outre-mer
4. une île où il y a beaucoup de maisons multicolores en bois

Une maison en bois, Pointe-à-Pitre, Guadeloupe

Lecture supplémentaire 2

Les noms de famille

En France les noms de famille ont des origines très variées. Certains évoquent une caractéristique physique: **Legrand, Lebrun, Petit.**

D'autres sont des noms de profession.

Médecin   Boucher   Charpentier

D'autres sont des noms d'endroits.

D'autres encore sont des termes géographiques.

Quel est votre nom de famille?
Il signifie quelque chose de spécial?

Après la lecture

Noms de famille américains Can you think of some American family names for each of the above categories? Can you think of any other categories for American family names?

La Belgique

La Tunisie

Le Maroc

Le Mali

CONNEXIONS

Les Beaux-Arts

Art et histoire

Art and history are often closely connected. Looking at a beautiful painting brings us much enjoyment. It can also teach us a great deal about the period in which the artist produced it. A portrait, for example, shows us how people looked and dressed at the time.

Today many families keep a photo album. Prior to the invention of photography many families had a portrait done. This was particularly true of the royal families, and King Louis XVI and his queen, Marie-Antoinette, were no exception.

Marie-Antoinette
à la rose

La portraitiste de Marie-Antoinette

Élisabeth Vigée-Lebrun est née[1] à Paris en 1775 (mille sept cent soixante-quinze). Elle étudie l'art auprès de son père, l'artiste Louis Vigée. La jeune Élisabeth a beaucoup de talent et en très peu de temps[2] elle a du succès.

Élisabeth Vigée-Lebrun est la portraitiste de Marie-Antoinette.

Marie-Antoinette

Voici un portrait de Marie-Antoinette avec ses quatre enfants. La reine est une mère dévouée. Elle adore ses enfants.

[1] née *born*
[2] en très peu de temps *in a short time*

Marie-Antoinette et
ses enfants

Versailles

Versailles

La famille royale habite dans le grand palais à Versailles. Mais Marie-Antoinette n'aime pas beaucoup la vie[3] au grand palais. Elle a un petit palais—le Petit Trianon. Pas loin du Petit Trianon Marie-Antoinette a un petit hameau où elle aime passer du temps. Le hameau est un petit village avec des maisonnettes (petites maisons) avec un toit de chaume. Là, Marie-Antoinette aime passer du temps avec les gens[4] simples.

La Révolution

Pendant la Révolution la famille royale est séparée et emprisonnée. Louis XVI et Marie-Antoinette sont guillotinés. *Les adieux de Louis XVI* est un tableau de l'artiste J.-J. Hauer de l'époque révolutionnaire.

[3] vie *life* [4] gens *folks, people*

Le hameau de Marie-Antoinette

Les adieux de Louis XVI

Après la lecture

La famille royale Donnez les informations suivantes. (*Give the following information.*)

1. le nom de la portraitiste de Marie-Antoinette
2. le nom du mari de Marie-Antoinette
3. la résidence officielle de la famille royale
4. le nom du petit palais de Marie-Antoinette
5. la destinée de la famille royale

C'est à vous

Use what you have learned

PARLER 1

Belle résidence

✔ *Describe a home or apartment*

You are trying to sell one of the apartments or houses listed in the ads. Say as much as you can to convince your client (your classmate) to buy one.

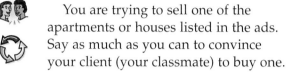

CHAUSSON IMMOBILIER
IMMOplus
• 33, av. de Foix - 09120 VARILHE
Tél. : 05.61.60.79.80 - Fax : 05.61.60.86

Près VARILHES : (09) MAISON campagne, 5 pièces, salle d'eau, wc, grandes dépendances (bergerie, étable, chai) aménageables. Cour, jardin. Proximité toutes commodités.

Région PAMI
(09) NID D'A
rénové, cu
campagnarde
jour-salon ch
née 65 m², bu
4 chambres,
de bains, wc.
confort. Grand
pendance. Sit
lé avec très be
vironnement.

Dans station thermale des PYRÉNÉES : près de ski, MAISON de maître, 12 pièces, bon ét son de gardien, garage, boxes à chevaux. 8 ha. Situation exceptionnelle.

PARLER 2

L'immeuble

✔ *Talk about families and where they live*

With a classmate, look at the apartment building. A different family lives on each floor. University students live in the garrets under the roof. Give each family and student a name. Say as much as you can about them and their lodgings.

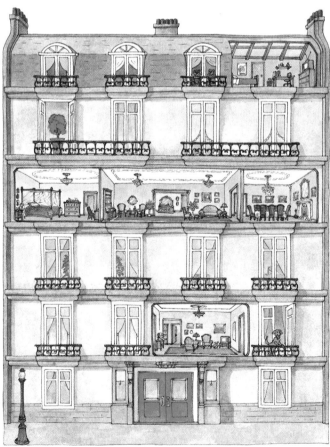

3 Quinze ans
✔ *Invite a friend to a birthday party*

A good friend will soon be fifteen. Write an invitation to his or her birthday party. You may wish to use the well-known French expression R.S.V.P.—**Répondez, s'il vous plaît.**

4 Ma famille et moi
✔ *Describe yourself and your family*

You plan to spend next year as an exchange student in Toulouse, France. You have to write a letter about yourself and your family to the agency in your community that selects the exchange students. Your letter must be in French. Make your description as complete as possible.

Writing Strategy

Ordering details There are several ways to order details when writing. The one you choose depends upon your purpose for writing. When describing a physical place, it is sometimes best to use spatial ordering. This means describing things as they actually appear—from left to right, from back to front, from top to bottom, or any other logical order that works.

5 La maison de mes rêves

Write a description of your dream house. Be as complete as you can.

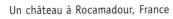

Un château à Rocamadour, France

Vocabulaire

1 Complétez. *(Complete.)*

*To review **Mots 1**, turn to pages 112–113.*

1. Mes parents sont ma _____ et mon _____.
2. Les parents de mes parents sont mes _____.
3. La sœur de ma mère est ma _____.
4. Le frère de mon père est mon _____.
5. Les enfants de mes oncles et de mes tantes sont mes _____ et mes _____.

2 Identifiez. *(Identify.)*

*To review **Mots 2**, turn to pages 116–117.*

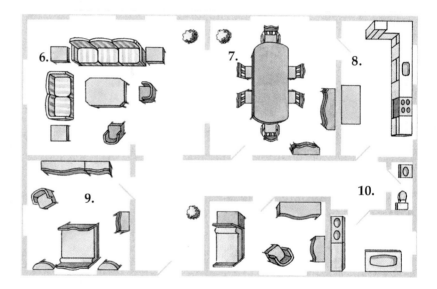

Structure

3 Complétez avec «avoir». *(Complete with avoir.)*

*To review the verb **avoir**, turn to page 120.*

11. J'_____ une petite famille.
12. Marc aussi _____ une petite famille.
13. Sa sœur _____ seize ans.
14. Les parents de Marc et sa sœur _____ un appartement à Paris.
15. Vous _____ une maison ou un appartement?
16. Et toi, tu _____ une petite ou une grande famille?

4 **Choisissez.** *(Choose.)*

17. Où est la voiture de Serge? ____ voiture est dans le garage?

    a. Sa **b.** Son **c.** Ses

18. Où est ____ maison?

    a. ta **b.** ton **c.** tes

19. ____ anniversaire est le 4 novembre.

    a. Ma **b.** Mon **c.** Mes

20. Paul et Marc sont les frères de Sandrine? Oui, ce sont ____ frères.

    a. leurs **b.** son **c.** ses

To review possessive adjectives, turn to page 123.

5 **Complétez.** *(Complete.)*

21. Il y a de très ____ maisons dans notre ____ quartier. (vieux, beau)

22. Nous avons un ____ appartement avec de ____ pièces. (nouveau, beau)

To review these adjectives, turn to page 126.

Culture

6 **Vrai ou faux?** *(True or false?)*

23. Les pavillons sont des petites maisons en banlieue.
24. Les H.L.M. sont généralement à l'extérieur des villes.
25. Beaucoup de Français qui habitent en ville, habitent dans une maison privée.

To review this cultural information, turn to pages 130–131.

Des H.L.M.

Vocabulaire

Identifying family members

la famille	la fille	la grand-mère	
les parents *(m. pl.)*	l'enfant *(m. et f.)*	les petits-enfants	le neveu
le père	le frère	*(m. pl.)*	la nièce
la mère	la sœur	le petit-fils	le/la cousin(e)
le mari	les grands-parents	la petite-fille	un chat
la femme	*(m. pl.)*	l'oncle	un chien
le fils	le grand-père	la tante	

Talking about family affairs or events

un anniversaire	donner
un cadeau	inviter
un gâteau	avoir… ans
une bougie	Quel âge… ?
une fête	

How well do you know your vocabulary?

- Find the sixteen cognates.
- Use as many of them as you can to write a story.

Identifying the rooms of a house

une pièce	une chambre à coucher
une salle de séjour	une salle de bains
une cuisine	des toilettes *(f. pl.)*
une salle à manger	

Talking about a home and the neighborhood

une maison	un garage	un code	(tout) près de
un appartement	une voiture	une cour	loin de
un immeuble	un balcon	un(e) voisin(e)	donner sur
un quartier	une vue	beau, belle	monter
une station de métro	le rez-de-chaussée	nouveau, nouvelle	à pied
une terrasse	un étage	vieux, vieille	en ascenseur
un jardin	un escalier	premier, première	
un arbre	un ascenseur	deuxième	
une fleur	une entrée	troisième	

Other useful words and expressions

une journée	il y a
tout le monde	C'est (pas) rigolo.
autour de (d')	

Technotour

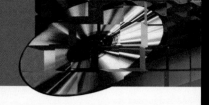

BON VOYAGE!

VIDÉO • Épisode 4

Avant de visionner

In this video episode, Christine and Mme Seguin, secretary at the International Youth Institute, take a trip to Giverny.

Christine a une surprise pour Mme Seguin.

Christine et Mme Seguin dans la cuisine de la maison de Monet

FRENCH ONLINE

À découvrir

Learn more about Monet's house and Giverny, a charming village northwest of Paris, online.

Les jardins autour de la maison de Monet

FRENCH *Online*

In the Chapter 4 Internet activity, you will have a chance to learn about renting or buying a house or an apartment in a French-speaking country. To begin your virtual adventure, go to the Glencoe French Web site: **french.glencoe.com**

Révision

Conversation

Un anniversaire

Sandrine: Bonjour, Christophe. Ça va?

Christophe: Oui, ça va. Et toi?

Sandrine: Pas mal. Qu'est-ce que tu as dans ton sac?

Christophe: J'ai un cadeau pour ma sœur. C'est son anniversaire aujourd'hui.

Sandrine: Ta sœur Mélanie? Elle a quel âge?

Christophe: Elle a seize ans. Et Sandrine, tu as ma nouvelle adresse?

Sandrine: Ta nouvelle adresse? Tu n'habites pas rue de l'Odéon?

Christophe: Non, maintenant on habite dans le 5e, tout près de la station de métro Maubert-Mutualité.

Le boulevard Hausmann, Paris

La station de métro Maubert-Mutualité

Après la conversation

Répondez. *(Answer.)*

1. Sandrine parle à qui?
2. Qu'est-ce qu'il y a dans son sac?
3. C'est l'anniversaire de qui?
4. C'est quand, son anniversaire?
5. Elle a quel âge?
6. Qui a une nouvelle adresse?
7. Il habite où maintenant?
8. Il habite près de quelle station de métro?

Structure

Les verbes au présent

1. Review the forms of regular **-er** verbs.

PARLER	je parle, tu parles, il/elle/on parle, nous parlons, vous parlez, ils/elles parlent
AIMER	j'aime, tu aimes, il/elle/on‿aime, nous‿aimons, vous‿aimez, ils‿/elles‿aiment

2. Review the irregular verbs you have learned so far.

ÊTRE	je suis, tu es, il/elle/on‿est, nous sommes, vous‿êtes, ils/elles sont
AVOIR	j'ai, tu as, il/elle/on‿a, nous‿avons, vous‿avez, ils‿/elles‿ont

3. Review the placement of **ne (n')… pas** when expressing a negative idea.

Je ne travaille pas.
Il n'habite pas à Paris.

1 **Historiette** **Flore habite à Paris.**
Inventez une histoire. *(Make up a story.)*

1. Flore habite à Paris?
2. Elle quitte la maison à quelle heure le matin?
3. Et toi, tu habites où?
4. Le matin, tu arrives à l'école à quelle heure?
5. Tu parles français ou anglais à l'école?
6. Et Flore, qu'est-ce qu'elle parle?
7. Flore quitte le collège à cinq heures de l'après-midi?
8. Tes copains et toi, vous quittez l'école à quelle heure?
9. Vous travaillez après les cours?
10. Les élèves français travaillent après les cours?

2 **Historiette** **Une famille**

Complétez. *(Complete.)*

1. Bonjour. Moi, je ____ français. Je ____ de Paris. (être)
2. Ma famille n'____ pas très grande. Nous ____ quatre. (être)
3. J'____ une sœur. (avoir)
4. Ma sœur ____ dix ans et moi, j'____ dix-sept ans. (avoir)
5. Et vous, vous ____ quel âge? (avoir)
6. Vous ____ américain(e) ou français(e)? (être)

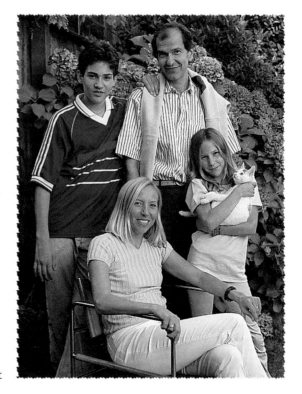

Une famille française avec leur chat

Les articles et les adjectifs

1. Review the following forms of the indefinite and definite articles.

un garçon	une fille	
des copains	des$_z$ écoles	

le garçon	la fille	l'ami(e)
les copains	les$_z$ écoles	les$_z$ ami(e)s

2. Adjectives that end in a consonant have four forms.

Le garçon est brun. **Les garçons sont bruns.**
La fille est brune. **Les filles sont brunes.**

Deux copains sympathiques à Paris

3. Adjectives that end in **e** have only two forms, singular and plural.

un ami sympathique **des amis sympathiques**
une amie sympathique **des amies sympathiques**

3 **Historiette** **La famille de Valentin** Complétez avec **un**, **une** ou **des**. *(Complete with* un, une, *or* des.*)*

Valentin a une grande famille. Il a __1__ père et __2__ mère. Il a __3__ frères et __4__ sœurs? Oui, il a trois frères et quatre sœurs. Il a aussi sept cousins, mais __5__ seule cousine. Il a __6__ chien, Tifou, et __7__ chat, Pompon.

Valentin et sa famille habitent dans __8__ grande maison à Pontchartrain. Valentin est élève dans __9__ lycée de la région. Valentin est __10__ élève excellent.

4 **C'est qui?** Complétez avec **le, la, l'** ou **les**.
(Complete with le, la, l', *or* les.*)*

1. Guillaume est _____ ami de Loïc.
2. Joanne est _____ sœur de Guillaume.
3. Mais Joanne n'est pas _____ amie de Loïc.
4. Justine et Mélanie sont _____ amies de Joanne et Guillaume.
5. Marc et Jean-Paul aussi sont _____ amis de Joanne et Guillaume.
6. Guillaume est _____ frère de Joanne et Christelle.
7. Christelle est _____ cousine de Loïc.

5 **Sa sœur aussi** Répondez d'après le modèle.
(Answer according to the model.)

—**Il est très intelligent.**
—**Sa sœur aussi est très intelligente.**

1. Il est content.
2. Il est amusant.
3. Il est sympathique.
4. Il est énergique.
5. Il est très intéressant.
6. Il est brun.

 # Les adjectifs possessifs

1. Review the forms of the possessive adjectives. The adjectives
mon, ton, and **son** have three forms.

mon ‿appartement	ma maison	mes ‿appartements	mes maisons
ton ‿appartement	ta maison	tes ‿appartements	tes maisons
son ‿appartement	sa maison	ses ‿appartements	ses maisons

2. The adjectives **notre, votre,** and **leur** have two forms—singular
and plural.

notre appartement	notre maison	nos ‿appartements	nos maisons
votre appartement	votre maison	vos ‿appartements	vos maisons
leur appartement	leur maison	leurs ‿appartements	leurs maisons

3. Remember that you use **mon, ton, son** before a feminine singular
noun that begins with a vowel or silent **h: mon‿adresse,
mon‿amie.**

La salle à manger de
la maison de Monet
à Giverny

6 **Qui?** Complétez. *(Complete.)*

Julien a un frère, Paul, et une sœur, Magali. __1__ parents ont donc trois enfants. __2__ trois enfants sont Julien, __3__ frère et __4__ sœur.

—Julien, __5__ frère a quel âge?

—Euh… __6__ frère a quinze ans et __7__ sœur a neuf ans.

—Julien et Paul, comment est __8__ prof de musique?

—Qui? __9__ prof de musique? Il est très sympa. Beaucoup de __10__ profs sont sympas.

École nationale de musique et de danse, Yerres

7 **Un(e) amie** Work with a classmate. Each of you will tell about a friend. Describe your friend, some things he or she does and where he or she lives.

8 **Une conversation** Have a conversation with a classmate. Talk about your school, classes, family, and house.

 LITERARY COMPANION *You may wish to read the adaptation of* **La petite Fadette**, *a novel by George Sand. You will find this literary selection on page 504.*

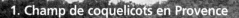

1. Champ de coquelicots en Provence
2. Quart de finale de la coupe de l'UEFA à Lens, dans le Nord
3. La cité médiévale de Carcassonne, dans le Languedoc
4. La Promenade des Anglais et l'hôtel Negresco à Nice, sur la Côte d'Azur
5. Fillette musulmane à Marseille
6. L'Hôtel du Palais à Biarritz, au Pays Basque
7. Homme en costume traditionnel de l'Auvergne

6

REFLETS

NATIONAL GEOGRAPHIC

de la France

7

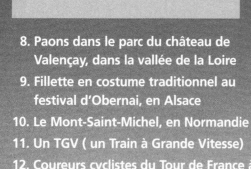

8

8. Paons dans le parc du château de
Valençay, dans la vallée de la Loire

9. Fillette en costume traditionnel au
festival d'Obernai, en Alsace

10. Le Mont-Saint-Michel, en Normandie

11. Un TGV (un Train à Grande Vitesse)

12. Coureurs cyclistes du Tour de France à
Vitré, en Bretagne

13. Rosace de la cathédrale Notre-Dame de
Reims, en Champagne

14. Jeune écolier et cycliste en Normandie

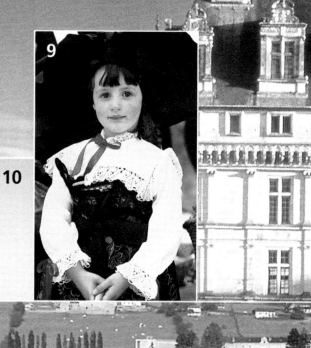

9

10

11

12

NATIONAL GEOGRAPHIC

REFLETS
de la France

14

Au café et au restaurant

Objectifs

In this chapter you will learn to:

✔ order food or a beverage at a café or restaurant

✔ tell where you and others go

✔ tell what you and others are going to do

✔ give locations

✔ tell what belongs to you and others

✔ describe more activities

✔ compare eating habits in the United States and in the French-speaking world

Vincent Van Gogh *Terrasse du café le soir*

Vocabulaire

Mots 1

À la terrasse d'un café 🎧

- une serveuse
- trouver une table
- une table libre
- une table occupée

Karim va au café avec Maïa.
Les deux copains y vont ensemble.
Ils trouvent une table libre.

- un serveur
- la carte

Le serveur arrive.
Il donne la carte à Karim.
Maïa regarde la carte.

- Vous désirez?
- Un coca, s'il vous plaît.
- Et pour moi, une limonade.

Karim prend un coca.
Maïa prend une limonade.
Ils commandent une boisson (une consommation).

J'ai soif. Je voudrais quelque chose à boire.

un citron pressé

un café (un express)

un crème

un jus de pomme

un jus d'orange

des tartines de
pain beurré

un croissant

une omelette
nature

une omelette aux
fines herbes

un sandwich
au jambon

un croque-monsieur

un sandwich
au fromage

une salade
verte

des frites

une soupe
à l'oignon

une saucisse de Francfort,
un hot-dog

J'ai faim. Je voudrais
quelque chose à manger.

une crêpe

une glace
au chocolat

une glace
à la vanille

VOCABULAIRE

cent cinquante-cinq ⚜ **155**

Commençons
Let's use our new words

1 **Historiette** **On va au café.**
Répondez d'après les indications.

(Answer according to the cues.)

1. Pierre va où? (au café)
2. Il va au café avec qui? (Chantal)
3. Ils vont au café quand? (après les cours)
4. Les deux copains y vont ensemble? (oui)
5. Qu'est-ce qu'ils trouvent?
   (une table libre)
6. Qui arrive? (le serveur)
7. Il donne la carte à qui? (à Chantal)
8. Qu'est-ce que les amis commandent?
   (une boisson)
9. Chantal prend une limonade? (oui)
10. Qu'est-ce que Pierre prend? (un coca)

Un café, Nice

2 **Tu as faim ou soif?** Suivez les modèles.
(Follow the models.)

une salade
Moi, j'ai faim. Je voudrais quelque chose à manger.

un coca
Moi, j'ai soif. Je voudrais quelque chose à boire.

1. un citron pressé
2. un petit crème
3. une omelette nature
4. une limonade
5. une glace à la vanille
6. un jus d'orange
7. un croque-monsieur
8. une crêpe

3 **Historiette** **Un beau café**
Répondez d'après le dessin.
(Answer according to the illustration.)

1. C'est la terrasse d'un café ou l'intérieur
   d'un café?
2. Il y a beaucoup de tables occupées?
3. Il y a une table libre?
4. Qui travaille dans le café?
5. Magali a soif. Qu'est-ce qu'elle commande?
6. Rémi a faim. Qu'est-ce qu'il commande?

4 **À la terrasse d'un café** Suivez le modèle.
(Follow the model.)

Client: Monsieur, s'il vous plaît!
Serveur: Oui, vous désirez?
Client: Une glace au chocolat, s'il vous plaît.

1.   2.   3.  4.

5.   6.  7.

5 **J'aime ça.** Work with a classmate. Tell what snack foods and beverages you like or don't like.

6 **Au café** Work in small groups. You're in a café in Honfleur, in Normandie. One of you will be the server. Have a conversation from the time you enter the café until you leave. You will get a table, order, and talk about your friends, family, and school. The waiter will have to interrupt once in a while.

Honfleur, Normandie

7 **Jeu** **Devinette** French people often tell you: **J'ai une faim de loup!** Can you guess whether it means they are very hungry or not? You also hear: **Elle mange comme un oiseau.** Can you guess whether it means she eats a lot or very little? Are there similar expressions in English? What are they?

 *For more practice using words from **Mots 1**, do Activity 13 on page H14 at the end of this book.*

Vocabulaire

Le couvert 🎧

une tasse

une nappe

une assiette

un verre

une serviette

une fourchette

un couteau

une cuillère

Au restaurant 🎧

Vous aimez votre steak comment?

Monsieur, s'il vous plaît! Je n'ai pas de serviette.

À point, s'il vous plaît.

Alexandre prend un steak frites.

Alexandre va au restaurant.
Il ne va pas au restaurant tout seul.
Il y va avec des copains.
Ils n'y vont pas en voiture.
Ils ne prennent pas le bus.
Ils y vont à pied.

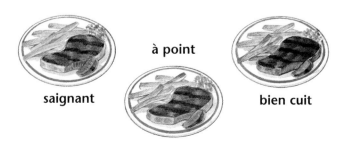

à point

saignant

bien cuit

L'addition, s'il vous plaît.

Alexandre n'invite pas ses copains.
Chacun paie pour soi.

un pourboire

de l'argent

Le service est compris.
Mais Alexandre laisse tout de même un petit pourboire.
Il laisse un peu d'argent pour le serveur.

Les trois repas de la journée 🎧

le petit déjeuner

le déjeuner

le dîner

On prend le petit déjeuner
le matin.

On déjeune entre midi
et deux heures.

On dîne le soir.

Commençons

Let's use our new words

8 **Historiette** **Au restaurant** Inventez une histoire. *(Make up a story.)*

1. Laurène va au restaurant?
2. Elle prend le bus pour aller au restaurant?
3. Elle a faim?
4. Elle regarde la carte?
5. Elle commande un steak frites?
6. Elle aime son steak comment?
7. Pour le dessert, elle prend une glace? À quel parfum? Au chocolat ou à la vanille?
8. Après le déjeuner, Laurène demande l'addition?
9. Le service est compris ou pas?
10. Laurène laisse un pourboire pour le serveur?
11. Elle laisse un peu d'argent ou beaucoup d'argent?

Laurène regarde la carte.

Un serveur

9 **Historiette** **Un dîner au resto** Choisissez. *(Choose.)*

1. Loïc ne va pas au restaurant _____. Il y va avec des copains.
   a. ensemble **b.** au cinquième **c.** tout seul
2. Ils n'y vont pas en voiture. Ils ne prennent pas le métro. Ils y vont _____.
   a. ensemble **b.** à pied **c.** après les cours
3. Loïc _____ un steak frites.
   a. prend **b.** laisse **c.** prépare
4. Après le dîner, Loïc demande _____.
   a. la carte **b.** le pourboire **c.** l'addition
5. Dans les restaurants en France, le service est _____.
   a. occupé **b.** compris **c.** libre
6. Le service est excellent et Loïc _____ un pourboire.
   a. laisse **b.** prend **c.** commande
7. Mais Loïc n'invite pas ses copains. _____ paie pour soi.
   a. L'addition **b.** Chacun **c.** Le serveur

10 **Madame, s'il vous plaît!** Demandez à la serveuse.
(Tell the waitress what you need.)

Une serviette, s'il vous plaît, madame!

1.   **2.**   **3.**   **4.**   **5.**

11 **Les repas** Vrai ou faux? *(True or false?)*

1. On dîne le matin.
2. En France, on déjeune entre midi et deux heures.
3. On prend une tartine et un grand crème pour le dîner.
4. On prend un croque-monsieur pour le déjeuner.
5. On prend une soupe à l'oignon pour le dessert.
6. Une fourchette, c'est pour la soupe.
7. Une assiette, c'est pour le café.
8. Une nappe, c'est pour la soupe.

12 **Au restaurant** Work with a classmate. Take turns asking each other questions about the illustration. Answer each other's questions.

13 **Qu'est-ce que tu manges?** With a classmate, take turns finding out what each of you eats for breakfast and lunch.

 *For more practice using words from **Mots 2**, do Activity 14 on page H15 at the end of this book.*

Structure

Telling and finding out where people go
Le verbe **aller** au présent

1. The verb **aller** *(to go)* is an irregular verb. Study the following forms.

ALLER	
je vais	nous‿allons
tu vas	vous‿allez
il/elle/on va	ils/elles vont

Je vais au café, mais mes parents vont au restaurant.
Tu vas au restaurant avec des copains?
Vous y allez en bus?

2. If you do not mention the place you are going to, you must put the word **y** before the verb **aller**. **Y** refers to a place already mentioned. **Aller** cannot stand alone.

   Tu vas au café?
   Oui, j'y vais et Laurent y va aussi.

> **Savez-vous que... ?**
>
> The expression **On y va!** means "Let's get going." As a question, it means "Should we go?"

3. As you already know, the verb **aller** is also used to express how you feel.

Ça va?	**Oui, ça va bien, merci.**
Comment tu vas?	**Très bien, merci. Et toi?**
Vous allez bien?	**Oui, je vais bien, merci. Et vous?**

Café de Flore, Paris

Continuons
Let's put our words together

14 **Au restaurant!** Répétez la conversation avec un copain ou une copine.
(Repeat the conversation with a classmate.)

15 **On va au Flore.** Complétez d'après la conversation.
(Complete according to the conversation.)

1. Marie _____ bien.
2. Où _____ Paul?
3. Il _____ au Café de Flore.
4. Il n'y _____ pas tout seul.
5. Son amie Marie y _____ aussi.
6. Les deux copains y _____ ensemble.
7. Ils n'y _____ pas en voiture.
8. Ils y _____ à pied.

16 Historiette **Oui, j'y vais.** Donnez des réponses personnelles. *(Give your own answers.)*

1. Tu vas souvent ou très peu au restaurant?
2. Tu y vas seul(e) ou avec ta famille?
3. Tu vas quelquefois dans un restaurant chinois ou italien?
4. Tu vas toujours dans le même restaurant?
5. Tu vas quelquefois au restaurant avec des copains?

17 Historiette **À l'école** Donnez des réponses personnelles. *(Give your own answers.)*

1. Tes copains et toi, vous allez à l'école?
2. Vous allez à quelle école?
3. Vous allez à l'école à quelle heure?
4. Vous y allez comment—à pied, en car scolaire ou en voiture?
5. Après les cours, vous allez au café?

Honfleur, Normandie

18 On dîne au restaurant. Complétez la conversation. *(Complete the conversation.)*

Anne: Ce soir, je dîne au restaurant.
Jean: Ah oui? Où est-ce que tu __1__?
Anne: Au Vieux Honfleur.
Jean: Excellente idée! On y __2__ ensemble.
Anne: Mais, euh… je n'y __3__ pas toute seule.
Jean: Ah bon, tu y __4__ avec qui?
Anne: Euh… avec Olivier.
Jean: Vous y __5__ à quelle heure?
Anne: Mais tu es bien indiscret!

Telling what's going to happen
Aller + infinitif

1. You use **aller** + an infinitive to express what is going to take place in the near future.

> **Demain on va avoir un examen.**
> **Les élèves vont étudier.**
> **Je vais passer l'examen.**
> **L'examen va être difficile, c'est sûr!**

2. To make a sentence negative, you put **ne… pas** around the conjugated form of **aller.**

> **Tu ne vas pas aller au café?**
> **Moi, je ne vais pas regarder la télé.**

Continuons
Let's put our words together

19 **Ce soir!** Donnez des réponses personnelles. *(Give your own answers.)*

1. Ce soir, tu vas regarder la télé?
2. Tu vas téléphoner à un copain ou une copine?
3. Tu vas préparer le dîner?
4. Tu vas aller en classe?
5. Tu vas inviter tes professeurs au restaurant?

20 **Absurdités** Mettez à la forme négative.
(Make the sentences negative.)

1. Nous allons en classe pendant le week-end.
2. Les chiens et les chats vont à l'école.
3. Demain le prof de maths va parler français.
4. Vous allez déjeuner pendant le cours de géographie.
5. Ce soir, je vais parler au téléphone avec Elvis Presley.

21 **Quand?** Work with a classmate. Tell each other some things you like to do. Then tell when you are going to do them—**ce soir, demain, demain matin, la semaine prochaine.**

Structure

Expressing direction and possession
Les contractions avec **à** et **de**

1. The preposition **à** can mean "to," "in," or "at." **À** is contracted with **le** and **les** to form one word—**au, aux.** Note that liaison occurs when **aux** is followed by a vowel.

Savez-vous que... ?

À is used in many food expressions.

une soupe à l'oignon
une omelette aux fines herbes

à + le	= au	Je vais au lycée.
à + les	= aux	Le prof parle aux͜élèves.
à + la	= à la	Tu vas à la cantine?
à + l'	= à l'	Vous allez à l'école à pied?

2. The preposition **de** can mean "of," "from," or "about." **De** contracts with **le** and **les** to form one word—**du, des.** Liaison occurs when **des** is followed by a vowel.

de + le	= du	Il y a une belle vue du balcon.
de + les	= des	On parle toujours des͜amis.
de + la	= de la	Il arrive de la cantine.
de + l'	= de l'	Je rentre de l'école.

3. The preposition **de** also indicates possession or ownership.

Le lycée **de** Vincent est à Paris.
C'est la voiture **du** professeur **de** Vincent.
Minou est le chat **des** voisins **de** Vincent.

Continuons
Let's put our words together

22 **Tu vas où?** Donnez des réponses personnelles. *(Give your own answers.)*

1. Quel est le nom de ton école?
2. Tu vas à l'école à quelle heure?
3. Tu vas au cours de français le matin ou l'après-midi?
4. Tu vas au cours d'anglais à quelle heure?
5. Tu aimes parler aux profs?
6. Tu aimes parler des profs aussi?
7. Tu habites près de l'école ou loin de l'école?
8. Tu rentres de l'école à quelle heure?
9. Comment est-ce que tu rentres de l'école?

23 **Historiette** **Je n'y vais pas.** Complétez avec **à.** (*Complete with* à.)

Ce soir, je ne vais pas ___1___ (le concert). Je ne vais pas ___2___ (le parc). Je ne vais pas ___3___ (le collège). Je ne vais pas ___4___ (le restaurant). Je ne vais pas parler ___5___ (les copains). Je ne vais pas ___6___ (l'anniversaire) de Julie. Je vais aller où, alors? Je vais rentrer ___7___ (la maison). Pourquoi? Je suis fatigué(e)!

24 **Au café** Suivez le modèle. (*Follow the model.*)

une tarte aux fruits / une tarte aux pommes
—Qu'est-ce que tu vas prendre?
—Je vais prendre une tarte.
—Une tarte aux fruits ou une tarte aux pommes?
—Oh, je vais prendre une tarte _____.

1. un sandwich au jambon / un sandwich au fromage
2. une omelette au fromage / une omelette aux fines herbes
3. une soupe à la tomate / une soupe à l'oignon
4. une glace au chocolat / une glace à la vanille
5. une crêpe au chocolat / une crêpe aux fruits

25 **Le dîner des copains** Combinez d'après le modèle. (*Combine according to the model.*)

c'est la voiture / les parents de Vincent
C'est la voiture des parents de Vincent.

1. je vais à la table / les amis de Marc
2. ils sont à la terrasse / le café
3. nous regardons la carte / le restaurant
4. c'est le coca / l'amie de Marc
5. voilà le pourboire / la serveuse

Cellia Saubry *Coin de rue*

Describing more activities
Le verbe **prendre**

1. The verb **prendre,** "to take," also means "to have" when used with foods. It is an irregular verb. Pay particular attention to both its spelling and pronunciation.

PRENDRE			
je	prends	nous	prenons
tu	prends	vous	prenez
il/elle/on	prend	ils/elles	prennent

Je prends le car scolaire pour aller à l'école.
Les voisins ne prennent pas l'ascenseur.
Je vais prendre un coca.

2. The verbs **apprendre** *(to learn)* and **comprendre** *(to understand)* are conjugated the same way as **prendre.**

> **On apprend beaucoup à l'école.**
> **Vous comprenez le français, n'est-ce pas?**

Les deux amis apprennent l'anglais.

Continuons
Let's put our words together

26 **Historiette** **Alexandre** Inventez une histoire. *(Make up a story.)*

1. Alexandre prend le car scolaire pour aller à l'école?
2. En classe, il prend des notes quand le professeur parle?
3. Il comprend bien le français?
4. Il apprend beaucoup de choses au cours de français?

Ils prennent leur petit déjeuner.

27 **À l'école** Donnez des réponses personnelles. *(Give your own answers.)*

1. Tu prends ton petit déjeuner à la maison ou à la cafétéria de l'école?
2. À l'école, tu prends l'escalier ou l'ascenseur pour monter au premier étage?
3. À la cafétéria de l'école, qu'est-ce que tu prends quand tu as soif?
4. Qu'est-ce que tu prends quand tu as faim?

28 **Toujours à l'école** Répondez. *(Answer.)*

1. La majorité des élèves prennent le car scolaire pour aller à l'école?
2. Les élèves prennent l'escalier ou l'ascenseur pour monter au premier étage?
3. En cours de français, tout le monde comprend bien quand le professeur parle?
4. Vous apprenez beaucoup de choses en cours de français?

29 **Au pluriel!** Mettez au pluriel. *(Make the sentences plural.)*

1. Je prends le car scolaire pour aller à l'école.
2. Je prends l'ascenseur pour monter au quatrième étage.
3. Tu prends le bus, le métro ou la voiture?
4. Tu prends beaucoup de notes en classe?
5. L'élève est très intelligent et il apprend beaucoup de choses.
6. Elle comprend bien la leçon.
7. Son copain prend un coca au café.
8. Et moi, je prends une glace au chocolat.

*For more practice using the verbs **aller** and **prendre**, do Activity 15 on page H16 at the end of this book.*

Vous êtes sur le bon chemin. Allez-y!

Conversation

Au restaurant

Claire: Tu as faim?

Loïc: Oui. J'ai hyper faim! Je vais prendre un bon steak frites.

Serveur: Vous désirez?

Loïc: Un steak frites, s'il vous plaît. Saignant.

Serveur: Et pour vous, mademoiselle?

Claire: Ben, un steak aussi, mais pas de frites. Une salade verte.

Serveur: Et vous aimez votre steak comment?

Claire: À point, s'il vous plaît.
(Après le dîner)

Loïc: L'addition, s'il vous plaît!

Serveur: Oui, monsieur, j'arrive!

Claire: On laisse quelque chose? Il est sympa, le serveur.

Loïc: Oh, écoute, le service est compris.

Après la conversation

Répondez. *(Answer.)*

1. Où sont Claire et Loïc?
2. Loïc a faim?
3. Qu'est-ce qu'il va prendre?
4. Et Claire, qu'est-ce qu'elle va prendre?
5. Qu'est-ce qu'elle commande avec le steak?
6. Claire et Loïc prennent leur steak comment?
7. Après le dîner, qui demande l'addition?
8. À votre avis *(In your opinion)*, est-ce qu'ils vont laisser un pourboire?

Parlons un peu plus
Let's talk some more

On commande? You and your friend are at a restaurant. Look at the menu and try to decide what to order. Then order. Another one of your classmates will be the server.

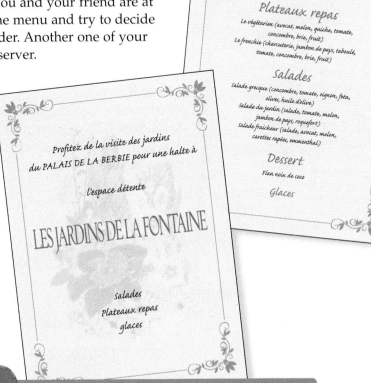

Profitez de la visite des jardins du PALAIS DE LA BERBIE pour une halte à

l'espace détente

LES JARDINS DE LA FONTAINE

salades
Plateaux repas
glaces

sandwichs
Jambon blanc, beurre, cornichons, salade verte, carottes rapées
Jambon de pays, beurre, cornichons

Plateaux repas
Le végétarien (avocat, melon, quiche, tomate, concombre, brie, fruit)
Le frenchie (charcuterie, jambon de pays, taboulé, tomate, concombre, brie, fruit)

salades
salade grecque (concombre, tomate, oignon, feta, olives, huile d'olive)
salade du jardin (salade, tomate, melon, jambon de pays, roquefort)
salade fraicheur (salade, avocat, melon, carottes rapées, emmenthal)

Dessert
Flan noix de coco

Glaces

Prononciation

Le son /r/ 🎧

The French sound /**r**/ is very different from the American /r/. When you say /**r**/, the back of your tongue should almost completely block the air going through the back of your throat. Repeat the following words and sentences.

le verre	toujours	la voiture	le pourboire
la carte	la tartine	la cuillère	la fourchette
pour	les crêpes	le serveur	le croque-monsieur
boire	les frites	le croissant	

Le serveur arrive avec un verre de jus d'orange.
Je voudrais laisser un pourboire pour la serveuse.

verre

Lectures culturelles

Reading Strategy

Making comparisons while reading

When you study a foreign language, you are often asked to compare customs in your country to those in another. As you read the passage, take note of similarities and differences between restaurants in France and those in the United States. Making these comparisons in your head or on paper will help clarify ideas and enable you to remember more of what you read.

Au restaurant? Vraiment?

Ce soir, Valentin va dîner dans un petit restaurant du coin[1]. Il invite ses deux amis Ahmed et Julie. Ils vont aller tous ensemble au restaurant.

Les copains arrivent au restaurant. Ils trouvent une table libre et ils prennent leur place. Tango prend sa place aussi, sous[2] la table. Sous la table? Oui. Mais qui est Tango? C'est le chien de Julie. Il est très bien élevé[3], Tango. Julie ne laisse pas Tango seul à la maison. Tango accompagne Julie partout, même au restaurant. Pourquoi pas? Un chien bien élevé est toujours le bienvenu[4]!

[1] du coin *local*
[2] sous *under*
[3] bien élevé *well-behaved*
[4] le bienvenu *welcome*

La Polynésie française

Tahiti

Haïti

Le serveur arrive. Les amis regardent la carte et ils commandent. Après le dîner, Valentin demande l'addition. Le serveur arrive et donne l'addition à Valentin. Valentin regarde l'addition et paie. D'habitude chacun paie pour soi, mais aujourd'hui, c'est exceptionnel. Valentin paie pour tout le monde parce qu'il invite ses copains. En France, «inviter», c'est «payer»!

Après la lecture

A Valentin va au restaurant? Vrai ou faux? *(True or false?)*
1. Valentin va au restaurant tout seul.
2. Les copains entrent dans le restaurant et demandent une table au serveur.
3. Tango est un chien bien élevé.
4. Tango aussi va au restaurant.
5. Ahmed et Julie demandent l'addition.
6. Les trois amis paient l'addition.

B Des différences culturelles In this reading, there are some interesting cultural differences between France and the United States. What are they?

Les repas en France

La façon de manger en France change assez vite[1]. Pour le petit déjeuner, ça ne change pas vraiment; on prend toujours le petit déjeuner à la maison. C'est toujours un petit déjeuner rapide et frugal: une tartine de pain beurré et un bol de café, de thé ou de chocolat. Quelquefois, les enfants mangent des céréales.

On déjeune entre midi et deux heures. Mais le déjeuner n'est plus[2] le repas principal parce que les enfants déjeunent à la cantine de l'école. Les parents déjeunent à la cafétéria de leur entreprise[3] ou dans un restaurant près de l'entreprise.

Le dîner est maintenant le repas principal pour beaucoup de Français. Un des parents (ou les deux) prépare le dîner dans la cuisine et la famille dîne ensemble. Souvent on mange des produits surgelés[4]. En France, il y a des plats surgelés excellents. Le dîner est un moment important pour la famille; c'est le seul moment de la journée où on est ensemble.

Un restaurant aux Champs-Élysées

[1] vite *fast*
[2] n'est plus *is no longer*
[3] entreprise *firm*
[4] surgelés *frozen*

Après la lecture

Les repas Répondez. *(Answer.)*
1. En France, comment est le petit déjeuner?
2. Qu'est-ce qu'on prend pour le petit déjeuner?
3. On déjeune à quelle heure?
4. On déjeune où?
5. Quel est le repas principal?
6. Qu'est-ce qu'on prépare souvent pour le dîner?
7. Le dîner est un moment important pour la famille? Pourquoi?

Un dîner en famille

Les goûts changent.

Beaucoup de Français sont de vrais gourmets. Ils aiment manger bien. La cuisine française est excellente. Elle est célèbre dans le monde entier. Les Français continuent à apprécier leur cuisine mais ils apprécient aussi les plats d'autres pays[1]. La cuisine asiatique est très populaire: la cuisine chinoise, la cuisine thaïlandaise et aussi la cuisine vietnamienne. En France, il y a beaucoup de restaurants vietnamiens. La cuisine vietnamienne ressemble un peu à la cuisine chinoise. Il y a aussi beaucoup de restaurants algériens, tunisiens et marocains où la spécialité est toujours le couscous.

Comme aux États-Unis, il existe en France des chaînes de restaurants et des chaînes de fast-food. Certaines sont américaines, d'autres sont européennes. Elles sont françaises ou belges, par exemple, comme *Léon de Bruxelles*. Sa spécialité: les moules[2] frites, c'est-à-dire[3] des moules avec toutes sortes de sauces et des frites. C'est un plat traditionnel en Belgique.

Et la pizza? La pizza est très appréciée en France! Tout le monde aime la pizza!

[1] pays *countries*
[2] moules *mussels*
[3] c'est-à-dire *that is to say*

Au restaurant *Léon de Bruxelles*

Les aliments préférés des jeunes de 7 à 14 ans sont:
le steak frites (51%), les hamburgers (51%), la pizza (49%), les gâteaux (37%), les spaghettis ou raviolis (32%), les sandwichs (17%). 71% des Français indiquent qu'ils préfèrent la cuisine française aux cuisines étrangères.

PIZZA VESUVIO

25, RUE QUENTIN-BAUCHARD
75008 PARIS

☎ 01 47 23 60 26
Fax 01 47 23 63 24

Après la lecture

Au restaurant en France Vrai ou faux? *(True or false?)*
1. Les Français aiment manger bien.
2. Les Français n'apprécient pas leur cuisine.
3. La cuisine asiatique est assez populaire en France.
4. Les restaurants asiatiques en France sont toujours des restaurants chinois.
5. Le couscous est une spécialité vietnamienne.
6. *Léon de Bruxelles* est une chaîne de restaurants belge en France.
7. Les Français n'aiment pas du tout la pizza.

La Belgique

La Tunisie

Le Maroc

Le Mali

CONNEXIONS

Les mathématiques

L'arithmétique

When we go shopping or out to eat, it is often necessary to do some arithmetic. We either have to add up the bill ourselves or check the figures someone else has done for us. In a café or restaurant we may want to figure out what we should leave for a tip, even if **le service est compris.**

We almost never do arithmetic in a foreign language. We normally do arithmetic in the language in which we learned it. However, it is fun to know some basic arithmetical terms in case we have to discuss a problem concerning a bill, for example, with a French-speaking person.

Before we learn some of these arithmetical terms in French, let's look at some differences in numbers. Note how the numbers 1 and 7 are written in French.

Note also that the thousands are indicated by a space or a period and the decimals are indicated by a comma.

1 000   2 000   3 000   4 000
1.000   2.000   3.000   4.000
210,75

L'arithmétique

additionner	+	soustraire	−
multiplier	×	diviser	÷

Pour additionner:
  Deux plus deux, ça fait quatre.
  $2 + 2 = 4$
Pour soustraire:
  Quatre moins deux, ça fait deux.
  $4 - 2 = 2$
Pour multiplier:
  Deux fois deux, ça fait quatre.
  $2 \times 2 = 4$
Pour diviser:
  Quatre divisé par deux, ça fait deux.
  $4 \div 2 = 2$
Dix pour cent (%) de 200 euros, c'est 20 euros.

A Ça fait combien? Faites les opérations

suivantes à voix haute. *(Solve the following problems aloud.)*

1. 2 + 2 =   5. 4 × 4 =
2. 14 + 6 =   6. 8 × 3 =
3. 30 − 8 =   7. 27 ÷ 9 =
4. 20 − 4 =   8. 80 ÷ 10 =

B L'addition, s'il vous plaît! You went out

to a restaurant with three friends. This is your bill.
Do the following.

1. Add up to see if the total is correct.
2. Add 10 percent, even though the tip is included.
3. Calculate how much each of you owes.

C Comment compter sur ses doigts Here

are three different ways people count on their fingers.
Which one is yours? With a classmate, choose a way
that is not yours and show each other numbers. Take
turns figuring out which number it is.

```
           LE BAR À HUÎTRES
          112, Bd du Montparnasse
               75014 PARIS
          TEL: 01 . 43 . 20 . 71 . 01

               6 Thomas
-------------------------------------------
Tbl 16/1        Fct 9919          Cts 5
          25 Jul   20:19
          *** Réimprimée ***
-------------------------------------------
              Prix en Frs
3 Salade de Thon                  126.00
1M. FRAICH                         98.00
3 Terrine Volaille                117.00
3 SOLE MEUNIÈRE                   393.00
1 Tout café                        36.00
1 Café Colombie                    18.00
1 Café Crème                       20.00
              Total en Frs

122.74  T. V. A.  20.60%          808.00
89.38 Service  15%                685.26
        Total du   808.00

              Total en Eur

18.71  T. V. A.  20.60%           123.18
13.63 Service  15%                104.47
        Total du   123.18

Toute l'équipe
Bar À Huîtres Montparnasse
vous remercie de votre visite.
À BIENTÔT
```

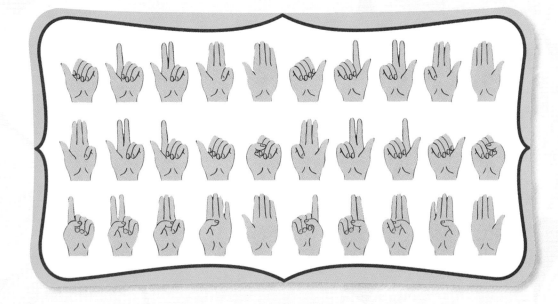

C'est à vous

Use what you have learned

PARLER

1 Au café

✔ *Order something to eat or drink in a café*

Work with a classmate. One of you is the customer and the other is the server. You order from the menu provided.

BUFFET CHAUD

CROQUE-POILÂNE	37		
SUPER CROQUE-POILÂNE (Jambon, fromage, tomate, œuf au plat)	44		
CROQUE-MONSIEUR	30	OMELETTE JAMBON ou FROMAGE	36
CROQUE-MADAME	34		
HOT-DOG FROMAGE	30	OMELETTE MIXTE (Jambon, fromage)	44
SAUCISSES FRITES (2 saucisses)	44	1/4 POULET FRITES	52
ŒUFS AU PLAT JAMBON	36	JAMBON DE PARIS FRITES	44
OMELETTE ou ŒUFS PLAT NATURE	30	QUICHE MAISON	48
		LASAGNES, SALADE	48

PARLER
ÉCRIRE

2 À la terrasse des Deux Magots

✔ *Talk about school and teachers as you order food and drinks*

Work in groups of three or four. You're all friends sitting on the **terrasse** of the famous café **Les Deux Magots** in Paris, watching the world go by. You talk about many things—school, teachers, friends, etc. One of you will play the role of the waiter. You have to interrupt the conversation once in a while to take the orders and serve.

ÉCRIRE

3 La carte

✔ *Plan a menu*

Write a menu in French for your school cafeteria.

Élodie prend le déjeuner
à la cantine.

Writing Strategy

Visualizing Many writers have a mental picture of what they want to write before they actually begin to write. The mental picture helps organize what they want to say. It also helps them visualize what they want to describe in their writing. Closing your eyes and visualizing what you want to write can make the writing experience more pleasant. When writing in a foreign language, you also have to restrict your mental picture to what you know how to say.

ÉCRIRE

4 Un restaurant

You have been asked to write a short article about a visit to a restaurant. Look at this illustration. Pretend this is the mental picture you have of the restaurant you are going to write about. Look at it for several minutes and then write a paragraph about it.

Assessment

Vocabulaire

1 Choisissez. *(Choose.)*

To review **Mots 1,** turn to pages 154–155.

1. Après les cours, Michel et Chantal vont au _____.
   a. café   **b.** ensemble

2. Ils trouvent _____ à la terrasse.
   a. une table libre   **b.** une tartine

3. Le serveur _____ la carte à Chantal.
   a. regarde   **b.** donne

4. Chantal a soif. Elle commande quelque chose à _____.
   a. manger   **b.** boire

5. Michel a faim. Il prend _____.
   a. un jus d'orange   **b.** une tartine de pain beurré

Deux amis au café

2 Choisissez. *(Choose.)*

To review **Mots 2,** turn to pages 158–159.

6. À midi, Henri va _____ au restaurant.
   a. dîner   **b.** déjeuner   **c.** payer

7. Il _____ le métro.
   a. prend   **b.** commande   **c.** laisse

8. Henri aime son steak _____.
   a. à pied   **b.** à point   **c.** ensemble

9. Après le déjeuner, Henri _____ l'addition.
   a. demande   **b.** invite   **c.** laisse

10. Dans les restaurants en France _____ est compris.
    a. le verre   **b.** l'addition   **c.** le service

Structure

3 **Complétez avec «aller».**
(Complete with the verb aller.)

11. Nous _____ à l'école en voiture?
12. Laurent, tu _____ au café?
13. Vous _____ bien, madame?

To review the verb **aller,** turn to page 162.

4 **Choisissez.** *(Choose.)*

14. Je vais _____ au café avec mes copains.
   a. déjeune   **b.** déjeuner
15. Ils vont _____ un pourboire pour le serveur.
   a. laisser   **b.** laissent

To review the use of **aller** + an infinitive, turn to page 165.

5 **Complétez avec «à» ou «de».**
(Complete with à or de.)

16. Les amis vont _____ café.
17. Vincent rentre _____ école à cinq heures.
18. C'est la voiture _____ père de Marie.
19. Le prof donne un examen _____ élèves.

To review the forms of **à** and **de,** turn to page 166.

6 **Complétez avec «prendre».**
(Complete with the verb prendre.)

20. Les copains _____ le métro.
21. Vous _____ le petit déjeuner à la maison?
22. Pour monter à l'appartement, on _____ l'ascenseur.
23. Tu _____ un sandwich à midi?

To review the verb **prendre,** turn to page 168.

Culture

7 **Complétez.** *(Complete.)*

24. Les copains _____ une table libre au restaurant.
25. Claire paie pour tout le monde. Elle _____ ses copains.

To review this cultural information, turn to pages 172–173.

Vocabulaire

Getting along in a café or restaurant

un café
la terrasse d'un café
une table
  occupée
  libre
un serveur
une serveuse

la carte
l'addition (f.)
l'argent (m.)
le pourboire
aller
trouver une table
commander

inviter
payer
laisser
prendre
déjeuner
dîner
avoir faim

avoir soif
Vous désirez?
je voudrais
quelque chose
  à manger
  à boire
Le service est compris.

Identifying snacks and beverages

une boisson
une consommation
un coca
une limonade
un café
un express
un crème
un citron pressé
un jus de pomme

un jus d'orange
une tartine de pain
  beurré
un croissant
un sandwich
  au jambon
  au fromage
un croque-monsieur

un steak
  saignant
  à point
  bien cuit
des frites (f. pl.)
une soupe à l'oignon
une omelette
  nature
  aux fines herbes

une saucisse de
    Francfort, un
    hot-dog
une salade verte
une glace
À quel parfum?
  au chocolat
  à la vanille
une crêpe

Identifying a place setting

le couvert
un verre
une tasse

une fourchette
un couteau
une cuillère

une assiette
une nappe
une serviette

> **How well do you know your vocabulary?**
> - Choose words for specific foods you enjoy.
> - Create a menu using these words.

Identifying meals

un repas
le petit déjeuner
le déjeuner
le dîner

Other useful words and expressions

tout(e) seul(e)
toujours
souvent

quelquefois
peu

Technotour

BON VOYAGE!

Avant de visionner

In this video episode, Christine and Chloé have lunch on the terrace of a café in Paris.

Chloé et Christine vont dans un café.

Elles commandent une boisson.

À découvrir

Learn more about café life in Paris online.

Un café, Paris

FRENCH *Online*

In the Chapter 5 Internet activity, you will have a chance to learn more about cafés and restaurants in the Francophone world. To begin your virtual adventure, go to the Glencoe French Web site: **french.glencoe.com**

CHAPITRE

6

La nourriture et les courses

Objectifs

In this chapter you will learn to:

✔ *identify more foods*

✔ *shop for food*

✔ *tell what you or others are doing*

✔ *ask for the quantity you want*

✔ *talk about what you or others don't have*

✔ *tell what you or others are able to do or want to do*

✔ *talk about French food-shopping customs*

Paul Cézanne *Nature morte au panier*

RÉPUBLIQUE FRANÇAISE
LA POSTE 1992 3,40
Pain et Céréales
CONGRÈS INTERNATIONAL

184

Vocabulaire

Mots 1

À la boulangerie-pâtisserie

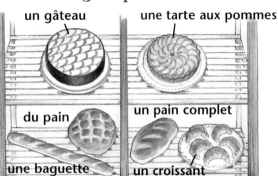

un gâteau

une tarte aux pommes

du pain

un pain complet

une baguette

un croissant

À la crémerie

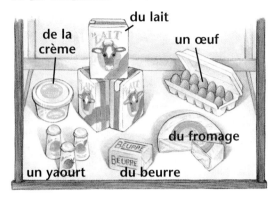

du lait

de la crème

un œuf

du fromage

un yaourt

du beurre

À la boucherie

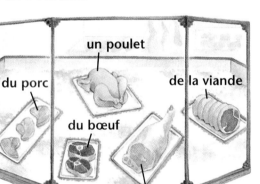

un poulet

du porc

de la viande

du bœuf

de l'agneau

À la poissonnerie

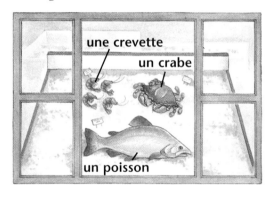

une crevette

un crabe

un poisson

À la charcuterie

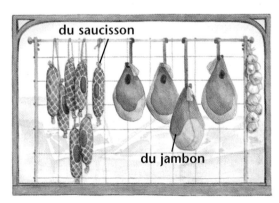

du saucisson

du jambon

À l'épicerie

de l'huile

du vinaigre

du poivre

du sel

un sac

Paul fait les courses.
Il va à la boulangerie.
Il va chercher du pain.

Je voudrais une baguette, s'il vous plaît.

Ah, je regrette, il n'y a plus de baguettes.

Paul est à la boulangerie.
Il veut acheter une baguette.
Il n'y a plus de baguettes.

Bon, alors un pain complet.

Et avec ça?

C'est tout, merci.

Il ne peut pas acheter de baguette.
Il achète un pain complet.

Commençons
Let's use our new words

1 **Historiette** **À la crémerie** Inventez une histoire. *(Make up a story.)*

1. Madame Cadet va chercher du beurre. Elle va à la crémerie ou à la boucherie?
2. Elle veut acheter aussi du lait. Elle va à la crémerie?
3. Elle veut des œufs aussi?
4. Elle peut acheter du fromage à la crémerie?
5. Elle va acheter des yaourts pour le dessert?

2 **Historiette** **On fait les courses.**
Répondez d'après les indications.
(Answer according to the cues.)

1. Qui fait les courses? (Élodie)
2. Elle fait les courses quand? (le samedi matin)
3. Elle a un sac? (oui)
4. Elle va au supermarché? (non)
5. Elle va où? (à la boulangerie)
6. Qu'est-ce qu'elle va acheter à la boulangerie? (du pain)
7. Elle veut une baguette? (oui)
8. Il n'y a plus de baguettes? (non)
9. Alors, qu'est-ce qu'elle achète? (un pain complet)

Une crémerie, Montgeron, France

3 **À l'épicerie** Complétez d'après la photo. *(Complete according to the photo.)*

On va acheter du __1__, des __2__, de la __3__, du __4__, de l' __5__, du __6__ et du __7__.

4 **On va où?** Complétez. *(Complete.)*

1. Pour acheter un poulet, du bœuf, du porc et de l'agneau, on va _____.
2. Pour acheter du lait, on va _____.
3. Pour acheter des croissants et un gâteau, on va _____.
4. Pour acheter de la viande, on va _____.
5. Pour acheter du saucisson et du jambon, on va _____.
6. Pour acheter de la crème et des œufs, on va _____.
7. Pour acheter du poisson et des crevettes, on va _____.
8. Pour acheter des yaourts, on va _____.
9. Pour acheter une tarte aux pommes, on va _____.
10. Pour acheter des crabes, on va _____.

Une poissonnerie, Paris

5   **Les courses** You're living in Arles with a French family. You offered to do the grocery shopping. Your host gives you this list. Find out from your French brother or sister (your partner) where you go for each item.

des crevettes et des crabes
du saucisson
4 tartes aux pommes
2 baguettes
un poulet
du fromage (du Camembert)
du lait
un gâteau au chocolat

For more practice using words from Mots 1, do Activity 16 on page H17 at the end of this book.

Au marché 🎧

le marchand de fruits et légumes

la marchande

Elle est bonne, ma salade!

Il est bon, mon melon!

le marchand

une salade

une pomme de terre

des haricots verts

une poire

une pomme

des fraises

C'est combien, les carottes?

Un euro le kilo.

Alors, un kilo, s'il vous plaît.

Vous voulez autre chose?

Oui, une livre de tomates et c'est tout.

Alors ça fait deux euros cinquante.

Ariane est au marché.
Elle veut acheter des légumes.
Elle va chez la marchande de fruits et légumes.

| un kilo = 1 000 (mille) grammes |
| une livre = 500 (cinq cents) grammes |

On achète des épinards?

Non.

Pourquoi?

Parce que je n'aime pas ça.

un chariot

Julien et son frère sont au supermarché.
Julien veut acheter de l'eau minérale et du lait.
Il achète une bouteille d'eau minérale et un litre de lait.

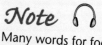

Note 🎧

Many words for foods in French are cognates.

un fruit   une carotte
une banane   une tomate
une orange   un oignon

un pot de moutarde

un paquet de légumes surgelés

un litre de lait

250 grammes de beurre

une tranche de jambon

une boîte de petits pois
une boîte de conserve

un pot de confiture

une bouteille d'eau minérale

une douzaine d'œufs

VOCABULAIRE

Vocabulaire

Commençons
Let's use our new words

6 **Fruit(s) ou légume(s)?** Identifiez d'après le modèle.
(Identify according to the model.)

 C'est une pomme. C'est un fruit.

1.   2.    3.   4.

5.   6.   7.   8.

7 **Historiette** **Mathilde va au marché.** Complétez. *(Complete.)*

Mathilde veut préparer une grande salade. Elle va au marché. Elle va chez la __1__ *(marchande)*. Elle achète une __2__ *(salade)*, des __3__ *(carottes)* et des __4__ *(tomates)*. La marchande demande: «Vous voulez autre chose?» Mathilde répond: «Non, merci, __5__ *(Madame)*.» Elle donne de l'argent à la __6__ *(marchande)*.

8 **Historiette** **Martin va au supermarché.** Complétez. *(Complete.)*

Martin veut acheter de la moutarde, de l'eau minérale, une boîte de petits pois et un paquet de légumes surgelés. Pour acheter tout ça, il va au supermarché. Au supermarché, il prend un chariot. Il achète deux __1__ *(bouteille)* d'eau minérale, un __2__ *(paquet)* de carottes surgelées et trois __3__ *(boîte)* de sardines. Et autre chose aussi—un __4__ *(pot)* de moutarde. Martin va à la caisse. Ça __5__ *(fait)* combien, les bouteilles d'eau minérale, le paquet de carottes surgelées, les __6__ *(boîtes)* de sardines et le __7__ *(pot)* de moutarde? Ça fait onze euros cinquante.

9 **C'est combien, s'il vous plaît?** Conversez d'après le modèle.
(Make up a conversation according to the model.)

—C'est combien, la boîte de petits pois?
—Un euro quatorze.

1.

2.

3.

4.

5.

6.

10 **Pourquoi pas?** Conversez d'après le modèle.
(Make up a conversation according to the model.)

1. Tu veux du saucisson?
2. Tu veux des fraises?
3. Tu veux des haricots verts?
4. Tu veux des petits pois?
5. Tu veux de la confiture de fraises?
6. Tu veux du poisson?

eau minérale
jambon
fraises
œufs
lait
beurre
frites surgelées

11 **À l'épicerie** You're in a grocery store in Paris. You want to buy the items on the list. Tell the clerk (your partner) how much you want of each item and find out how much it costs.

For more practice using words from Mots 2, do Activity 17 on page H18 at the end of this book.

Structure

Telling and finding out what people do
Le verbe **faire** au présent

1. The verb **faire** (*to do, to make*) is an irregular verb. Study the following forms.

FAIRE	
je fais	nous faisons
tu fais	vous faites
il/elle/on fait	ils/elles font

2. You will use the verb **faire** a great deal in French. **Faire** is used in many expressions that take a different verb in English. Such expressions that cannot be translated directly from one language to another are called "idiomatic expressions." **Faire les courses** (*to go grocery shopping*) and **faire ses devoirs** (*to do homework*) are examples of idiomatic expressions. The following are some others.

> **Maman prépare un bon dîner. Elle aime beaucoup faire la cuisine.**
> **Les copains vont faire un pique-nique.**
> **Moi, je fais de l'allemand et ma sœur fait de l'espagnol.**

Continuons
Let's put our words together

12 **On fait les courses.**
Répétez la conversation.

(Repeat the conversation.)

Éric: Salut, Anne! Ça va?
Anne: Ça va. Qu'est-ce que tu fais?
Éric: Je fais les courses.
Anne: Ben, moi aussi. Je vais au marché de la rue Dejean. On fait nos courses ensemble?
Éric: Merci, mais j'ai beaucoup de choses différentes à acheter. Je vais aller au supermarché.
Anne: Ben, je vais avec toi. C'est dans la même direction.
Éric: D'accord.

Rue Dejean, Paris

13 **Qu'est-ce qu'ils font?** Complétez et répondez d'après la conversation. *(Complete and answer according to the conversation.)*

1. Qu'est-ce qu'il ____, Éric?
2. Qu'est-ce qu'elle ____, Anne?
3. Qu'est-ce qu'ils ____, Anne et Éric?
4. Est-ce qu'ils ____ les courses ensemble?

14 **Et toi?** Donnez des réponses personnelles. *(Give your own answers.)*

1. Tu fais quelquefois la cuisine chez toi?
2. Tu fais tes études dans un lycée français ou dans une école secondaire américaine?
3. Tu fais tes devoirs devant la télévision?
4. Tu fais du français?

15 **À chacun son travail** Suivez le modèle. *(Follow the model.)*

Moi, je fais le dîner. Et vous deux, qu'est-ce que vous faites?

Nous aussi, on fait le dîner.

1. Moi, je fais les courses.
2. Moi, je fais la cuisine.
3. Moi, je fais le déjeuner.
4. Moi, je fais les sandwichs.
5. Moi, je fais le gâteau.

16 **Historiette** **Mon copain Hugo** Complétez. *(Complete.)*

Hugo et moi, on est copains. Il est très intelligent. Hugo __1__ du russe. Moi aussi, je __2__ du russe. Nous __3__ du russe ensemble. Hugo et moi, nous __4__ quelquefois nos devoirs ensemble.

Hugo et son amie Marie __5__ de l'histoire avec Madame Delcourt. Qu'est-ce qu'ils __6__ au cours d'histoire? Ils apprennent beaucoup de nouvelles choses. Vous __7__ du français, n'est-ce pas? Vous __8__ du français avec qui?

17 **Nous sommes gentils.** Get together with a classmate. Discuss the things you do to help around the house. Decide who is the most helpful.

*For more practice using the verb **faire**, do Activity 18 on page H19 at the end of this book.*

Talking about all or some
Le partitif et l'article défini

1. In French, you use the definite article (**le, la, l', les**) when talking about something in a general sense.

Les enfants aiment le lait.	*Children like milk.*
Je déteste les œufs.	*I hate eggs.*
Je n'aime pas la salade.	*I don't like lettuce.*

2. The partitive expresses an unspecified amount. English uses "some," "any," or no word at all to express the partitive.

Do you have (any) toast?
Yes, I do. Would you like (some) jam with your toast?

3. In French, you use **de** + the definite article to express the partitive. Remember that **de** contracts with **le** and **les** to form one word, **du** and **des**.

de + le = du	Tu as du lait et du beurre?
de + les = des	Je vais acheter des fruits et des légumes.
de + la = de la	Je voudrais de la crème.
de + l' = de l'	Je voudrais de l'eau.

4. Study the following chart. It contrasts the use of a noun in the general sense with the partitive.

General Sense	Partitive
J'aime le poulet.	Je voudrais du poulet.
J'aime la viande.	Je voudrais de la viande.
J'aime l'eau minérale.	Je voudrais de l'eau minérale.
J'aime les pommes.	Je voudrais des pommes.

Note that verbs indicating likes and dislikes are followed by the definite article. All other verbs are followed by the partitive.

Il déteste la viande.	**Elle va acheter de la viande.**
J'adore le fromage.	**Tu prends du fromage?**

Continuons
Let's put our words together

18   **Qu'est-ce que je vais acheter?** Répondez d'après le modèle.
(Answer according to the model.)

Tu veux des fruits?

Oui, je vais acheter des fruits. J'aime les fruits.

1. Tu veux du pain?
2. Tu veux du fromage?
3. Tu veux des bananes?
4. Tu veux de la glace?

19 **J'aime tout!** Conversez d'après le modèle.
(Make up a conversation according to the model.)

 la crème
—**J'aime beaucoup la crème.**
—**D'accord. Je vais chercher de la crème.**

1. le saucisson   3. l'eau minérale   5. le jambon
2. le lait   4. la limonade   6. les pommes

20 **Historiette** **Des provisions** Complétez. *(Complete.)*

Au marché, Jean-Marc achète __1__ pain, __2__ jambon, __3__ fromage, __4__ fraises et __5__ crème. Il va préparer __6__ sandwichs au jambon et au fromage. Pour le dessert, il va préparer __7__ fraises avec __8__ crème.

21 **Historiette** **Des différences**
Complétez. *(Complete.)*

Isabelle Marquet a une sœur, Sophie. Quand les deux sœurs vont au restaurant, Isabelle commande toujours __1__ poisson. Elle aime bien __2__ poisson. Mais Sophie n'aime pas du tout __3__ poisson. Elle aime __4__ viande et elle commande toujours __5__ viande. Elle commande toujours __6__ bœuf. Et elle aime son bœuf à point, pas bien cuit!

Expressing what people don't have
Le partitif au négatif

1. All forms of the partitive, **du, de la, de l'**, and **des**, change to **de (d')** after a negative.

Affirmatif		Négatif	
Je veux	du pain. de la crème. de l'eau. des carottes.	Je ne veux pas	de pain. de crème. d'eau. de carottes.

Note that the same is true after **ne... plus.**

> **Je ne mange plus de viande.**

2. Remember that the definite article does not change in the negative.

> **J'aime les carottes. Je n'aime pas les carottes.**

Continuons
Let's put our words together

22 **Non, merci.** Conversez d'après le modèle.
(Make up a conversation according to the model.)

de l'eau
—**Vous voulez de l'eau?**
—**Non, merci. Pas d'eau pour moi.**

1. du pain	**3.** du porc	**5.** du lait
2. de l'agneau	**4.** des crevettes	**6.** de la limonade

23 **Qu'est-ce que tu as?** Conversez d'après le modèle.
(Make up a conversation according to the model.)

des livres
—**Tu as des livres?**
—**Non, je n'ai pas de livres. / Oui, j'ai des livres.**

1. un ami	**3.** un chat	**5.** des frères
2. une amie	**4.** des cousines	**6.** des sœurs

24 **Je voudrais...** Conversez d'après le modèle.
(Make up a conversation according to the model.)

Je voudrais du jambon, s'il vous plaît.

Je regrette, mais il n'y a plus de jambon.

1. Je voudrais de l'eau minérale, s'il vous plaît.
2. Je voudrais de la glace à la vanille, s'il vous plaît.
3. Je voudrais des croissants, s'il vous plaît.
4. Je voudrais des fraises, s'il vous plaît.
5. Je voudrais du fromage, s'il vous plaît.

25 **Juliette fait les courses.** Répondez d'après le modèle.
(Answer according to the model.)

—Elle va acheter du poisson à la boucherie?
—**Non, elle ne va pas acheter de poisson à la boucherie.
Elle va acheter de la viande.**

1. Elle va acheter du pain à la boucherie?
2. Elle va acheter du fromage à la boulangerie?
3. Elle va acheter des légumes à la charcuterie?
4. Elle va acheter de la viande à la crémerie?
5. Elle va acheter des œufs chez le marchand de fruits et légumes?

Une charcuterie, Conques, France

26 **Je n'aime pas ça!**
Répondez d'après le modèle.
(Answer according to the model.)

—Tu as de la confiture?
—**Non, je n'ai pas de confiture. Je n'aime pas la confiture.**

1. Tu as du saucisson?
2. Tu as du fromage?
3. Tu as du café?
4. Tu as de la limonade?
5. Tu as des épinards?
6. Tu as des sardines?

27 Historiette Au supermarché Complétez. *(Complete.)*

Quand je vais au supermarché, je n'achète pas __1__ fruits. Je n'aime pas __2__ fruits du supermarché. J'achète __3__ fruits au marché, chez le marchand de fruits et légumes. Je n'achète pas __4__ café au supermarché. Je n'achète pas __5__ viande. Je n'achète pas __6__ légumes, pas __7__ oignons. Qu'est-ce que j'achète au supermarché? J'achète seulement __8__ boîtes de conserve, __9__ bouteilles d'eau minérale, __10__ sel, __11__ poivre, __12__ vinaigre et __13__ huile.

28 Dans le frigidaire

 Work with a classmate. Ask him or her for something you'd like to eat or drink. Your partner will check to see whether or not it's in the refrigerator. Use the model as a guide.

—**Tu as de la glace au chocolat? J'adore la glace au chocolat.**

—**Je regrette, il n'y a plus de glace au chocolat.**

29 Un sandwich extraordinaire

Work with a classmate. Discuss what would be a great sandwich. You may (or may not) want to use some of the following ingredients.

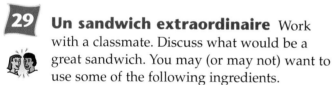

du beurre de cacahouète

de la mayonnaise

du chocolat

de la gelée de raisin

des cornichons

des sardines

Attention!

Pay special attention to the spelling and pronunciation of the following adjectives that double the consonant in the feminine.

FÉMININ	MASCULIN
bonne(s)	bon(s)
canadienne(s)	canadien(s)
gentille(s)	gentil(s)
quelle(s)	quel(s)

Complétez. (*Complete.*)

1. Tu fais de la ____ cuisine? (bon)
2. Tu fais de ____ sandwichs? (bon)
3. Tu as des amis ____ et ____? (canadien, vietnamien)
4. Tu as des amies ____? (tunisien)
5. Tu aimes les filles qui sont ____? (gentil)
6. Tu aimes ____ profs? (quel)

Telling what one can do or wants to do
Les verbes **pouvoir** et **vouloir**

1. Study the forms of the verbs **pouvoir** (*to be able to*) and **vouloir** (*to want*).

POUVOIR		VOULOIR	
je	peux	je	veux
tu	peux	tu	veux
il/elle/on	peut	il/elle/on	veut
nous	pouvons	nous	voulons
vous	pouvez	vous	voulez
ils/elles	peuvent	ils/elles	veulent

Savez-vous que... ?

Je voudrais is a polite form of **je veux.** It means "I would like."

Je voudrais une livre de haricots verts, s'il vous plaît.

Michel ne peut pas aller au marché à pied.
Il veut acheter des légumes et des fruits.
Vous voulez manger maintenant?
Vous pouvez si vous voulez.

2. In the negative, you put **ne... pas** around the verbs **pouvoir** and **vouloir**.

Je ne veux pas manger de frites.
Ils ne peuvent pas aller au restaurant ce soir.

Continuons
Let's put our words together

30 **Je veux bien, mais je ne peux pas.** Conversez d'après
le modèle. *(Make up a conversation according to the model.)*

—**Tu veux aller au restaurant?**

—**Je veux bien, mais je ne peux pas.**

1. Tu veux aller au café?
2. Tu veux dîner avec Caroline?
3. Tu veux travailler après l'école?
4. Ta sœur veut faire les courses?

5. Elle veut aller au marché?
6. Elle veut préparer le dîner?
7. Elle veut inviter des amis?

Un marché,
Saint-Rémy-de-Provence, France

31 **Si vous voulez, vous pouvez.** Conversez d'après le modèle.
(Make up a conversation according to the model.)

Nous voulons travailler.

Si vous voulez travailler, vous pouvez travailler.

1. Nous voulons manger maintenant.
2. Nous voulons inviter des amis.
3. Nous voulons aller au restaurant.
4. Nous voulons commander de la pizza.
5. Nous voulons regarder le film.
6. Nous voulons écouter nos CD.

32 **Historiette** **Pas assez d'argent** Complétez avec **pouvoir** ou **vouloir**. *(Complete with* pouvoir *or* vouloir.)

Pierre et son frère ont faim. Ils __1__ aller dans un restaurant où ils __2__ dîner rapidement. Ils __3__ commander deux hamburgers chacun, mais ils ne __4__ pas. Pierre insiste, mais son frère ne __5__ pas: «Pas question! On n'a pas assez d'argent! Tu __6__ commander seulement un hamburger aujourd'hui.»

33 **Qui peut préparer le dîner?** Complétez. *(Complete.)*

Marie: Je voudrais bien faire le dîner ce soir, mais vraiment, je ne __1__ (pouvoir) pas.

Julien: Tu ne __2__ (pouvoir) pas? Pourquoi?

Marie: Je __3__ (être) très fatiguée! Je __4__ (être) vraiment crevée.

Julien: On __5__ (pouvoir) aller au restaurant, si tu __6__ (vouloir).

Marie: Oh, je ne __7__ (vouloir) pas aller au restaurant ce soir.

Julien: On __8__ (pouvoir) faire des sandwichs.

Marie: Oui, ou… toi, tu __9__ (pouvoir) faire le dîner.

Julien: Je __10__ (vouloir) bien, mais ce n'__11__ (être) pas une très bonne idée.

Marie: Pourquoi?

Julien: Parce que je __12__ (faire) très mal la cuisine!

34 **Pourquoi pas?** Work with a classmate. Tell each other some things you or you and your friends want to do but can't. When possible, give reasons.

 *For more practice using the verbs **pouvoir** and **vouloir**, do Activity 19 on page H20 at the end of this book.*

Vous êtes sur le bon chemin. Allez-y!

Conversation

Au marché

Marchand: Et maintenant, je suis à vous, madame. Comment allez-vous ce matin?

Mme Brun: Très bien, merci. Et vous?

Marchand: Oh, comme ci, comme ça! Enfin… Qu'est-ce que vous désirez aujourd'hui?

Mme Brun: Je voudrais des haricots verts et des carottes. C'est combien, les haricots verts?

Marchand: Quatre euros le kilo. Et ils sont bons!

Mme Brun: Alors, un kilo, s'il vous plaît, et une livre de carottes.

Marchand: Et avec ça, madame?

Mme Brun: C'est tout, merci. Ça fait combien?

Marchand: Alors, un kilo de haricots verts, une livre de carottes… Ça fait quatre euros cinquante.

Mme Brun: Voilà, monsieur.

Marchand: Merci, madame. Et à samedi prochain.

Après la conversation

Répondez. *(Answer.)*

1. Mme Brun fait ses courses?
2. Le marchand va bien?
3. Mme Brun fait ses courses au supermarché?
4. Elle parle au marchand de légumes?
5. Qu'est-ce qu'elle veut acheter?
6. Elle veut des haricots verts?
7. Ça fait combien, les haricots verts et les carottes?

Parlons un peu plus
Let's talk some more

Qu'est-ce qu'on va manger?

Work with a classmate. Prepare a menu in French for tomorrow's meals—**le petit déjeuner, le déjeuner et le dîner.** Based on your menus, prepare a shopping list. Be sure to include the quantities you need.

Une poissonnerie, Abidjan, Côte d'Ivoire

Prononciation

Les sons /œ/ et /œ/

1. Listen to the difference in the vowel sounds in **peut** and **peuvent.** The sound /œ/ in **peut** is a closed vowel sound and the sound /œ/ in **peuvent** is an open vowel sound. Repeat the following words with the sound /œ/.

> il peut il veut des œufs deux

2. Repeat the following words with the sound /œ/.

> ils peuvent ils veulent un œuf
> leur sœur du beurre

3. Now repeat the following pairs of words. Be sure to distinguish between the two vowel sounds.

> il peut / ils peuvent
> il veut / ils veulent

4. Now repeat the following sentences.

> Elle veut faire les courses, mais ils ne veulent pas.
> Elle veut du beurre et des œufs.
> Leur sœur est sérieuse.

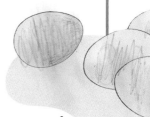

un œuf

des œufs

Lectures culturelles

Les courses

C'est aujourd'hui mardi. À dix heures du matin, comme tous les matins, excepté le lundi quand les magasins sont fermés[1], Mme Lelong quitte son appartement. Elle a son sac et elle va faire les courses. Elle fait les courses dans différents petits magasins. Elle achète du pain tous les jours. Elle va à la boulangerie où elle achète une baguette. Si elle veut de la viande, elle va à la boucherie. Si elle veut du poisson, elle peut aller à la poissonnerie, mais elle est très loin. Pour un pot de confiture ou une bouteille d'eau minérale, l'épicerie n'est pas loin.

Après le déjeuner, si elle n'a pas assez de pain pour le soir, elle peut acheter une autre baguette. Mais pas avant 16 heures. Les petits magasins sont fermés tous les jours de 13 heures à 16 heures, et bien sûr le dimanche!

[1] fermés *closed*

Une boulangerie-pâtisserie, Paris

Un marchand de fruits, Paris

Haïti

Une boucherie, Domme, France

Une boulangerie, Paris

Les Français aiment bien aller chez les petits commerçants du quartier—l'épicier, le boucher, le boulanger, etc. Leurs prix sont un peu plus chers[2] qu'au supermarché, mais la qualité de leurs produits est très bonne. Il y a aussi le côté humain[3]. Les Français aiment bavarder (converser) un peu avec le marchand ou la marchande. On trouve ça sympa.

[2] Leurs prix sont un peu plus chers *Their prices are a little more expensive*
[3] côté humain *human dimension*

Après la lecture

A Madame Lelong Répondez. *(Answer.)*

1. Mme Lelong quitte son appartement à quelle heure?
2. Qu'est-ce qu'elle prend pour faire ses courses?
3. Elle fait ses courses où?
4. Elle va où pour acheter du pain?
5. Si elle veut de la viande, elle va où?
6. Si elle veut du poisson, elle peut aller où?
7. Qu'est-ce qu'elle achète à l'épicerie?
8. Quand est-ce que les magasins sont fermés?

B Stratégie de lecture Reread the Reading Strategy on page 206. You don't know the meaning of the word **commerçants**. Using the suggestion given in the Reading Strategy, can you figure out the meaning of this word?

C Les petits commerçants Expliquez. *(Explain.)*

1. Qui sont les petits commerçants du quartier?
2. Comment est la qualité de leurs produits?
3. En général, comment sont leurs prix?
4. Qu'est-ce que les Français aiment faire avec les commerçants?

Les grandes surfaces

Beaucoup de Français font leurs courses dans les petits magasins de leur quartier. Mais beaucoup d'autres Français—surtout les gens[1] qui travaillent ou qui n'habitent pas en ville—font leurs courses dans les grandes surfaces.

Les grandes surfaces sont de grands supermarchés ou hypermarchés. Ils sont généralement situés à la périphérie des villes. Il y a toujours un grand parking parce que les clients y vont en voiture.

Dans un hypermarché on peut tout acheter: de la nourriture, mais aussi des vêtements[2], des bicyclettes, des livres, des disques et même des ordinateurs[3]. Les clients prennent des chariots pour transporter leurs achats[4]. Les grandes chaînes ont pour nom Leclerc et Carrefour.

[1] gens *people*
[2] vêtements *clothes*
[3] ordinateurs *computers*
[4] achats *purchases*

Un hypermarché, Nantes

L'intérieur d'un hypermarché

Après la lecture

Les courses Vrai ou faux? *(True or false?)*
1. Les supermarchés et les hypermarchés sont des grandes surfaces.
2. Les grandes surfaces sont situées surtout dans les grandes villes.
3. Les clients vont presque toujours à pied dans les grandes surfaces.
4. Dans un hypermarché on peut acheter toutes sortes de marchandises.

Les marchés

Sarlat-la-Canéda, Dordogne

Dans les villes et les villages de France, il y a toujours un marché. Dans les grandes villes, il y a des marchés permanents temporaires. Les marchés temporaires ont lieu[1] en général deux fois par semaine, le mercredi ou le jeudi et le samedi. Ils ont lieu dans la rue ou sur une place.

Les marchés existent dans les autres pays francophones. Voici un très joli marché à Dakar. Et voici un marché à Fort-de-France. Les fruits et les légumes ont l'air[2] très bons, n'est-ce pas? Ils sont délicieux!

[1] ont lieu *take place*　　[2] ont l'air *look*

Dakar, Sénégal

Après la lecture

Les marchés Complétez. (*Complete.*)

1. Dans les villes et les villages de France, il y a toujours un _____.
2. Les marchés peuvent être temporaires ou _____.
3. Ils peuvent avoir lieu dans _____ ou _____.
4. Ils ont lieu le _____ ou le _____ et le _____.
5. Il y a aussi des marchés dans _____.

Fort-de-France, Martinique

Maroc

Le Mali

CONNEXIONS

Les mathématiques

Les conversions

When you travel in many of the French-speaking countries, or almost anywhere in Europe, you need to make many mathematical conversions. The metric system, rather than the English system, is used for distance, weights, and measures.

soupe d'été

Je trouve sympa de présenter la soupe avec tous ces petits morceaux de légumes. Parfois, je la sers accompagnée de croûtons de pain à l'ail et de gruyère coupé en dés. On se régale tous. Au menu, j'ai prévu une salade crue (pour la vitamine C) avec un œuf dur (pour les éléments bâtisseurs: les protéines). 1 œuf, cela peut remplacer 50 g de viande ou de poisson.

LES USTENSILES
- 1 planche à découper
- 1 cocotte
- 1 couteau de cuisine en acier inoxydable
- 1 cuillère à soupe
- 1 cuillère en bois

LES INGREDIENTS POUR 4 PERSONNES
- Pommes de terre : 250 g — 3 moyennes
- Courgettes : 250 g — 2 moyennes
- Tomates : 3 moyennes
- Oignons : 2
- Huile : 1 cuillerée à soupe
- Eau : 1 litre

Le système métrique

Le système métrique est un système décimal: il a pour base 10. Les mesures ont pour base le mètre et les poids ont pour base le gramme. Pour les liquides, la base est le litre. Les unités supérieures et inférieures sont formées avec les préfixes suivants:

kilo = × 1 000	un kilogramme = 1 000 grammes
hecto = × 100	un hectomètre = 100 mètres
déca = × 10	un décalitre = 10 litres
déci = ÷ 10	un décimètre = 1 mètre ÷ 10
centi = ÷ 100	un centilitre = 1 litre ÷ 100
milli = ÷ 1 000	un milligramme = 1 gramme ÷ 1 000

Un kilogramme (un kilo) est équivalent à environ[1] deux livres[2]. Une livre est équivalente à un peu moins[3] d'un demi-kilo. Un mile américain est équivalent à environ un kilomètre et demi. Un litre est équivalent à environ un quart américain.

[1] environ *about*
[2] livres *pounds*
[3] un peu moins *a little less*

Après la lecture

Poids et mesures

Vrai ou faux? *(True or false?)*

1. Le système anglais de poids et mesures a pour base 10.
2. Les poids ont comme unité de base le litre.
3. Il y a 1 000 grammes dans un kilo.
4. Un kilo est l'équivalent d'environ deux livres anglaises.
5. Une livre américaine est l'équivalent de 500 grammes.
6. On mesure les liquides en quarts en France.
7. En France, on mesure les liquides en litres.

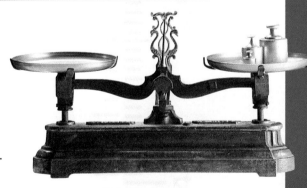

C'est à vous

Use what you have learned

PARLER

1 **Au marché**

✔ *Buy food from a vendor at the market*

Work with a classmate. You are spending a semester studying in Belgium. You are going to prepare a dinner for your Belgian family. Decide what you need to buy at the market and in what quantities. Then have a conversation with your classmate, who will be the vendor at the market.

PARLER

2 **Je veux bien, mais je ne peux pas parce que...**

✔ *Talk about what you want to do but can't*

Work in groups of three or four. Tell some things you want to do but can't do because you are going to do something else. Tell what you are going to do.

PARLER
ECRIRE

3 **Une compétition**

✔ *Express quantities*

Compete with a classmate. You each have two minutes. See which one of you can make up the most phrases using the following words.

un kilo de · une livre de · un litre de · une bouteille de · une boîte de · six tranches de · un paquet de

4 Une publicité

✔ *Write an advertisement for a supermarket*

Using these French supermarket ads as a guide, write similar food advertisements in French for your local supermarket. Choose any four foods you like to advertise.

Writing Strategy

Ordering ideas You can order ideas in a variety of ways when writing. Therefore, you must be aware of the purpose of your writing in order to choose the best way to organize your material. When describing an event, it is logical to put the events in the order in which they happen. Using a sensible and logical approach helps readers develop a picture in their minds.

5 On fait les courses.

Your class is planning a French meal. Describe the trip you take with your class to the local market or supermarket to buy the ingredients. Tell what you buy, whom you buy it from, and how much everything costs.

Un supermarché, Dakar, Sénégal

Assessment

Vocabulaire

1 Identifiez. *(Identify each item.)*

To review **Mots 1,** turn to pages 186–187.

1.

2.

3.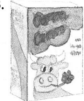

4.

2 Choisissez. *(Choose.)*

To review **Mots 2,** turn to pages 190–191.

5. Une pomme et une poire sont des _____.
     a. fraises   **b.** légumes   **c.** fruits

6. C'est _____, un kilo de carottes?
     a. comment   **b.** combien   **c.** un marchand

7. Il va acheter _____ de moutarde.
     a. un paquet   **b.** une boîte   **c.** un pot

8. Je voudrais six _____ de jambon, s'il vous plaît.
     a. bouteilles   **b.** tranches   **c.** litres

Structure

To review the verb **faire,** turn to page 194.

3 Complétez avec «faire». *(Complete with faire.)*

9. Je _____ les courses le matin.
10. Mon frère _____ du latin.
11. Vous _____ vos devoirs?
12. Les élèves ne _____ pas la cuisine.

4 **Choisissez.** *(Choose.)*

13. Moi, j'aime beaucoup ____ lait.
    a. le   **b.** du   **c.** de

14. Je voudrais ____ eau.
    a. d'   **b.** de l'   **c.** du

15. Il va acheter ____ fruits et ____ légumes.
    a. des   **b.** de   **c.** les

To review the partitive and the definite article, turn to pages 196, 198.

5 **Récrivez au négatif.** *(Rewrite the sentences in the negative.)*

16. Je vais acheter du pain.
17. Je voudrais de la crème.

To review these special adjectives, turn to page 201.

6 **Récrivez les phrases.** *(Rewrite the sentences.)*

18. Les carottes sont très bonnes.
    Le poisson ____.
19. Tu veux quel sandwich?
    Tu veux ____ salade?

To review the verbs *pouvoir* and *vouloir,* turn to page 201.

7 **Complétez.** *(Complete.)*

20. Je ____ faire le travail. (pouvoir)
21. Vous ____ aller au restaurant? (vouloir)
22. Tu ____ aller au marché. (pouvoir)
23. Ils ____ parler au prof. (vouloir)

Culture

8 **Répondez.** *(Answer.)*

24. Beaucoup de magasins sont fermés quel jour en France?
25. On peut aller où pour acheter un pot de confiture ou une bouteille d'eau minérale?

To review this cultural information, turn to pages 206–207.

Vocabulaire

Shopping for food

faire les courses (f. pl.)	une poissonnerie	le/la marchand(e)
une boulangerie	une charcuterie	un sac
une pâtisserie	une épicerie	surgelé(e)
une crémerie	un marché	
une boucherie	un supermarché	

Identifying some food

du pain	de la viande	de l'eau minérale	un légume
un pain complet	du bœuf	de la moutarde	une salade
un croissant	de l'agneau (m.)	des petits pois (m. pl.)	une carotte
une baguette	du porc	un fruit	une pomme de terre
une tarte aux pommes	du jambon	une banane	des haricots verts
de la crème	du saucisson	une pomme	des épinards (m. pl.)
du lait	du poisson	une orange	une tomate
du beurre	une crevette	une poire	un oignon
du fromage	un crabe	une fraise	
de la confiture	du sel	un melon	
un œuf	du poivre		
un yaourt	de l'huile (f.)		
un poulet	du vinaigre		

Identifying quantities

un paquet	un litre
un pot	une douzaine
un gramme	une boîte
un kilo(gramme)	une bouteille
une livre	une tranche

> **How well do you know your vocabulary?**
> - Choose two foods that you like from the list.
> - Tell how you buy each, for example, *une douzaine, une bouteille*, etc.

Other useful words and expressions

aller chercher	C'est combien?	Vous voulez autre chose?	C'est tout.
il n'y a plus de	Ça fait combien?	Et avec ça?	Pourquoi?
je regrette	bon(ne)		parce que

Technotour
BON VOYAGE!

Avant de visionner

In this video episode, Vincent and Manu go food shopping. Manu demonstrates once again how he turns a routine task into fun.

Vincent et Manu font les courses.

Manu «prépare» un repas fabuleux.

FRENCH ONLINE

À découvrir

Learn more about markets in Paris online.

Marché Poncelet, Paris

In the Chapter 6 Internet activity, you will have a chance to learn more about food in the Francophone world. To begin your virtual adventure, go to the Glencoe French Web site: **french.glencoe.com**

Les vêtements

Objectifs

In this chapter you will learn to:

✔ *identify and describe articles of clothing*

✔ *state color and size preferences*

✔ *shop for clothing*

✔ *describe people's activities*

✔ *compare people and things*

✔ *express opinions and make observations*

✔ *discuss clothes and clothes shopping in the French-speaking world*

Un tissu de la Côte d'Ivoire

ROYAUME DU MAROC

AIT MOUHAD

0.15 POSTES

Vocabulaire

Les vêtements sport

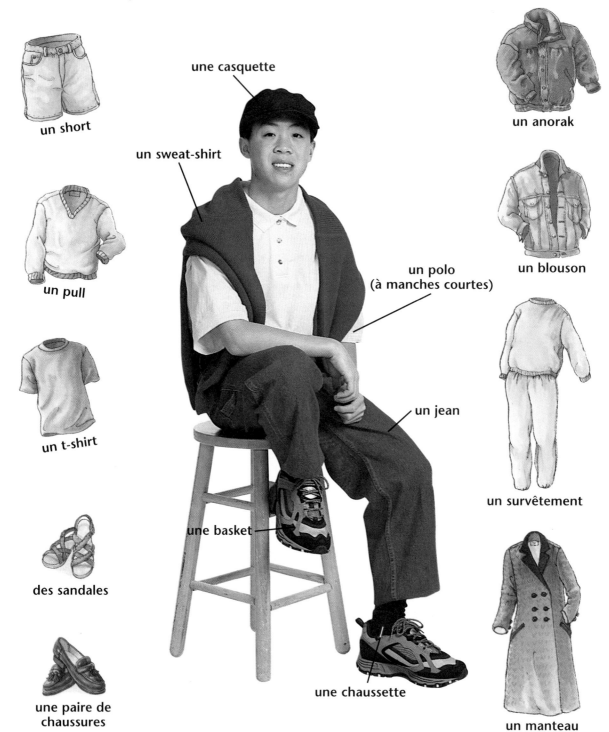

un short

une casquette

un anorak

un sweat-shirt

un pull

un blouson

un polo
(à manches courtes)

un t-shirt

un jean

un survêtement

des sandales

une basket

une paire de
chaussures

une chaussette

un manteau

Les vêtements pour hommes 🎧

un centre commercial

une boutique

une chemise (à manches longues)

un complet

une veste

une cravate

un pantalon

Marc porte des sandales.
Il voit des chaussures
dans la vitrine.
Il entre dans la boutique.

plus cher

le prix

35€

20€

moins cher

Les prix sont moins chers
quand il y a des soldes.

Les vêtements pour femmes 🎧

Johanne va au grand magasin.
Elle voit beaucoup de chemisiers.
Elle voit des chemisiers au rayon des
vêtements pour femmes.
Tous les chemisiers sont en solde!

Qu'est-ce que je vais
mettre samedi?

une robe sport

un chemisier

un tailleur

une jupe plissée

une
vendeuse

une robe
habillée

Commençons
Let's use our new words

1 **Chloé et Adrien** Répondez d'après les photos. (*Answer according to the photos.*)

1. Qu'est-ce que Chloé porte?
2. Et Adrien? Qu'est-ce qu'il porte?

2 **Qu'est-ce qu'on va mettre?**
Répondez. (*Answer.*)

1. Ce soir M. Ben Azar va aller dans un restaurant chic. Qu'est-ce qu'il va mettre?
2. Qu'est-ce que sa femme va mettre?
3. Qu'est-ce que tu portes à l'école?
4. Qu'est-ce que tu portes à la maison?
5. Qu'est-ce qu'on porte en juillet et en août?
6. Qu'est-ce qu'on porte en décembre et janvier?
7. Qu'est-ce qu'une femme porte quand elle va travailler?
8. Qu'est-ce qu'un homme porte quand il va au travail?

Chloé   **Adrien**

3 **Sport ou habillé?** Identifiez. (*Tell whether each item is casual or formal.*)

1. des baskets
2. un tailleur
3. un jean
4. un complet
5. un blouson
6. une cravate
7. un polo à manches courtes
8. une chemise à manches longues
9. un survêtement
10. une jupe plissée

La vitrine d'une boutique, Paris

4 **Historiette Au rayon des chemisiers** Inventez une histoire. *(Make up a story.)*

1. Mélanie entre dans un grand magasin ou dans une boutique?
2. La boutique est dans une rue ou dans un centre commercial?
3. Il y a des soldes aujourd'hui?
4. Il y a des chemisiers dans la vitrine?
5. Elle va au rayon des chemisiers?
6. Elle voit beaucoup de chemisiers?
7. Elle parle à la vendeuse?
8. Elle veut un chemisier à manches courtes ou à manches longues?
9. Elle veut un chemisier habillé ou sport?
10. Les chemisiers sont en solde?
11. Les vêtements sont moins chers quand ils sont en solde?

5 **C'est qui?** Work with a classmate. One of you describes what someone in the class is wearing and the other has to guess who it is. Take turns.

6 **Mon ensemble favori** Work with a classmate. Discuss what you consider an ideal outfit for school. Tell what you like to wear and what you don't like to wear. See if you are on the same wavelength.

Des jeunes habillés sport

For more practice using words from Mots 1, do Activity 20 on page H21 at the end of this book.

Vocabulaire

On fait des courses.

> Il est joli, le pantalon vert. Tu ne trouves pas?

> Si, j'aime beaucoup!

le shopping

> Vous faites quelle pointure?

> Je fais du 38.

une cabine d'essayage

> Ça va, le pantalon?

> Non, il est trop grand. Il est trop large. Je voudrais la taille au-dessous.

> Vous faites quelle taille?

> Je fais du 38.

> Non, il est trop petit. Il est trop serré. Je voudrais la taille au-dessus.

essayer

Julien essaie le pantalon.

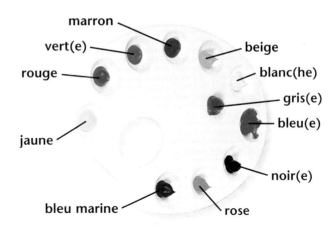

marron
vert(e)
rouge
jaune
beige
blanc(he)
gris(e)
bleu(e)
noir(e)
bleu marine
rose

De quelle couleur est la jupe?
Elle est verte.

Et les chaussures?
Elles sont marron.

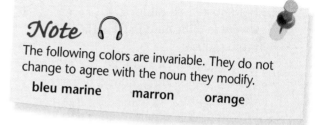

Note 🎧

The following colors are invariable. They do not change to agree with the noun they modify.

bleu marine   **marron**   **orange**

À mon avis, la robe rouge est plus jolie que la (robe) verte.

Moi, je crois que j'aime mieux la (robe) verte.

Moi, le rouge, c'est ma couleur favorite.

Vocabulaire

Commençons
Let's use our new words

7 **Historiette** **Olivier fait des courses.** Inventez une histoire.
(Make up a story.)

1. Olivier fait des courses?
2. Il veut acheter un blue jean?
3. Il voit un jean qu'il aime dans la vitrine?
4. Il entre dans le grand magasin?
5. Il fait quelle taille?
6. Il va essayer le jean?
7. Il est comment, le pantalon—grand, petit, juste à sa taille?
8. Il veut la taille au-dessus ou la taille au-dessous?
9. Les jeans sont en solde?
10. Ils sont moins chers quand ils sont en solde?
11. Olivier trouve que les jeans sont chers?
12. Olivier va acheter le jean?

Rayon des vêtements pour hommes, Galeries Lafayette, Paris

8 **Ta couleur favorite** Donnez des réponses personnelles.
(Give your own answers.)

1. De quelle couleur est ton blouson favori?
2. De quelle couleur est ton jean favori?
3. De quelle couleur est ta chemise favorite ou ton chemisier favori?
4. Qu'est-ce que tu portes aujourd'hui? De quelle couleur sont tes vêtements?

9 **Mes préférences** Donnez des réponses personnelles.
(Give your own answers.)

1. Tu aimes mieux les vêtements sport ou habillés?
2. Les baskets ou les chaussures?
3. Les chemises ou les chemisiers à manches longues ou à manches courtes?
4. Les vêtements un peu serrés ou larges?
5. Les couleurs sombres ou les couleurs claires?
6. Les vêtements chers ou pas chers?

10 **De petits problèmes** Répondez. *(Answer.)*

1. Les chaussures sont trop petites ou trop grandes?

2. La jupe est trop longue ou trop courte?

3. Le pantalon est un peu serré ou un peu large?

4. Les manches sont trop longues ou trop courtes?

5. Le tailleur est joli ou pas?

11 **Les couleurs** Complétez d'après la couleur. *(Complete with the color.)*

1. Aurélien va acheter un pantalon _____.

4. Justine va acheter une robe _____.

2. Anne va acheter un chemisier _____.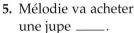

5. Mélodie va acheter une jupe _____.

3. Fred va acheter une chemise _____.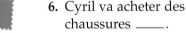

6. Cyril va acheter des chaussures _____.

12 **Jeu** **Qui porte une jupe bleue?** Study the clothing of all the students in the next row for several minutes. Then turn your back to that row. One of your classmates will mention an item of clothing and ask you who is wearing it. If you don't remember, your classmates can help you out by giving hints such as: **La personne est blonde. Elle est très amusante.**

 For more practice using words from Mots 2, do Activity 21 on page H22 at the end of this book.

Structure

Describing people's activities
Le verbe **mettre**

1. Study the forms of the verb **mettre** (*to put, to put on*) in the present tense.

METTRE	
je mets	nous mettons
tu mets	vous mettez
il/elle/on met	ils/elles mettent

2. Note that **mettre** has various meanings.

> **Il met une chemise et une cravate pour aller au travail.**
> **Les serveurs mettent la table au restaurant.**
> **On met la télévision pour regarder un film.**

For more information about shopping for clothing in the Francophone world, go to the Glencoe French Web site: french.glencoe.com

Continuons
Let's put our words together

13 **Qu'est-ce qu'on met?** Répondez. (*Answer.*)

1. Tu mets un survêtement quand tu fais du jogging?
2. Tu mets la table pour le dîner?
3. Ton père met la télé le matin pendant le petit déjeuner?
4. Ta mère met la radio pour écouter les informations?
5. Tes copains mettent une cravate pour aller à l'école?
6. Tes copines mettent une jupe plissée pour aller à l'école?

Des amis devant l'école

14 **Dans le sac à dos** Complétez avec **mettre** d'après les dessins.
(Complete with mettre *according to the illustrations.)*

1. Qu'est-ce qu'ils _____ dans leur sac à dos?
   Ils _____.

2. Qu'est-ce que tu _____ dans ton sac à dos?
   Je _____.

3. Qu'est-ce que vous _____ dans votre sac à dos?
   On _____.

15 **Qu'est-ce que vous mettez?** Work with a classmate. Compare what you wear on different occasions.

- pour aller à l'école
- quand vous allez dîner chez des amis de vos parents
- pour aller au cinéma le samedi soir
- pour aller à un mariage
- pour aller dans un restaurant chic

Complétez et prononcez.
(Complete and pronounce aloud.)

1. sérieux
   un élève _____ et une élève _____
2. long
   une jupe _____ et un manteau _____
3. favori
   mon pull _____ et ma robe _____
4. blanc
   une chemise _____ et un chemisier _____
5. long
   des pantalons _____ et des manches _____

Attention!

Pay particular attention to the spelling and pronunciation of the following adjectives. Note that the final consonant sound is pronounced in the feminine forms but not in the masculine forms.

Féminin	Masculin
sérieuse(s)	sérieux
longue(s)	long(s)
favorite(s)	favori(s)
blanche(s)	blanc(s)

Note that all forms of **cher—chère(s)**, **cher(s)**—sound alike.

For more practice using the verb **mettre**, *do Activity 22 on page H23 at the end of this book.*

Comparing people and things
Le comparatif des adjectifs

1. When you compare two or more people or things, you use **plus (+)... que, moins (−)... que,** and **aussi (=)... que.** Study the following chart.

> Le jean est plus cher que le pantalon.
> Le jean est aussi cher que le pantalon.
> Le jean est moins cher que le pantalon.

> **Les sandales sont moins confortables que les baskets.**
> **Mais elles sont plus confortables que les chaussures.**

Attention!

Note the liaison with **plus** and **moins.**
plus‿intéressant(e)
moins‿élégant(e)

2. You use the stress pronouns **moi, toi, lui, elle, nous, vous, eux,** and **elles** after **que (qu')** when comparing people.

> Elle est plus sympa que moi.
> Elle est aussi sympa que lui.
> Elle est moins sympa que vous.

> **Il est aussi intelligent que moi.**
> **Mais il est plus intelligent qu'eux.**

Continuons
Let's put our words together

16 **À mon avis** Donnez des réponses personnelles. *(Give your own answers.)*

1. Le français, c'est plus difficile ou plus facile que les maths?
2. Le professeur de français est plus strict, moins strict ou aussi strict que les autres professeurs?
3. Le football américain est plus amusant ou moins amusant que le basket-ball?
4. Ton école secondaire est plus grande ou moins grande que ton école primaire?
5. Ta classe de français est aussi grande ou plus petite que ta classe de sciences?

17 Plus ou moins que l'autre

Plus ou moins que l'autre Répondez d'après les dessins. Suivez le modèle. *(Answer according to the illustrations.)*

—**Le blouson bleu est aussi grand que le blouson noir?**
—**Oui, le blouson bleu est aussi grand que le blouson noir.**

1. Le blouson bleu est aussi cher que le blouson noir?
2. Le blouson bleu est moins beau que le blouson noir?
3. La jupe jaune est moins chère que la jupe grise?
4. La jupe grise est plus courte que la jupe jaune?

18 Ma famille et mes copains

Ma famille et mes copains Donnez des réponses personnelles. *(Give your own answers.)*

1. Ta sœur, elle est plus petite ou plus grande que toi?
   Tu es plus grand(e) ou plus petit(e) qu'elle?
2. Tu es plus patient(e) ou moins patient(e) que ton frère?
   Il est plus patient ou moins patient que toi?
3. Tes grands-parents sont aussi stricts que tes parents?
   Ils sont vraiment moins stricts qu'eux?
4. Tes copains sont plus sociables que toi?
   Tu es plus timide qu'eux?

19 Comparaisons

Comparaisons Work with a classmate. Compare people you know. You may want to use the following words.

grand   petit   sociable   intéressant   dynamique

amusant   beau   sympa   sérieux

Seeing and believing
Les verbes **voir** et **croire**

Study the forms of the verbs **voir** (*to see*) and **croire** (*to believe*).

VOIR		CROIRE	
je	vois	je	crois
tu	vois	tu	crois
il/elle/on	voit	il/elle/on	croit
nous	voyons	nous	croyons
vous	voyez	vous	croyez
ils/elles	voient	ils/elles	croient

Savez-vous que... ?

When **voir** and **croire** are followed by a clause, you must use **que (qu')**.
Je vois que vous êtes content.
Je crois qu'il est content aussi.

Continuons
Let's put our words together

20 **À votre avis** Répondez que oui. (*Answer yes.*)

1. Vos parents croient que vous êtes intelligents?
2. Votre professeur de français croit que vous travaillez bien?
3. Vos camarades de classe croient que vous êtes sympathiques?
4. Vos grands-parents croient que vous êtes adorables?

21 **Dans une boutique**
Répondez que oui. (*Answer yes.*)

1. Tu vois des choses que tu aimes dans la vitrine?
2. Tu crois qu'on peut entrer dans la boutique?
3. Tu crois que tu vas acheter le pantalon noir?
4. Tu crois qu'ils vont avoir ta taille?
5. Tu vois le prix?

22 **Vraiment?** Conversez d'après le modèle.
(*Make up a conversation according to the model.*)

—Il va bientôt arriver.
—Vous croyez?

1. Il va bientôt téléphoner.
2. Il va bientôt payer.
3. Il va bientôt rentrer.
4. Il va bientôt acheter une maison.

23 **Des opinions différentes!** Complétez avec **croir.**
(Complete with croire.*)*

1. Il ____ que tout est moins cher pendant les soldes. Et vous, vous ____ ça aussi?
2. Julien ____ que l'examen va être facile, mais nous, on ____ qu'il va être difficile.
3. Tu ____ que les chats sont plus intelligents que les chiens, mais moi, je ____ que les chiens sont plus intelligents que les chats.
4. Alice ____ que Paris est près de Nice, mais nous, nous ____ que c'est loin de Nice.
5. Moi, je ____ que la cousine de Sandra est française, mais mes copains ____ qu'elle est italienne.

Attention!

Pay particular attention to the spelling of verbs that end in –**yer**.

ESSAYER j'essaie / nous essayons
tu essaies / vous essayez
il essaie / ils essaient

PAYER je paie / nous payons
tu paies / vous payez
il paie / ils paient

Complétez. *(Complete.)*

1. Vous ____ où? (payer)
2. On ____ à la caisse. (payer)
3. Je ____ parce que j'invite. (payer)
4. Il va ____ la chemise? (essayer)
5. Non, mais il ____ le pantalon. (essayer)

*For more practice using the verbs **voir** and **croire**, do Activity 23 on page H24 at the end of this book.*

Vous êtes sur le bon chemin. Allez-y!

Conversation

Dans une petite boutique

Vendeur: Bonjour, monsieur. Vous voulez voir quelque chose?

Fabien: Bonjour. Oui, je voudrais un jean, s'il vous plaît.

Vendeur: Oui, vous faites quelle taille?

Fabien: Je fais du 36.

Vendeur: Voilà un 36. La cabine d'essayage est juste là.
(Fabien essaie le jean dans la cabine d'essayage.)

Vendeur: Ça va, la taille?

Fabien: Pas vraiment. Je crois que c'est un peu petit.

Vendeur: Vous voulez la taille au-dessus?

Fabien: Oui, je veux bien.
(Fabien essaie l'autre jean.)

Fabien: Ah oui, c'est bien.

Vendeur: Vous désirez autre chose?

Fabien: Oui, un polo bleu marine ou blanc.

Vendeur: Vous avez de la chance. Ils sont en solde.

Après la conversation

Répondez. *(Answer.)*

1. À qui parle Fabien?
2. Qu'est-ce qu'il veut voir?
3. Il fait quelle taille?
4. Où est-ce qu'il essaie son jean?
5. Le jean est trop grand ou trop petit?
6. Il veut la taille au-dessus ou la taille au-dessous?
7. Il veut acheter autre chose?

Parlons un peu plus
Let's talk some more

A **Au magasin** Work with a classmate. Take turns playing the role of the salesperson and the customer in the following situations.

- **Au rayon des vêtements pour hommes** You want to buy a shirt as a gift for your father or a friend. They have his size but not the color you want.

- **Au rayon des chaussures** You are looking for a pair of brown shoes. The ones the salesperson shows you are quite expensive.

B **Jeu** **Qu'est-ce qu'il/elle porte?** Have one student leave the room while others choose a classmate to describe. The student who left comes back in and has to guess which classmate the others have chosen by asking questions about his or her clothes.

Prononciation

Les sons /sh/ et /zh/

It is important to make a distinction between the sounds /sh/ as in **chat** and /zh/ as in **joli.** Put your fingers on your throat. When you say the sound /zh/ as in **joli,** you should feel a vibration, but not when you say /sh/ as in **chat.** Repeat the following words with the sound /sh/.

acheter	chaussure	chemise
chemisier	achat	short

chemise
orange

Now repeat the following words with the sound /zh/.

large	jupe	orange
beige	joli	

Now repeat the following sentences that combine both sounds.

J'achète toujours mes chaussures au marché.
Le t-shirt jaune est joli, mais le short orange est moins cher.

CONVERSATION

deux cent trente-cinq 🔶 **235**

Lectures culturelles

Rue du Faubourg-Saint-Honoré, Paris

On fait des courses où, à Paris?

Chez les grands couturiers[1]

Les noms des grands couturiers français—Yves Saint-Laurent, Dior, Cardin, Givenchy, Coco Chanel—sont célèbres dans le monde entier. On peut voir les boutiques élégantes des grands couturiers dans l'avenue Montaigne ou dans la rue du Faubourg-Saint-Honoré. C'est là que les gens aisés (riches) vont acheter leurs vêtements et accessoires.

Magasin de la Samaritaine, Paris

Les petites boutiques et les grands magasins

Mais la plupart (la majorité) des Parisiens ne font pas leurs achats chez les grands couturiers. Partout à Paris, il y a de petites boutiques qui sont beaucoup moins chères que les boutiques des grands couturiers. Il y a aussi des grands magasins. À Paris, les grands magasins du Printemps et des Galeries Lafayette sont les plus renommés (célèbres). Il y a aussi des chaînes de magasins bon marché[2] comme le Prisunic.

Dans les grands magasins, on peut aller d'un rayon à un autre. Il y a souvent des articles en promotion[3] et deux fois par an il y a des soldes—début janvier et début juillet.

[1] grands couturiers *designers*
[2] bon marché *inexpensive*
[3] en promotion *on special*

Haïti

Les marchés aux puces[4]

Les adolescents aiment bien aller aux puces. Ils y vont pendant le week-end parce que les marchés aux puces sont fermés[5] pendant la semaine.

Les marchés aux puces sont de grands marchés où on trouve de tout—des vêtements, de la nourriture, des tables, des chaises, etc. On peut trouver un vêtement ou un accessoire avec la griffe[6] d'un grand couturier très bon marché… ou très cher!

[4] marchés aux puces *flea markets*
[5] fermés *closed*
[6] griffe *label*

Marché aux puces, Saint-Ouen, Paris

Après la lecture

A Des informations Donnez les informations suivantes. *(Give the following information.)*
1. les noms de quelques grands couturiers français
2. les noms de quelques rues très élégantes à Paris
3. là où la plupart des Parisiens vont faire leurs achats
4. le nom d'un grand magasin parisien assez élégant
5. le nom d'une chaîne de magasins aux prix plus modestes
6. là où les adolescents aiment faire leurs achats

B Les achats Vrai ou faux? *(True or false?)*
1. La plupart des Parisiens font leurs achats chez les grands couturiers.
2. Les petites boutiques sont plus chères que les boutiques des grands couturiers.
3. Les Galeries Lafayette, c'est le nom d'un grand magasin à Paris.
4. Les grands magasins n'ont pas de soldes.
5. On va souvent au marché aux puces le lundi.
6. On peut acheter beaucoup de marchandises différentes dans un marché aux puces.

Marché aux puces, Nice

Les vêtements

En Afrique du Nord

Dans les pays du Maghreb (le Maroc, l'Algérie et la Tunisie), beaucoup de gens[1] vont dans les souks pour acheter leurs vêtements. Un souk est un grand marché, souvent situé dans la médina, le vieux quartier d'une ville arabe. Dans les pays du Maghreb, beaucoup d'hommes portent un pull et un jean.

Deux hommes en djellaba, Tunisie

Beaucoup de femmes portent une jupe et un chemisier. Mais on voit souvent des vêtements plus traditionnels. On voit des hommes qui portent une djellaba, par exemple. En Tunisie, beaucoup de femmes ont un sifsari. Le sifsari est un type de voile[2]. Le sifsari n'a pas de signification religieuse.

Un souk, Marrakech, Maroc

En Afrique Occidentale

Dans les pays d'Afrique Occidentale, les femmes portent souvent un boubou. Un boubou est une longue tunique ample. Les boubous sont très jolis. Les hommes aussi portent un boubou. Ils portent un boubou par-dessus[3] un pantalon et une chemise.

[1] gens *people*
[2] voile *veil*
[3] par-dessus *on top of, over*

Deux femmes en boubou, Sénégal

Après la lecture

Quel est le mot? Identifiez le mot. *(Identify the word.)*

1. un marché arabe
2. le vieux quartier d'une ville arabe
3. un vêtement masculin des pays du Maghreb
4. un type de voile tunisien
5. un vêtement porté par les hommes et les femmes en Afrique Occidentale

Les tailles

En France et dans les autres pays d'Europe, les pointures et les tailles ne sont pas les mêmes qu'aux États-Unis. Voici des tableaux qui indiquent les correspondances.

FEMMES				
Chaussures				
États-Unis	6	7	8	9	
France	36	37	38	39	
Robes, Tailleurs, Pulls, Chemisiers				
États-Unis	6	8	10	12	14
France	38	40	42	44	46

HOMMES				
Chaussures				
États-Unis	9	10	11	12	
France	40	41	42	43	
Chemises				
États-Unis	$14\frac{1}{2}$	15	$15\frac{1}{2}$	16	$16\frac{1}{2}$
France	37	38	39	40	41

Si vous trouvez des chaussures que vous aimez et que vous voulez acheter, vous allez demander quelle pointure?

Si vous voyez une chemise ou un chemisier que vous voulez acheter, vous allez demander quelle taille?

Après la lecture

Moi Donnez des réponses personnelles.
(Give your own answers.)
1. Vous êtes en France. Vous voulez des chaussures. Vous faites quelle pointure?
2. Vous voulez une chemise ou un chemisier. Quelle est votre taille?

CONNEXIONS

Les lettres

La poésie

A poem is a literary piece most often written in verse. The poet uses images, meter, rhythm, and sounds to evoke or suggest ideas, sensations, and emotions in the reader. Many poets say a great deal in very few words. The poem we are about to read by the French poet Apollinaire is an example.

Apollinaire (1880–1918)

Guillaume Apollinaire a une vie[1] bohème. Sa poésie reflète sa vie. Il visite beaucoup de pays européens. Les mouvements intellectuels et artistiques de son époque intéressent Apollinaire. C'est une période (avant la guerre[2] de 1914) très riche en idées. Les poètes et les artistes peintres échangent leurs nouvelles idées. Apollinaire discute ses idées avec son bon ami, le peintre Picasso.

Apollinaire est un des premiers grands poètes modernes français. Certains de ses poèmes sont des calligrammes. Le poème a la forme de l'objet que le poète décrit[3]. Le poème «La cravate» est un exemple de calligramme.

[1] vie *life*
[2] guerre *war*
[3] décrit *describes*

Pablo Picasso

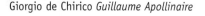

Giorgio de Chirico *Guillaume Apollinaire*

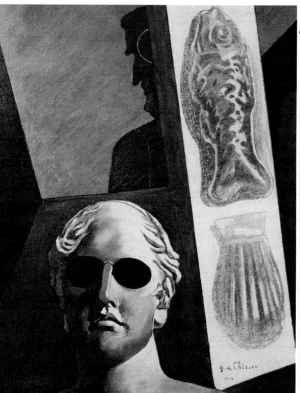

LA CRAVATE
DOU
LOU
REUSE°
QUE TU
PORTES
ET QUI T'
ORNE Ô CI
VILISÉ
ÔTE- TU VEUX
LA° BIEN
SI RESPI
RER°

doulOureuse *painful*

ôte-la *take it off*

respirer *breathe*

Paris vers 1900

Après la lecture

A Mes idées Répondez. *(Answer.)*

1. Si tu es un garçon, tu aimes mettre une cravate?
2. Si tu es une fille, tu trouves que c'est une bonne idée d'obliger un garçon à porter une cravate?
3. Apollinaire aime les cravates?
4. Il croit qu'on peut bien respirer si on porte une cravate?
5. Il croit que l'homme civilisé porte une cravate?

B Explication du texte Explain in English Apollinaire's ideas and tell whether you agree with him.

C'est à vous

Use what you have learned

1 PARLER

Une fête
✔ *Identify and describe articles of clothing*

You are talking with a friend after school. You are both invited to a party, but you don't know what to wear. Discuss what kind of a party it is and what would be appropriate.

2 PARLER

Un nouveau look
✔ *State your color and style preferences in clothes*

You and your partner have decided that you are going to change your style of clothes. Discuss what the new "you" is going to look like.

Des amies à Ouagadougou, Burkina Faso

3 PARLER ÉCRIRE

Des cadeaux
✔ *Shop for clothing*

You have just spent a few weeks in France and want to buy some gifts for family and friends back home. Make a list of what you want to buy. Go to different stores to buy the items you want. With a classmate, take turns being the customer and salesperson at the stores where you are purchasing the items on your list.

ÉCRIRE

4 On commande des vêtements.
✔ *Order clothing from a catalogue and give color preferences and size*

You want to order from the catalogue to the right. Write a letter stating which items you want, what color, what size.

ÉCRIRE

5 Le catalogue
✔ *Write descriptions of clothing*

Write five descriptions for an online clothing catalogue. Describe the items, tell the sizes they come in, the colors, the occasions they could be worn for, and the prices.

REVUE DE DÉTAILS
NEWS MODE Repéré aux quatre coins de la mode, tout ce qui nous plaît. De la tête aux pieds.

Coloris: noir, beige.
Tailles: du 36 au 40 pour la femme; du 40 au 45 pour l'homme.

modèle femme
du 36 au 40   499 FRF   76,07 €

modèle homme
du 40 au 45   499 FRF   76,07 €

99F**90** l'une
15,23 €

Chemise
77% viscose, 23% polyester.
Coloris assortis.
Du 37/38 au 43/44.

99F**90** l'une
15,23 €

Cravate
100% soie.
Coloris assortis.

(1) Robe en velours (150 €, 5 tailles, 8 coloris).
(2) Veste sur jupe en taffetas de soie (75 €, 3 tailles, 5 coloris (veste) et 150 €, du 36 au 42, en noir ou bronze (jupe)).

Writing Strategy

Clustering   Most writers brainstorm ideas before they begin to write. The next logical step is to "cluster" these ideas. This is done by writing down your main ideas and drawing a box around each one. Then draw a line indicating which ideas are connected to each other. Once you do this, it is easy to add other details to each cluster of ideas. When beginning to write, sort out your clusters and present each in a logical and organized paragraph.

ÉCRIRE

6 Le look de ton école

Write a note to your French friend describing **le look** at your school. Tell him or her what boys and girls usually wear to school and what types of clothing and colors are "in" **(à la mode).**

Quel est leur look?

Assessment

Vocabulaire

To review **Mots 1**, turn to pages 220–221.

1 Identifiez. *(Identify.)*

1.   2.   3.   4.

To review **Mots 2**, turn to pages 224–225.

2 Complétez. *(Complete.)*

5. —_____, le pantalon?
   —Non, il est trop grand.
6. —Vous faites quelle ____?
   —Je fais du 38, pour les chemises.
7. —De quelle ____ est la jupe?
   —Elle est grise.
8. —Le jean est trop petit.
   —Je voudrais la taille ____.

Structure

To review the verb **mettre**, turn to page 228.

3 Complétez avec «mettre». *(Complete with* mettre.*)*

9. Les garçons ne ____ pas de cravate pour aller à l'école.
10. Après le dîner je ____ la télé.
11. Qu'est-ce que vous ____ quand vous faites du jogging?
12. Qu'est-ce que tu ____ dans ton sac à dos?

To review the forms of these adjectives, turn to page 229.

4 Complétez. *(Complete.)*

13. C'est ma boutique ____. (favori)
14–15. La chemise est ____ et le pantalon est ____ aussi. (blanc)
16. Elle met une robe ____. (long)

5 Complétez. *(Complete.)*

17. —Jean est très sympa.
—Oui. Mais il n'est pas ____ sympa ____ toi.

18. —Ce jean ne coûte pas cher.
—Non, il est ____ cher ____ les autres.

19. —Les deux frères sont très intelligents.
—C'est vrai. Paul est ____ intelligent ____ Loïc.

To review the comparative of adjectives, turn to page 230.

6 Récrivez chaque phrase. *(Rewrite each sentence.)*

20. Je crois que oui.
Vous ____.

21. Elle voit de jolies chaussures dans la vitrine.
Elles ____.

22. Vous voyez ça?
Tu ____?

To review the verbs **voir** and **croire**, turn to page 232.

Culture

7 Vrai ou faux? *(True or false?)*

23. Les boutiques des grands couturiers sont très chères.

24. Un grand magasin a beaucoup de rayons différents.

25. On trouve les marchés aux puces dans les quartiers élégants de Paris.

To review this cultural information, turn to pages 236–237.

La boutique d'un grand couturier, Paris

Vocabulaire

Identifying articles of clothing

les vêtements (m. pl.)	une veste	un polo	une basket
un jean	un pantalon	un manteau	une chaussure
un short	un t-shirt	un anorak	une chaussette
une casquette	une sandale	un blouson	
un pull	un sweat-shirt	un survêtement	

Identifying men's clothing

une chemise
une cravate
un complet

Identifying women's clothing

une jupe plissée	une robe
un chemisier	un tailleur

How well do you know your vocabulary?

- Choose words that describe an outfit you would like to have.
- Describe your shopping trip to look for the outfit.

Shopping

une boutique	un vendeur	cher (chère)	trouver
un centre commercial	une vendeuse	faire des courses	mettre
un grand magasin	un rayon	essayer	
une vitrine	des soldes (m. pl.)	entrer (dans)	
une cabine d'essayage	le prix	porter	

Describing clothes

large	sport	à manches	la pointure
serré(e)	joli(e)	longues	la taille
habillé(e)	favori(te)	courtes	au-dessus
			au-dessous

Identifying colors

De quelle couleur?	noir(e)	rouge	marron
blanc(he)	gris(e)	beige	orange
brun(e)	bleu(e)	rose	
vert(e)	jaune	bleu marine	

Other useful words and expressions

Vous faites quelle taille?	en solde	voir
Je fais du 40.	à mon avis	croire

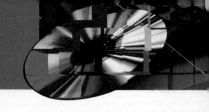

Technotour
BON VOYAGE!

Avant de visionner

In this video episode, Christine and Chloé organize a fashion show featuring Chloé's designs.

Christine et Chloé veulent acheter une robe.

Chloé essaie une robe.

À découvrir

Learn more about the world of fashion in Paris online.

Un défilé de mode à Paris

FRENCH Online

In the Chapter 7 Internet activity, you will have a chance to learn more about clothing and shopping in the Francophone world. To begin your virtual adventure, go to the Glencoe French Web site: **french.glencoe.com**

Conversation

Faire la cuisine!

Julie: Tu vas préparer le déjeuner?

Miéna: Moi? Préparer le déjeuner? Tu rigoles!
Je déteste faire la cuisine.

Julie: Tu veux aller au resto, alors?

Miéna: Non, je ne peux pas. Je n'ai pas le
temps. Je vais manger une tranche de
pizza.

Julie: Tu n'as pas le temps d'aller au resto?
Pourquoi?

Miéna: Je veux acheter quelque chose pour
samedi. Je vais à une fête chez une amie.

Julie: Qu'est-ce que tu vas acheter?

Miéna: Je crois que je vais acheter une robe.

Julie: Près de chez moi, il y a des soldes dans
une petite boutique sympa.

Miéna: Merci, mais je vais aller aux Galeries.
Je trouve toujours quelque chose là.

Galeries Lafayette, Paris

Après la conversation

Répondez. (*Answer.*)

1. Miéna va préparer le déjeuner?
2. Elle aime faire la cuisine?
3. Elle veut aller déjeuner au
   restaurant?
4. Elle ne peut pas aller au restaurant?
5. Qu'est-ce qu'elle va manger?
6. Qu'est-ce qu'elle veut acheter?
7. Elle va où samedi?
8. Elle va aller dans quel magasin?

Structure

Les verbes irréguliers au présent

1. Review the following irregular verbs.

ALLER	je vais, tu vas, il/elle/on va, nous_z_allons, vous_z_allez, ils/elles vont
PRENDRE	je prends, tu prends, il/elle/on prend, nous prenons, vous prenez, ils/elles prennent
FAIRE	je fais, tu fais, il/elle/on fait, nous faisons, vous faites, ils/elles font
POUVOIR	je peux, tu peux, il/elle/on peut, nous pouvons, vous pouvez, ils/elles peuvent
VOULOIR	je veux, tu veux, il/elle/on veut, nous voulons, vous voulez, ils/elles veulent
METTRE	je mets, tu mets, il/elle/on met, nous mettons, vous mettez, ils/elles mettent
CROIRE	je crois, tu crois, il/elle/on croit, nous croyons, vous croyez, ils/elles croient
VOIR	je vois, tu vois, il/elle/on voit, nous voyons, vous voyez, ils/elles voient

2. Note that for all the preceding verbs except **aller,** the three singular
forms sound alike. For all these verbs except **faire,** the **nous** and
vous stems are the same.

1 **Historiette** **On fait des courses.** Répondez d'après les indications. *(Answer according to the cues.)*

1. Tu vas aller où? (aux Galeries Lafayette)
2. Qu'est-ce que tu vas faire? (acheter un cadeau)
3. Qu'est-ce que tu veux acheter? (une chemise blanche)
4. C'est pour qui, la chemise? (mon père)
5. Il fait quelle taille? (du 39)
6. Tu vois un chemisier pour ta mère? (oui)
7. Qui met le chemisier dans un sac? (le vendeur)

2 **Historiette** **À l'école** Mettez au pluriel. *(Make the sentences plural.)*

1. Je vais à l'école.
2. Je prends le car pour aller à l'école.
3. Je veux poser une question.
4. L'élève peut poser des questions.
5. Sandrine croit qu'elle a la bonne réponse.
6. Elle prend ses cahiers.

Galeries Lafayette, Paris

Des pâtisseries

Les contractions **au** et **du**

The prepositions **à** and **de** contract with **le** to form **au** and **du,** and with **les** to form **aux** and **des.**

à + le = au	Il va au collège.
à + les = aux	Le prof parle aux élèves.
de + le = du	Il rentre du collège.
de + les = des	Il parle des élèves.

3 **Où?** Répondez d'après les indications. *(Answer according to the cues.)*

1. On achète des tartes où? (pâtisserie)
2. Et du saucisson? (charcuterie)
3. Et de l'eau minérale? (épicerie)
4. Et du poisson? (marché)
5. On parle a qui au marché? (marchands)

4 **D'où?** Complétez en utilisant **de** + un article défini. *(Answer with* de *+ a definite article.)*

1. Mon frère rentre _____ lycée.
2. Mon autre frère rentre _____ collège.
3. Ma sœur rentre _____ école.
4. Mon autre sœur rentre _____ cantine.
5. Nous parlons tous _____ professeurs.

 # Le partitif

1. Remember that the partitive, "some," "any," is expressed in French by **de** + the definite article. **De** contracts with **le** to form **du** and with **les** to form **des**. In the negative, **du, de la, de l'**, and **des** all become **de** or **d'**.

Je veux de l'argent.	**Je ne veux pas d'argent.**
J'ai des croissants.	**Je n'ai pas de croissants.**

2. Remember that **un** and **une** also become **de** or **d'** after a negative expression.

Tu veux un couteau?	**Tu ne veux pas de couteau?**
J'ai une serviette.	**Je n'ai pas de serviette.**

5 **Dans le chariot** Dites ce qu'il y a dans le chariot. *(Tell what is in the cart.)*

6 **Pas dans le chariot** Dites ce qu'il n'y a pas dans le chariot de l'Activité 5. *(Tell what is not in the cart in Activity 5.)*

7 **J'ai faim** Répondez d'après le modèle.
(*Answer according to the model.*)

—**Tu veux du poisson?**

—**Non, je ne veux pas de poisson. Je n'aime pas le poisson!**

1. Tu veux du bœuf?
2. Tu veux des œufs?
3. Tu veux des carottes à la crème?
4. Tu veux du poulet?
5. Tu veux de la salade?
6. Tu veux du gâteau au chocolat?

Le comparatif

1. You use the comparative to compare two people or two items.

> **Aurélie est plus (aussi, moins) sportive que son frère.**
> **Le pantalon est plus (aussi, moins) cher que le jean.**

2. You use the stress pronouns **moi, toi, lui, elle, nous, vous, eux,** and **elles** after **que (qu')** when comparing people.

> **Il est moins sympa qu'elle (que toi, qu'eux).**

8 **Cyril et moi** Répondez d'après le modèle.
(*Answer according to the model.*)

Cyril est très sérieux.

—**Il est plus sérieux que moi?**

—**Non, il est aussi sérieux que toi.**

1. Cyril est très timide.
2. Cyril est très grand.
3. Cyril est très amusant.
4. Cyril est très patient.
5. Cyril est très beau.
6. Cyril est très sympathique.

Marie est plus fatiguée que sa sœur.

9 **Christelle et moi** Remplacez Cyril par Christelle dans l'Activité 8. *(Replace* Cyril *with* Christelle *in Activity 8.)*

10 **Au restaurant** With a classmate, make up a conversation between a waiter or a waitress and a customer.

Un restaurant, Paris

11 **Qu'est-ce que tu fais?** Work with a classmate. Ask each other questions about the things you do or want to do. Use the following words in the conversation.

prendre vouloir pouvoir croire faire aller

12 **Des courses** Work with a classmate. Each of you will make up a grocery list. Exchange lists. Then tell each other where you are going to go and what you are going to do.

 LITERARY COMPANION *You may wish to read the poem «Dors mon enfant», by Elolongué Epanya Yondo, who was born in Cameroun and studied in Paris. This poem is found on page 510.*

1. Maisons du pays Dogon au Mali
2. Masque sénoufo de la Côte d'Ivoire
3. Danse rituelle et tambourinaires du Burundi
4. Une petite fille du Mali
5. Dakar, la capitale du Sénégal
6. Youssou N'dour, le célèbre chanteur pop
   du Sénégal
7. Un griot raconte aux jeunes du village
   l'histoire de leurs ancêtres

1

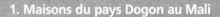

2

3

4

5

6

■ NATIONAL
GEOGRAPHIC

REFLETS
de l'Afrique

7

8. Baobab à Madagascar
9. Cueillette du thé au Burundi
10. Mosquée à Djenné, au Mali
11. Abidjan en Côte d'Ivoire
12. Match de la Coupe d'Afrique des Nations au Burkina Faso
13. Femme adioukrou en Côte d'Ivoire
14. Marchande de pain à Cotonou, au Bénin

8

10

9

11

12

13

REFLETS
de l'Afrique

14

 # Literary Companion

These literary selections develop reading and cultural skills and introduce students to French literature.

La petite Fadette 504
George Sand

«Dors mon enfant» 510
Elolongué Epanya Yondo

La petite Fadette **George Sand**

Vocabulaire

des frères jumeaux · · · les yeux

forts

Les jumeaux sont semblables.
Ils ont les yeux bleus.
Ils sont forts.

Il y a deux autres garçons dans la famille.
L'aîné a cinq ans.
Le cadet a deux ans.

pleurer · · ·

Le petit garçon a peur.

Il est triste. Il pleure.

un paysan

un champ

Les paysans travaillent dans les champs.
La petite fille est très pauvre.

Elle est (tombe) malade.

Activités

A **Historiette** **Les jumeaux**
Répondez.

1. Les deux frères sont jumeaux?
2. Ils sont très semblables?
3. Ils ont les yeux bleus?
4. Ils sont forts ou faibles?
5. Le cadet a cinq ans ou deux ans?
6. Et l'aîné, il a quel âge?

B **Quel est le mot?** Complétez.

1. Des ＿＿ sont des frères qui ont le même âge.
2. Le petit garçon est triste. Il ＿＿.
3. Il pleure aussi quand il a ＿＿.
4. Les jumeaux sont blonds et ils ont les yeux bleus. Ils sont très ＿＿.
5. M. et Mme Gaillard ont deux enfants. L'＿＿ a quinze ans et le
   ＿＿ a huit ans.
6. M. et Mme Gaillard ＿＿ dans les champs. M. et Mme Gaillard
   sont des ＿＿.
7. La petite fille n'est pas riche. Elle est ＿＿.
8. La petite fille est ＿＿. Elle a la grippe.

Le Berry, France

INTRODUCTION Le vrai nom de George Sand (1804–1876) est Aurore Dupin. Elle est née[1] à Paris, mais elle passe son enfance à Nohant, dans le Berry. Le Berry est une région rurale.

George Sand a un mariage malheureux. Séparée de son mari, elle rentre à Paris avec ses deux enfants. Ses romans les plus connus[2] sont des romans champêtres[3]. Dans ses romans, elle montre un grand intérêt pour les paysans du Berry. *La petite Fadette* est un roman champêtre publié en 1849.

[1] née *born*
[2] romans les plus connus *best-known novels*
[3] champêtres *pastoral*

La petite Fadette

1

Le père Barbeau habite à la Cosse. Le père Barbeau est un homme important. Il a deux champs. Il cultive ses deux champs pour nourrir° sa famille. Il a aussi une maison avec un jardin. C'est un homme courageux et bon. Il aime beaucoup sa famille—sa femme, la mère Barbeau, et ses trois enfants.

C'est alors que le père Barbeau et la mère Barbeau ont deux garçons à la fois°: deux beaux jumeaux. Il est impossible de distinguer les jumeaux l'un de l'autre parce qu'ils° sont très semblables. Sylvinet est l'aîné et Landry est le cadet.

nourrir *to feed*

à la fois *at the same time*
parce qu'ils *because they*

2

Les deux garçons grandissent° sans problème. Ils sont blonds avec de grands yeux bleus. Ils parlent avec la même voix°. Ils sont très amis. Ils sont toujours ensemble.

Les enfants ont maintenant 14 ans. Le père Barbeau dit qu'ils ont l'âge de travailler. Mais il n'y a pas assez de travail pour les deux garçons chez les Barbeau. Le père décide d'envoyer° un des garçons chez un voisin, le père Caillaud. Le père Caillaud habite à la Priche.

grandissent *grow up*
voix *voice*

envoyer *to send*

Les jumeaux sont très tristes. Être séparés, c'est horrible. Sylvinet commence à pleurer et Landry pleure aussi.

—Mais, le père Caillaud n'habite pas très loin, dit Landry.

—C'est vrai. Je vais chez le père Caillaud…

—Non, Sylvinet. Pas toi, moi! Je vais chez le père Caillaud!

Donc Landry quitte la maison de son père… Maintenant, il travaille chez le père Caillaud. Le père Caillaud est content que Landry travaille pour lui. Landry est très fort.

Le père Caillaud aime beaucoup Landry. Il traite Landry comme un de ses enfants. Landry aussi aime beaucoup le père Caillaud. Il est content de travailler à la Priche. Mais Sylvinet n'est pas content. Il est jaloux de Landry.

3

Françoise Fadet est une petite fille très pauvre. Elle habite avec sa grand-mère et son petit frère handicapé. Ils habitent près de la rivière°, pas très loin de la Priche. On appelle Françoise «la petite Fadette». La petite Fadette est très solitaire. Elle n'est pas comme les autres enfants. Elle est assez différente des autres. Les autres enfants ont peur de la petite Fadette. Certains détestent la petite fille.

rivière *river*

Un jour, Landry rentre à la Priche et rencontre° la petite Fadette qui pleure.

—Pourquoi° tu pleures comme ça?

—Parce qu'on me déteste.

—C'est un peu ta faute°, Fadette.

—Ma faute? Pourquoi?

—Parce que tu es toujours très sale° et désagréable avec les autres.

rencontre *meets*
Pourquoi *Why*

faute *fault*

sale *dirty*

Émile Lambinet *Écouen, près de Paris*

Landry, lui, ne trouve° pas la petite Fadette désagréable. Il trouve même qu'elle est intelligente et intéressante. La petite Fadette trouve Landry très beau. Elle aime Landry. Landry et la petite Fadette sont souvent ensemble et Landry change la personnalité de la petite Fadette.

Le jumeau de Landry, Sylvinet, est très jaloux de Landry et la petite Fadette. Il tombe très malade. Sa famille est désespérée. Mais qui sauve Sylvinet? La petite Fadette, l'amie de son frère Landry. Maintenant, tout° est possible, même le mariage de Landry et de la petite Fadette.

trouve *finds*

tout *everything*

William Bouguereau *Jeune fille au panier de fruits*

Après la lecture

A Les enfants Barbeau Répondez.

1. M. et Mme Barbeau ont combien d'enfants?
2. Ils ont des jumeaux?
3. L'aîné, c'est Sylvinet ou Landry?
4. Et le cadet?
5. Comment sont les jumeaux?
6. Ils sont bruns ou blonds?
7. Ils ont les yeux de quelle couleur?
8. Ils ont la même voix?

B Le père Barbeau Décrivez le père Barbeau.

C Les jumeaux Décrivez les jumeaux Barbeau.

D Séparation Complétez.

1. Quand les enfants ont ____ ans, le père Barbeau dit qu'ils ont l'âge de ____.
2. Le père Barbeau décide d'envoyer un enfant chez un ____, le père Caillaud.
3. Le père Caillaud ____ à la Priche.
4. Les jumeaux sont très ____ parce qu'ils vont être séparés.
5. Ils sont très tristes et ils ____.
6. ____ travaille chez le père Caillaud.
7. Le père Caillaud ____ beaucoup Landry. Il ____ Landry comme un de ses enfants.

E La petite Fadette Répondez.

1. Avec qui habite la petite Fadette?
2. Elle habite où?
3. Comment est la petite Fadette?
4. Qui a peur de la petite Fadette?
5. La petite Fadette pleure. Pourquoi?
6. Elle parle à qui?
7. Landry trouve la petite Fadette comment?
8. Qui change la personnalité de la petite Fadette?
9. Qui tombe malade?
10. Qui sauve Sylvinet?

«*Dors mon enfant*» Elolongué Epanya Yondo

Vocabulaire

un écrivain

un oranger fleuri

une revue un magazine
l'avenir le futur

Activité

Un oranger Répondez.

1. Un oranger, c'est un fruit ou un arbre?
2. L'orange, c'est le fruit de l'oranger?
3. Tu aimes les oranges?
4. Tu aimes le jus d'orange?
5. Il y a des orangers dans les régions tropicales?
6. C'est beau un oranger fleuri?

Gerard Sekoto *Jeune fille à l'orange*

INTRODUCTION La poésie africaine francophone est la poésie écrite par des Africains de langue française. La poésie africaine francophone est riche et variée. Deux écrivains de langue française célèbres sont Léopold Sédar Senghor et Aimé Césaire. Ces deux écrivains créent dans les années 30 le mouvement de «la négritude». La négritude, c'est «l'ensemble des valeurs culturelles de l'Afrique noire.»

En 1947, Alioune Diop fonde à Paris la revue *Présence Africaine*. La revue publie les œuvres[1] d'écrivains africains francophones et diffuse le concept de la négritude.

[1] œuvres *works*

Aujourd'hui, *Présence Africaine* est une maison d'édition[2] qui publie les œuvres d'écrivains africains.

«Dors mon enfant» est tiré de[3] *Kamérun! Kamérun!* du poète Elolongué Epanya Yondo. Elolongué Epanya Yondo est né au Cameroun en 1930. Il va étudier à Paris où il habite chez Alioune Diop. Elolongué Epanya Yondo veut inspirer un esprit de solidarité chez ses compatriotes pour établir un avenir[4] solide sans oublier[5] les traditions passées.

[2] maison d'édition *publishing house*
[3] tiré de *taken from*
[4] avenir *future*
[5] sans oublier *without forgetting*

«Dors mon enfant»

Dors° mon enfant dors	Dors *Sleep*
Quand tu dors	
Tu es beau	
Comme un oranger fleuri…	
Dors mon enfant dors	
Tu es si° beau	si *so*
Quand tu dors…	
Mon beau bébé noir dors	

Après la lecture

Dors mon enfant Répondez.

1. Qui parle dans le poème?
2. La mère trouve son enfant beau?
3. Elle compare son enfant à quel arbre?
4. Un oranger est un bel arbre?
5. Un oranger est beau surtout quand il fleurit?
6. La mère compare son enfant à un bel oranger fleuri?
7. Le petit enfant est de quelle race?
8. C'est un bébé ou un petit garçon?

Elizabeth Barakah Hodges *Madone noire*

Handbook

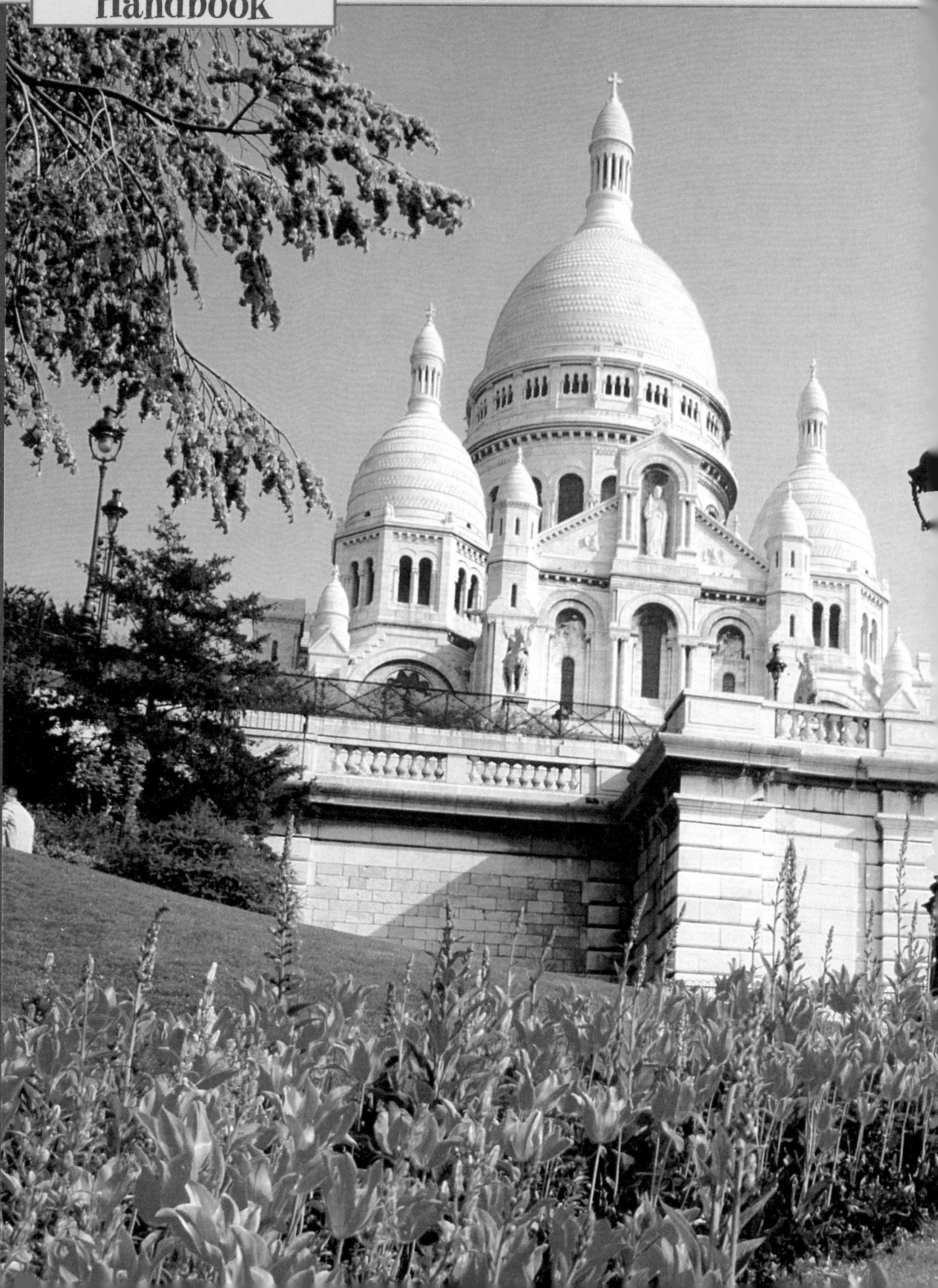

InfoGap Activities H2
These communicative activities review and reinforce the vocabulary and structure just learned

Study Tips H51
These helpful study hints aid in the learning of new material

Verb Charts H68

French-English Dictionary H72

English-French Dictionary H85

Index H120

InfoGap

Activity 1

CHAPITRE 1, Mots 1, pages 18–19

Olivier / Nice

Luc / Lyon

Élève A Ask your partner the following questions. Correct answers are in parentheses.

1. Comment est Sophie, petite ou grande?
   (Sophie est petite.)

2. Comment est Sylvie?
   (Elle est grande.)

3. Il est d'où, Olivier?
   (Il est de Nice.)

4. Luc est américain ou français?
   (Il est français.)

5. Comment est Olivier, brun ou blond?
   (Il est brun.)

6. Qui est de Montréal?
   (Sylvie est de Montréal.)

Sophie / Paris

Sylvie / Montréal

Élève A Answer your partner's questions based on the pictures below.

Élève B Answer your partner's questions based on the pictures below.

Sophie / Paris

Sylvie / Montréal

Olivier / Nice

Luc / Lyon

Élève B Ask your partner the following questions. Correct answers are in parentheses.

1. Comment est Olivier, petit ou grand?
   (Olivier est petit.)

2. Comment est Luc?
   (Luc est grand.)

3. Elle est d'où, Sophie?
   (Elle est de Paris.)

4. Qui est de Lyon?
   (Luc est de Lyon.)

5. Sophie est française ou américaine?
   (Elle est française.)

6. Comment est Luc, brun ou blond?
   (Il est blond.)

Activity 2

CHAPITRE 1, Mots 2, pages 22–23

Bruno Lapierre

Carol Smith

Nathalie Simonet et
Philippe Latour

Nathalie et
Luc Simonet

Élève A Answer your partner's questions based on the pictures below.

Élève A Ask your partner the following questions. Correct answers are in parentheses.

1. Qui est Luc?
   (Luc est le frère de Nathalie.)

2. Qui est Philippe?
   (Philippe est l'ami de Nathalie.)

3. Carol est élève dans une école américaine?
   (Oui, Carol est élève dans une école américaine.)

4. Bruno est élève dans un collège français?
   (Oui, Bruno est élève dans un collège français.)

Élève B Answer your partner's questions based on the pictures below.

Élève B Ask your partner the following questions. Correct answers are in parentheses.

1. Qui est Nathalie?
   (Nathalie est la sœur de Luc.)

2. Nathalie est sympathique?
   (Oui, Nathalie est très sympathique.)

3. Carol est américaine?
   (Oui, Carol est américaine.)

4. Bruno est français?
   (Oui, Bruno est français.)

Nathalie et
Luc Simonet

Nathalie Simonet et
Philippe Latour

Carol Smith

Bruno Lapierre

Activity 3

Napoléon Bonaparte

Oprah Winfrey

Charles de Gaulle

Meg Ryan

Élève A Correct your partner's statements based on the pictures below.

Élève A Read your partner the following false statements. Correct answers are in parentheses.

1. Meg Ryan est brune.
   (Non, elle n'est pas brune. Elle est blonde.)

2. Charles de Gaulle est américain.
   (Non, il n'est pas américain. Il est français.)

3. Oprah Winfrey est timide.
   (Non, elle n'est pas timide. Elle est sociable.)

4. Napoléon est très grand.
   (Non, il n'est pas très grand. Il est assez petit.)

Élève B Correct your partner's statements based on the pictures below.

Meg Ryan

Charles de Gaulle

Oprah Winfrey

Napoléon Bonaparte

Élève B Read your partner the following false statements. Correct answers are in parentheses.

1. Meg Ryan est timide.
   (Non, elle n'est pas timide. Elle est dynamique.)

2. Charles de Gaulle est petit.
   (Non, il n'est pas petit. Il est grand.)

3. Oprah Winfrey est française.
   (Non, elle n'est pas française. Elle est américaine.)

4. Napoléon est américain.
   (Non, il n'est pas américain. Il est français.)

Activity 4

Élève A Ask your partner the following questions. Correct answers are in parentheses.

1. Le cours de français est facile?
   (Oui, le cours de français est facile.)

2. Le prof est très sympathique?
   (Oui, le prof est très sympathique.)

3. Les élèves sont françaises ou américaines?
   (Les élèves sont françaises.)

4. Les élèves sont amies?
   (Oui, les élèves sont amies.)

Élève A Answer your partner's questions based on the picture below.

Élève B Answer your partner's questions based on the picture below.

Élève B Ask your partner the following questions. Correct answers are in parentheses.

1. Les élèves sont dans le même lycée?
   (Oui, les élèves sont dans le même lycée.)

2. Les élèves sont dans la salle de classe?
   (Oui, les élèves sont dans la salle de classe.)

3. Les élèves sont sympathiques?
   (Oui, les élèves sont sympathiques.)

4. Le cours de français est difficile?
   (Non, le cours de français n'est pas difficile.) or
   (Non, le cours de français est facile.)

Activity 5

Élève A Ask your partner the following questions. Correct answers are in parentheses.

1. Guy est fort en mathématiques?
   (Oui, il est fort en mathématiques.)

2. Guy est très fort en sciences naturelles?
   (Non, il n'est pas fort en sciences naturelles.) or *(Non, il est mauvais en sciences naturelles.)*

3. Il est mauvais en géométrie?
   (Non, il n'est pas mauvais en géométrie.) or *(Non, il est fort en géométrie.)*

4. L'économie est une science naturelle?
   (Non, l'économie n'est pas une science naturelle.) or *(Non, l'économie est une science sociale.)*

Élève A Answer your partner's questions based on the report card below.

Marie Dauphin

Les langues:	
Le français	A−
L'anglais	B+
Les sciences sociales:	
L'histoire	D
La géographie	C+
D'autres matières:	
La musique	A

Élève B Answer your partner's questions based on the report card below.

Guy Laurent

Les sciences naturelles:	
La biologie	C−
La chimie	D
Les mathématiques:	
La géométrie	A
Le calcul	B+
Les sciences sociales:	
L'économie	B

Élève B Ask your partner the following questions. Correct answers are in parentheses.

1. Marie est très forte en sciences sociales?
   (Non, elle est mauvaise en sciences sociales.) or *(Elle n'est pas forte en sciences sociales.)*

2. Le cours de français est très difficile?
   (Non, le cours de français est très facile.) or *(Non, le cours de français n'est pas difficile.)*

3. Marie est mauvaise en histoire?
   (Oui, Marie est mauvaise en histoire.)

4. L'anglais est une science sociale?
   (Non, l'anglais est une langue.) or *(Non, l'anglais n'est pas une science sociale.)*

Activity 6

Élève A Answer your partner's questions in complete sentences, using either **Oui** or **Non.**

Élève A Ask your partner the following questions. Correct answers are in parentheses.

1. La salle de classe est petite?
   (Oui, la salle de classe est petite.) or *(Non, la salle de classe n'est pas petite.)*

2. Les élèves sont intelligents?
   (Oui, les élèves sont intelligents.) or *(Non, les élèves ne sont pas intelligents.)*

3. Le lycée est grand?
   (Oui, le lycée est grand.) or *(Non, le lycée n'est pas grand.)*

4. Vous deux, vous êtes élèves dans un lycée français?
   (Oui, nous sommes élèves dans un lycée français.) or *(Non, nous ne sommes pas élèves dans un lycée français.)*

5. Tu es fort(e) en maths?
   (Oui, je suis fort[e] en maths.) or *(Non, je ne suis pas fort[e] en maths.)*

Élève B Answer your partner's questions in complete sentences, using either **Oui** or **Non.**

Élève B Ask your partner the following questions. Correct answers are in parentheses.

1. La prof est patiente?
   (Oui, la prof est patiente.) or *(Non, la prof n'est pas patiente.)*

2. Les élèves sont sympas?
   (Oui, les élèves sont sympas.) or *(Non, les élèves ne sont pas sympas.)*

3. Le prof est intéressant?
   (Oui, le prof est intéressant.) or *(Non, le prof n'est pas intéressant.)*

4. Vous êtes copains?
   (Oui, nous sommes copains.) or *(Non, nous ne sommes pas copains.)*

5. Tu es fort(e) en histoire?
   (Oui, je suis fort[e] en histoire.) or *(Non, je ne suis pas fort[e] en histoire.)*

Activity 7

Élève A Answer your partner's questions based on the picture below.

Élève A Ask your partner the following questions. Correct answers are in parentheses.

1. Les élèves sont où?
   (Les élèves sont dans la cour.)

2. Ils parlent entre les cours?
   (Oui, ils parlent entre les cours.)

3. Ils étudient dans la cour?
   (Non, ils n'étudient pas dans la cour.)

4. Les copains rigolent?
   (Oui, ils rigolent.)

Élève B Answer your partner's questions based on the picture below.

Élève B Ask your partner the following questions. Correct answers are in parentheses.

1. Les élèves passent la journée à l'école?
   (Oui, ils passent la journée à l'école.)

2. Ils regardent la prof?
   (Oui, ils regardent la prof.)

3. Un élève pose une question?
   (Oui, il pose une question.)

4. Les élèves déjeunent pendant le cours?
   (Non, ils ne déjeunent pas pendant le cours.)

Activity 8

Sophie

Marc

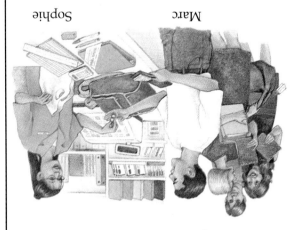

Élève A Ask your partner the following questions. Correct answers are in parentheses.

1. Camille est à la papeterie?
   (Oui, elle est à la papeterie.)

2. Elle achète des fournitures scolaires?
   (Oui, elle achète des fournitures scolaires.)

3. Elle achète un classeur et une calculatrice?
   (Oui, elle achète un classeur et une calculatrice.)

4. Elle paie où?
   (Elle paie à la caisse.)

Élève A Answer your partner's questions based on the picture below.

Élève B Answer your partner's questions based on the picture below.

Camille

Élève B Ask your partner the following questions. Correct answers are in parentheses.

1. Sophie travaille après les cours?
   (Oui, elle travaille après les cours.)

2. Elle travaille où?
   (Elle travaille dans une papeterie.)

3. Marc achète un sac à dos?
   (Oui, il achète un sac à dos.)

4. Il achète un classeur?
   (Oui, il achète un classeur.)

Activity 9

Élève A Answer your partner's questions using the correct form of the verb below.

1. arriver

2. poser

3. rigoler

4. parler

5. travailler

Élève A Ask your partner the following questions. Possible responses are in parentheses.

1. Tu quittes la maison à quelle heure le matin?
   (Je quitte la maison à sept heures et demie.)

2. Qui écoute quand le prof parle?
   (Les élèves écoutent quand le prof parle.)

3. On parle français en Belgique?
   (Oui, on parle français en Belgique.)

4. Vous étudiez quelle langue?
   (Nous étudions le français.)

5. Vous détestez les examens?
   (Oui, nous détestons les examens.) or
   (Non, nous ne détestons pas les examens.)

Élève B Answer your partner's questions using the correct form of the verb below.

1. quitter

2. écouter

3. parler

4. étudier

5. détester

Élève B Ask your partner the following questions. Possible responses are in parentheses.

1. On arrive à l'école à quelle heure?
   (On arrive à l'école à huit heures.)

2. Qui pose des questions?
   (Les élèves posent des questions.) or
   (Le prof pose des questions.)

3. Vous rigolez dans la cour?
   (Oui, nous rigolons dans la cour.) or
   (Non, nous ne rigolons pas dans la cour.)

4. Tu parles beaucoup au téléphone?
   (Oui, je parle beaucoup au téléphone.) or
   (Non, je ne parle pas beaucoup au téléphone.)

5. Tu travailles après les cours?
   (Oui, je travaille après les cours.) or
   (Non, je ne travaille pas après les cours.)

Élève A Read your partner the following statements. He or she will fill in the blank. Correct answers are in parentheses.

1. Le frère de mon père est mon ———.
   (oncle)

2. La mère de mon cousin est ma ———.
   (tante)

3. Le mari de ma mère est mon ———.
   (père)

4. La mère de mon père est ma ———.
   (grand-mère)

5. Le fils de ma tante est mon ———.
   (cousin)

Élève A Complete your partner's statements with the name of the relative.

Élève B Complete your partner's statements with the name of the relative.

Élève B Read your partner the following statements. He or she will fill in the blank. Correct answers are in parentheses.

1. La sœur de ma mère est ma ———.
   (tante)

2. La femme de mon père est ma ———.
   (mère)

3. La fille de mes parents est ma ———.
   (sœur)

4. Les parents de ma mère sont mes ———.
   (grands-parents)

5. Les enfants de mon oncle sont mes ———.
   (cousins)

Activity 11

Élève A Ask your partner the following questions. Correct answers are in parentheses.

1. On regarde la télé dans la salle de bains ou la salle de séjour?
   (*On regarde la télé dans la salle de séjour.*)

2. On dîne dans la chambre à coucher ou la salle à manger?
   (*On dîne dans la salle à manger.*)

3. Le balcon donne sur la cour ou sur la cuisine?
   (*Le balcon donne sur la cour.*)

4. On habite au troisième étage d'un immeuble ou d'une maison?
   (*On habite au troisième étage d'un immeuble.*)

5. La voiture est dans la cuisine ou le garage?
   (*La voiture est dans le garage.*)

Élève A Now answer your partner's questions.

Élève B Answer your partner's questions.

Élève B Ask your partner the following questions. Correct answers are in parentheses.

1. On parle avec les voisins dans la cour ou la salle de bains?
   (*On parle avec les voisins dans la cour.*)

2. On prépare le dîner dans l'ascenseur ou la cuisine?
   (*On prépare le dîner dans la cuisine.*)

3. On monte à l'appartement dans le métro ou l'ascenseur?
   (*On monte à l'appartement dans l'ascenseur.*)

4. Les toilettes sont dans l'appartement ou dans la cour?
   (*Les toilettes sont dans l'appartement.*)

5. On habite dans un quartier ou dans une entrée?
   (*On habite dans un quartier.*)

Activity 12

Élève A Ask your partner the following questions. Correct answers are in parentheses.

1. Marc a quel âge?
   (Il a quinze ans.)

2. Tes grands-parents ont une maison?
   (Non, ils ont un joli appartement.)

3. Tu as quel âge, toi?
   (J'ai —— ans.)

4. Qui a deux chiens?
   (La prof de maths a deux chiens.)

5. Quel âge ont tes grands-parents?
   (Ils ont quatre-vingts ans.)

Élève A Use the chart below to answer your partner's questions. Reminder: **toi** is you.

Paul	15 ans	Une sœur
Tes grands-parents	75 ans	Un chien
Toi	?	Des profs intéressants
Tes cousines	16 ans	Deux chats
Marie	14	Une petite famille

Élève B Ask your partner the following questions. Correct answers are in parentheses.

1. Qui a des profs intéressants?
   (Moi, j'ai des profs intéressants.)

2. Tes cousines ont combien de chats?
   (Mes cousines ont deux chats.)

3. Tes grands-parents ont quel âge?
   (Mes grands-parents ont soixante-quinze ans.)

4. Qui a une petite famille?
   (Marie a une petite famille.)

5. Paul a un frère ou une sœur?
   (Paul a une sœur.)

Élève B Use the chart below to answer your partner's questions. Reminder: **toi** is you.

Marc	15 ans	Une sœur
Tes grands-parents	80 ans	Un joli appartement
Toi	?	Des profs intéressants
La prof de maths	35	Deux chiens
Sophie	14	Une petite famille

Activity 13

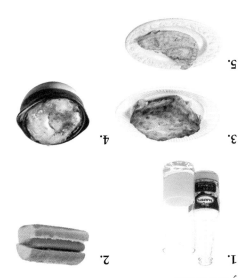

Élève A You are the server in a French café. Ask your partner what he or she wants to order. Correct answers are in parentheses.

1. Vous désirez?
   (*Un citron pressé, s'il vous plaît.*)

2. Vous désirez?
   (*Un croissant, s'il vous plaît.*)

3. Vous désirez?
   (*Une salade verte, s'il vous plaît.*)

4. Vous désirez?
   (*Un café, s'il vous plaît.*) or (*Un express, s'il vous plaît.*)

5. Vous désirez?
   (*Une tartine de pain beurré, s'il vous plaît.*)

Élève A Now your partner is the server. Use the following picture menu to give your order.

1.

2.

3.

4.

5.

Élève B Your partner is the server in a French café. Use the following picture menu to give your order.

1.

2.

3.

4.

5.

Élève B Now you are the server. Ask your partner what he or she wants to order. Correct answers are in parentheses.

1. Vous désirez?
   (*Un jus d'orange, s'il vous plaît.*)

2. Vous désirez?
   (*Une saucisse de Francfort, s'il vous plaît.*) or (*Un hot-dog, s'il vous plaît.*)

3. Vous désirez?
   (*Un croque-monsieur, s'il vous plaît.*)

4. Vous désirez?
   (*Une soupe à l'oignon, s'il vous plaît.*)

5. Vous désirez?
   (*Une omelette nature, s'il vous plaît.*)

Activity 14

Élève A Ask your partner the following questions. Correct answers are in parentheses.

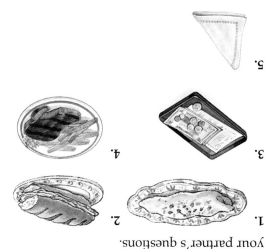

1. Un couteau, c'est pour la soupe?
   (Non, une cuillère, c'est pour la soupe.)

2. Un verre, c'est pour le café?
   (Non, une tasse, c'est pour le café.)

3. Une soupe à l'oignon, c'est pour le dessert?
   (Non, une glace au chocolat, c'est pour le dessert.)

4. Un couteau, c'est pour le steak?
   (Oui, un couteau, c'est pour le steak.)

5. Un verre, c'est pour la limonade?
   (Oui, un verre, c'est pour la limonade.)

Élève A Use the pictures below to answer your partner's questions.

Élève B Use the pictures below to answer your partner's questions.

1.

2.

3.

4.

5.

Élève B Now ask your partner the following questions. Correct answers are in parentheses.

1. On prend un croissant pour le dîner?
   (Non, on prend une omelette pour le dîner.)

2. On prend une crêpe pour le déjeuner?
   (Non, on prend un sandwich au jambon pour le déjeuner.)

3. C'est un pourboire ou une fourchette?
   (C'est un pourboire.)

4. C'est un steak saignant ou bien cuit?
   (C'est un steak bien cuit.)

5. C'est une assiette ou une serviette?
   (C'est une serviette.)

Activity 15

Élève A Ask your partner the following questions. Correct answers are in parentheses.

1. Les copains vont où?
   (Ils vont à l'école.)

2. Ils y vont comment?
   (Ils y vont en voiture.)

3. Tu vas où?
   (Je vais à la papeterie.)

4. Tu y vas à pied?
   (Non, j'y vais en bus.)

Élève A Answer your partner's questions based on the cues below.

1. l'école

2. à pied

3. le café

4. le métro

Élève B Answer your partner's questions based on the cues below.

1. l'école

2. en voiture

3. la papeterie

4. en bus

Élève B Ask your partner the following questions. Correct answers are in parentheses.

1. Vous allez où?
   (Nous allons à l'école.)

2. Vous y allez comment?
   (Nous y allons à pied.)

3. Tu vas où?
   (Je vais au café.)

4. Tu prends le bus pour aller au café?
   (Non, je prends le métro.)

Activity 16

CHAPITRE 6, Mots 1, pages 186–187

Élève A Ask your partner the following questions. Correct answers are in parentheses.

1. Pour acheter du pain, on va où?
   (On va à la boulangerie-pâtisserie.)

2. Pour acheter du lait, on va où?
   (On va à la crèmerie.)

3. Pour acheter une tarte aux pommes, on va où?
   (On va à la boulangerie-pâtisserie.)

4. Pour acheter du jambon, on va où?
   (On va à la charcuterie.)

5. Pour acheter de la crème, on va où?
   (On va à la crèmerie.)

Élève A Use the following pictures to answer your partner's questions.

Élève B Answer your partner's questions based on the pictures below.

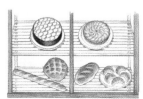

Élève B Ask your partner the following questions. Correct answers are in parentheses.

1. Pour acheter de la viande, on va où?
   (On va à la boucherie.)

2. Pour acheter du poisson, on va où?
   (On va à la poissonnerie.)

3. Pour acheter du poivre, on va où?
   (On va à l'épicerie.)

4. Pour acheter du porc, on va où?
   (On va à la boucherie.)

5. Pour acheter des crevettes, on va où?
   (On va à la poissonnerie.)

Activity 17

Élève A You play the part of the vendor. Ask your partner the following questions. Correct answers are in parentheses.

1. Vous voulez de la confiture?
(Oui, je voudrais un pot de confiture, s'il vous plaît.)

2. Vous voulez des légumes surgelés?
(Oui, je voudrais un paquet de légumes surgelés, s'il vous plaît.)

3. Vous voulez des petits pois?
(Oui, je voudrais une boîte de petits pois, s'il vous plaît.)

4. Vous voulez du lait?
(Oui, je voudrais un litre de lait, s'il vous plaît.)

5. Vous voulez du jambon?
(Oui, je voudrais une tranche de jambon, s'il vous plaît.)

Élève A Answer your partner's questions based on the information below.

 une bouteille

 250 grammes
 une douzaine

une boîte

un pot

Élève B Answer your partner's questions based on the information below.

 un pot
 un paquet

 une boîte
 un litre

 une tranche

Élève B Now you are the vendor. Ask your partner the following questions. Correct answers are in parentheses.

1. Vous voulez de la moutarde?
(Oui, je voudrais un pot de moutarde, s'il vous plaît.)

2. Vous voulez du beurre?
(Oui, je voudrais deux cent cinquante grammes de beurre, s'il vous plaît.)

3. Vous voulez des œufs?
(Oui, je voudrais une douzaine d'œufs, s'il vous plaît.)

4. Vous voulez des petits pois?
(Oui, je voudrais une boîte de petits pois, s'il vous plaît.)

5. Vous voulez de l'eau minérale?
(Oui, je voudrais une bouteille d'eau minérale, s'il vous plaît.)

Élève A Ask your partner the following questions. Correct answers are in parentheses.

1. Qui fait le déjeuner?
   (Moi, je fais le déjeuner.)

2. Qui fait du français?
   (Nous faisons du français.)

3. Qui fait des études?
   (Tu fais des études.)

4. Qui fait les exercices?
   (Alain et Eric font les exercices.)

5. Qui fait le gâteau?
   (Vous faites le gâteau.)

Élève A Use the information in the chart below to answer your partner's questions.

Qui?	Activité
Moi, je	(faire) les courses
Hugo et Marie	(faire) un pique-nique
Nous	(faire) de l'allemand
Vous	(faire) la cuisine
Tu	(faire) les devoirs

Élève B Use the information in the chart below to answer your partner's questions.

Qui?	Activité
Moi, je	(faire) le déjeuner
Nous	(faire) du français
Tu	(faire) des études
Alain et Eric	(faire) les exercices
Vous	(faire) le gâteau

Élève B Ask your partner the following questions. Correct answers are in parentheses.

1. Qui fait les courses?
   (Moi, je fais les courses.)

2. Qui fait un pique-nique?
   (Hugo et Marie font un pique-nique.)

3. Qui fait de l'allemand?
   (Nous faisons de l'allemand.)

4. Qui fait la cuisine?
   (Vous faites la cuisine.)

5. Qui fait les devoirs?
   (Tu fais les devoirs.)

Activity 19

Élève A Ask your partner the following questions. Correct answers are in parentheses.

1. Qui veut aller au restaurant?
   (*Moi, je veux aller au restaurant.*)

2. Qui peut travailler après l'école?
   (*Il peut travailler après l'école.*)

3. Qui veut inviter des amis?
   (*Tu veux inviter des amis.*)

4. Qui veut manger maintenant?
   (*Nous voulons manger maintenant.*)

5. Qui peut regarder le film?
   (*Vous pouvez regarder le film.*)

6. Qui veut aller au marché?
   (*Pierre veut aller au marché.*)

7. Qui veut écouter des CD?
   (*Eric et Michel veulent écouter des CD.*)

Élève A Use the information in the chart below to answer your partner's questions.

Qui?	Activité
Moi, je	(pouvoir) regarder le film
Elle	(vouloir) aller au restaurant
Nous	(pouvoir) faire des sandwichs
Ils	(vouloir) écouter des CD
Tu	(pouvoir) manger maintenant
Alain	(pouvoir) aller au marché
Hugo et Marie	(pouvoir) inviter des amis

Élève B Use the information in the chart below to answer your partner's questions.

Qui?	Activité
Moi, je	(vouloir) aller au restaurant
Il	(pouvoir) travailler après l'école
Tu	(vouloir) inviter des amis
Nous	(vouloir) manger maintenant
Vous	(pouvoir) regarder le film
Pierre	(vouloir) aller au marché
Eric et Michel	(vouloir) écouter des CD

Élève B Ask your partner the following questions. Correct answers are in parentheses.

1. Qui peut regarder le film?
   (*Moi, je peux regarder le film.*)

2. Qui veut aller au restaurant?
   (*Elle veut aller au restaurant.*)

3. Qui peut faire des sandwichs?
   (*Nous pouvons faire des sandwichs.*)

4. Qui veut écouter des CD?
   (*Ils veulent écouter des CD.*)

5. Qui peut manger maintenant?
   (*Tu peux manger maintenant.*)

6. Qui peut aller au marché?
   (*Alain peut aller au marché.*)

7. Qui peut inviter des amis?
   (*Hugo et Marie peuvent inviter des amis.*)

Activity 20

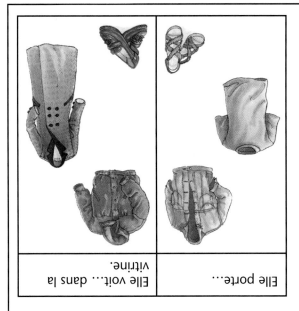

Elle voit… dans la vitrine.	Elle porte…

Élève A Use the information in the chart below to answer your partner's questions.

Élève A Ask your partner the following questions. Correct answers are in parentheses.

1. Marc porte un anorak?
   (Oui, il porte un anorak.)

2. Marc porte un blouson?
   (Non, il voit un blouson dans la vitrine.)

3. Marc porte un pull?
   (Oui, il porte un pull.)

4. Marc porte un t-shirt?
   (Non, il voit un t-shirt dans la vitrine.)

5. Marc porte une paire de chaussures?
   (Oui, il porte une paire de chaussures.)

6. Marc porte un survêtement?
   (Non, il voit un survêtement dans la vitrine.)

Élève B Use the information in the chart below to answer your partner's questions.

Il porte…	Il voit… dans la vitrine.

Élève B Ask your partner the following questions. Correct answers are in parentheses.

1. Chloé porte des sandales?
   (Oui, elle porte des sandales.)

2. Chloé porte un anorak?
   (Non, elle voit un anorak dans la vitrine.)

3. Chloé porte un blouson?
   (Oui, elle porte un blouson.)

4. Chloé porte une paire de chaussures?
   (Non, elle voit une paire de chaussures dans la vitrine.)

5. Chloé porte un t-shirt?
   (Oui, elle porte un t-shirt.)

6. Chloé porte un manteau?
   (Non, elle voit un manteau dans la vitrine.)

Activity 21

Élève A Find out your partner's opinion of different clothing items. Correct answers are in parentheses.

1. Il est joli, le pull bleu. Tu ne trouves pas?
   (Non, il est trop serré.)

2. Il est joli, le manteau gris. Tu ne trouves pas?
   (Non, il est trop long.)

3. Il est joli, l'anorak rouge. Tu ne trouves pas?
   (Non, il est trop cher.)

4. Elle est jolie, la jupe verte. Tu ne trouves pas?
   (Non, elle est un peu courte.)

5. Elles sont jolies, les chaussures marron. Tu ne trouves pas?
   (Oui, c'est ma couleur favorite.)

Élève A Use the information below to answer your partner's questions.

un peu large

Oui, c'est ma couleur favorite.

trop chères   trop petit   trop grand

Élève B Use the information below to answer your partner's questions.

trop serré   trop long   trop cher

un peu courte   Oui, c'est ma couleur favorite.

Élève B Find out your partner's opinion of different clothing items. Correct answers are in parentheses.

1. Il est joli, le short vert. Tu ne trouves pas?
   (Non, il est trop grand.)

2. Il est joli, le t-shirt orange. Tu ne trouves pas?
   (Non, il est trop petit.)

3. Elles sont jolies, les sandales bleues. Tu ne trouves pas?
   (Non, elles sont trop chères.)

4. Il est joli, le survêtement jaune. Tu ne trouves pas?
   (Non, il est un peu large.)

5. Il est joli, le blouson bleu. Tu ne trouves pas?
   (Oui, c'est ma couleur favorite.)

Activity 22

Élève A Ask your partner the following questions. Correct answers are in parentheses.

1. Qui met un short?
   (*Moi, je mets un short pour faire du jogging.*)

2. Qui met la radio le matin?
   (*Mes copains mettent la radio le matin.*)

3. Qui met une cravate?
   (*Mon père met une cravate pour aller au travail.*)

4. Qui met la table?
   (*Vous mettez la table pour le dîner.*)

5. Qui met un jean?
   (*Tu mets un jean pour aller au cinéma.*)

6. Qui met un complet?
   (*Nous mettons un complet pour aller à un mariage.*)

Élève A Use the information in the chart below to answer your partner's questions.

Qui?	Activité
Moi, je	(mettre) la télé le matin
Les serveurs	(mettre) la table au restaurant
Ma mère	(mettre) une jupe pour aller au marché
Nous	(mettre) des chaussettes rouges
Tu	(mettre) des baskets pour faire du jogging
Vous	(mettre) un pantalon pour aller à l'école

Élève B Use the information in the chart below to answer your partner's questions.

Qui?	Activité
Moi, je	(mettre) un short pour faire du jogging
Mes copains	(mettre) la radio le matin
Mon père	(mettre) une cravate pour aller au travail
Vous	(mettre) la table pour le dîner
Tu	(mettre) un jean pour aller au cinéma
Nous	(mettre) un complet pour aller à un mariage

Élève B Ask your partner the following questions. Correct answers are in parentheses.

1. Qui met la télé?
   (*Moi, je mets la télé le matin.*)

2. Qui met la table?
   (*Les serveurs mettent la table au restaurant.*)

3. Qui met une jupe?
   (*Ma mère met une jupe pour aller au marché.*)

4. Qui met des chaussettes rouges?
   (*Nous mettons des chaussettes rouges.*)

5. Qui met des baskets?
   (*Tu mets des baskets pour faire du jogging.*)

6. Qui met un pantalon?
   (*Vous mettez un pantalon pour aller à l'école.*)

Activity 23

Élève A Read the statements about clothing to your partner. Your partner does not agree with what you believe to be true. Correct answers are in parentheses.

1. Moi, je crois que le polo est plus grand que le t-shirt.
   (Non, je vois que le t-shirt est plus grand que le polo.) or *(Non, je vois que le polo est plus petit que le t-shirt.)*

2. Moi, je crois que la chemise est plus grande que le polo.
   (Non, je vois que la chemise est aussi grande que le polo.)

3. Moi, je crois que la jupe plissée est moins élégante que le chemisier.
   (Non, je vois que la jupe plissée est aussi élégante que le chemisier.)

Élève A Your partner tells you what he or she thinks about articles of clothing. Use the chart below to give your partner the correct information. Begin your response with **Non, je vois que…**

cher	l'anorak $ $ $	le blouson $	le manteau $ $ $ $ $ $
confortables	les baskets + +		les chaussures + +

Élève B Your partner tells you what he or she thinks about articles of clothing. Use the chart below to give your partner the correct information. Begin your response with **Non, je vois que…**

grand(e)	le t-shirt + + + + +	la chemise + + +	le polo + + +
élégant(e)	la jupe plissée + +		le chemisier + +

Élève B Read the statements about clothing to your partner. Your partner does not agree with what you believe to be true. Correct answers are in parentheses.

1. Moi, je crois que les chaussures sont moins confortables que les baskets.
   (Non, je vois que les chaussures sont aussi confortables que les baskets.)

2. Moi, je crois que le blouson est aussi cher que l'anorak.
   (Non, je vois que le blouson est moins cher que l'anorak.) or *(Non, je vois que l'anorak est plus cher que le blouson.)*

3. Moi, je crois que l'anorak est plus cher que le manteau.
   (Non, je vois que le manteau est plus cher que l'anorak.) or *(Non, je vois que l'anorak est moins cher que le manteau.)*

This guide is designed to help you achieve success as you embark on the adventure of learning another language. There are many ways to learn new information. You may find some of these suggestions more useful than others, depending upon which style of learning works best for you. Before you begin, it is important to understand how we acquire language.

Receptive Skills

Each day of your life you receive a great deal of information through the use of language. In order to obtain (get, receive) this information, it is necessary to understand the language being used. It is necessary to understand the language in two different ways. First you must be able to understand what people are saying when they speak to you. This is referred to as oral or listening comprehension. Oral comprehension or listening comprehension is the ability to understand the spoken language.

You must also be able to understand what you read. This is referred to as reading comprehension. Reading comprehension is the ability to understand the written language.

Listening comprehension and reading comprehension are called the *receptive skills.* They are receptive skills because as you listen to what someone else says or read what someone else has written you receive information without having to produce any language yourself.

It is usually very easy to understand your native language or mother tongue. It is a bit more problematic to understand a second language that is new to you. As a beginner, you are still learning the sounds of the new language, and you recognize only a few words. Throughout **Bon voyage!** we will give you hints or suggestions to help you understand when people are speaking to you in French or when you are reading in French. Following are some general hints to keep in mind.

HINTS FOR LISTENING COMPREHENSION

When you are listening to a person speaking French, don't try to understand every word. It is not necessary to understand everything to get the idea of what someone is saying. Listen for the general message. If some details escape you,

it doesn't matter. Also, never try to translate what people are saying in French into English. It takes a great deal of experience and expertise to be a translator. Trying to translate will hinder your ability to understand.

HINTS FOR READING COMPREHENSION

Just as you will not always understand every word you hear in a conversation, you will not necessarily understand every word you encounter in a reading selection, either. In **Bon voyage!,** we have used only words you know or can easily figure out in the reading selections. This will make reading comprehension much easier for you. However, if at some time you wish to read a newspaper or magazine article in French, you will most certainly come across some unfamiliar words. Do not stop reading. Continue to read to get the "gist" of the selection. Try to guess the meanings of words you do not know.

Productive Skills

There are two productive skills in language. These two skills are speaking and writing. They are called productive skills because it is you who has to produce the language when you say or write something. When you speak or write, you have control over the language and which words you use. If you don't know how to say something, you don't have to say it. With the receptive skills, on the other hand, someone else produces the language that you listen to or read, and you have no control over the words they use.

There's no doubt that you can produce your native language easily. You can say a great deal in your "mother tongue." You can write, too, even though you may sometimes make errors in spelling or punctuation. In French, there's not a lot you can say or write as a beginner. You can only talk or write about those topics you have learned in French class.

Study Tips

HINTS FOR SPEAKING Try to be as accurate as possible when speaking. Try not to make mistakes. However, if you do, it's not the end of the world. French people will understand you. You're not expected to speak a language perfectly after a limited time. You have probably spoken with people from other countries who do not speak English perfectly, but you can understand them. Remember:
* Keep talking! Don't become inhibited for fear of making a mistake.
* Say what you know how to say. Don't try to branch out in the early stages and attempt to talk about topics or situations you have not yet learned in French.

HINTS FOR WRITING There are many activities in each lesson of **Bon voyage!** that will help you speak and write in French. When you have to write something on your own, however, without the guidance or assistance of an activity in your book, be sure to choose a topic for which you know the vocabulary in French. Never attempt to write about a topic you have not yet studied in French. Write down the topic you are going to write about. Then think of the

words you know that are related to the topic. Be sure to include some action words (verbs) that you will need.

From your list of words, write as many sentences as you can. Read them and organize them into a logical order. Fill in any gaps. Then proof your paragraph(s) to see if you made any errors. Correct any that you find.

When writing on your own, be careful not to rely heavily, if at all, on a bilingual dictionary. It's not that bilingual dictionaries are bad, but when you look up a word you will very often find that there are several or many translations for the same word. As a beginning language student, you do not know which translation to choose; the chances are great that you will pick the wrong one.

As a final hint, never prepare your paragraph(s) in English and attempt to translate word for word. Always write from scratch in French.

*In each chapter of **Bon voyage!**, you will learn how to say and write new words. In Chapter 1, you learn how to describe a person. It won't be long before you'll be able to talk about many things in French. **Bon voyage!***

CHAPITRE 1
Vocabulaire

Mots 1 & 2 *(pages 18–25)*

1. Repeat each new word in the **Mots** section as many times as possible. The more you use a word, the more apt you are to remember it and keep it as part of your active vocabulary.
2. Read the words as you look at the illustrations.
3. If you're the type who has to write something down in order to remember it, copy each word once or twice.
4. Do these activities diligently. They provide you with the opportunity to use your new words many times.

5. This may sound strange, but it's a good idea to read these exercises aloud at home or when using the CD-ROM.
6. When doing the vocabulary activities by yourself or for homework, try to do each item orally before writing the answer.
7. After doing any activity that says **Historiette,** read all the answers aloud. Each time you do this, you will be telling a story in French. It's an excellent way to keep using the material you are learning.

CLASSROOM SUGGESTION Listen to what your classmates say when they respond in class. Do not tune them out. Paying attention to them allows you additional opportunities to hear your new words. The more you hear them, the more likely you are to learn and retain them.

Structure
Les adjectifs (page 28)
Pay particular attention to the final sound of many of the descriptive words you are learning. Remind yourself that you hear the final consonant sound of many descriptive words when you are describing a girl. You do not hear the sound when describing a boy.

HINT FOR SPELLING What letter do you delete from the feminine form? Remember that you delete the **e** that follows the consonant when referring to a male.

Le verbe être (pages 30–33)
1. **Être** is the first verb you are learning in French. Throughout your study of French, you will continue to learn many more verbs. Verbs are extremely important in French. At this point, you know three verb forms:
   je suis when talking about yourself
   tu es when talking to someone
   il/elle est when talking about someone

Get off to a good start! Learn these three simple forms and remember them.

2. As you do the activities, don't try to use words you don't know in French. For example, you may want to talk about someone who is very outgoing, but you don't know a French equivalent for "outgoing." Give the message using what you do know. For example, you can say: **Jean n'est pas timide, pas du tout.** You can also say: **Marie, elle est timide? Non, pas du tout. Marie n'est pas timide.** Using **ne… pas** with a word you know, you can convey the meaning you wish even though you do not know the precise word.

CLASSROOM SUGGESTION Listen to your classmates as they respond to the structure activities. Remember, the more you hear a form, the more readily you will be able to use it.

3. After doing any activity that says **Historiette**, read all the answers aloud. Each time you do this, you will be telling a story in French. It's an excellent way to keep using the material you are learning.

Lecture culturelle
Un garçon et une fille (pages 36–37)
1. Always read the Reading Strategy at the beginning of the **Lecture culturelle.** Practice these strategies and try applying them to other selections you read in French. The Reading Strategy on page 36 talks about cognates and how they help you guess the meanings of words you do not know. For example, you read: **Jean est un garçon français. Il est très intelligent, très capable.** You have probably never seen or used the word **capable** in French. However, you can guess its meaning because it is a cognate of the English word *capable.*

   In addition, it is used in apposition to **intelligent.** When you see a word or expression followed by a comma and then another word (in apposition), the word in apposition almost always clarifies the precise word and has the same or similar meaning.

2. Let's look at another way to guess meaning: **Jean est intelligent et il est aussi très sage. Il est prudent.** You don't know the word **sage,** but its meaning is clarified by **prudent.** Which of the following do you think **sage** means? *Talented? Wise, smart? Nice?* Hopefully you chose *wise, smart.* Think about how and why you arrived at this correct answer.

HINTS FOR WRITING As you complete your first chapter in French, you are able to write a description of a person. At this point, you cannot tell what the person does because you don't have the necessary vocabulary. So avoid this. However, you are able to tell what he or she is like. Write down the words you know in order to write your description. Do not think of words in English. Try to think only of the words you know in French. Begin to write your description. Remember what you learned about **e** if your description is of a female.

VOCABULAIRE *(page 46)*

As you complete the chapter, look at the reference vocabulary list. If there are several words you don't remember, go back to the **Mots 1** and **Mots 2** sections and review. If there are only one or two, you can choose to look them up in the dictionaries beginning on page H72 at the end of this book.

CHAPITRE 2

Get off to a good start! Do your French homework diligently and study for a short period of time each day. Do not skip some days and then try to cram. It doesn't work when studying a foreign language.

In each lesson of **Bon voyage!** you will learn a very manageable amount of new material. Since French is a romance language, much of the new material will involve word endings. Study each small set of new endings on a daily basis, and you'll have no problem. Don't wait until you have lots of them and try to cram them in all at once.

Vocabulaire

Mots 1 & 2 *(pages 50–57)*

1. In Chapter 1, you learned that adjectives describing something feminine end in **e**. The final consonant is pronounced. The **e** is dropped and the consonant is not pronounced when describing something masculine. In Chapter 2, you have four new words that reinforce the same concept: **fort, mauvais, strict,** and **intéressant.**

> **Elle est forte en maths.**
> **Il est fort en maths.**
> **La classe est intéressante.**
> **Le cours est intéressant.**

HINT FOR PRONOUNCING NEW WORDS

Imitate the pronunciation of your teacher or the audiocassettes or CDs to the best of your ability. Try to acquire the best pronunciation possible. However, don't be worried if you have a slight American accent. There are three levels of pronunciation.

* **Near-native** Try to pronounce like a native. Strive for a near-native pronunciation.
* **Accented but comprehensible** Many people have an accent when they speak a foreign language. You can tell they are not native speakers, but in spite of their accent, you can understand them. If you have such an accent, don't be concerned.
* **Very accented and incomprehensible** Some people have such a strong accent that it's impossible to understand what they're saying. If you have such a strong accent, it will be necessary to repeat and imitate more carefully.

Always remember to listen carefully, repeating as accurately as possible, and you'll succeed in acquiring acceptable pronunciation.

HINT FOR SPEAKING

Listen to your teacher pronounce new words or phrases and then repeat them several times. Once you know how to pronounce the words, read the words in your book. If you try to read a word in French before ever having pronounced it, the spelling will most probably interfere with your pronunciation. Always try to listen, repeat, and then read.

2. The vocabulary in **Mots 2** should be very easy to recognize and learn because many words are cognates. A cognate is a word that looks alike in both English and French and has the same meaning in both languages. In the early lessons of **Bon voyage!** we have used many cognates to help you acquire a substantial vocabulary quickly and easily.

However, be careful with the pronunciation of cognates. Even though they look alike and mean the same thing in both languages, they can be pronounced very differently.

Structure
Le pluriel: articles, noms et adjectifs
(pages 58–60)
When listening, you will not hear the **s** ending for the plural of a descriptive word. When speaking, you will not pronounce the **s.** However, when writing, you have to remember to write the **s** for plural words.

Les garçons intelligents
Les filles intelligentes

Le verbe être au pluriel *(pages 60–63)*
In this lesson, you learn three new verb forms:
nous sommes when talking about yourself and someone else
vous êtes when talking to two or more people
ils/elles sont when talking about two or more people
Go over these three forms until you feel confident that you know them.

Conversation
(page 66)
When you listen to people speak, you will notice that they often use little words or expressions that you will never see in written form. *Yeah* and *ya' know* are examples in English. You can often guess the meaning of these expressions by the speaker's tone of voice. In this conversation, listen to the tone of voice when the young woman says **Ben oui.** Do you think **Ben oui** means *No* or *Yeah?*

Lecture culturelle
Le français aux États-Unis *(pages 68-69)*
1. Read the Reading Strategy at the beginning of the **Lecture culturelle.** Look at the title of the reading on page 68. It lets you know immediately the general topic you'll be reading about.

2. Read the three subtitles or heads in the passage. They give you a more specific idea of what you'll be reading. Without having read the reading selection, you now have some understanding of what the reading is about. This will make comprehension much easier.

3. After looking at the title and subtitles, you may very quickly skim the reading. Rather than trying to remember all the information, look at the comprehension questions that follow it. Then go back to the reading and look for the specific factual information called for.

CHAPITRE 3
Vocabulaire
Mots 1 & 2 *(pages 82-89)*

1. Look at each photo or illustration carefully.
2. Read the labels. What does each word refer to?
3. Each word is then used in a meaningful context in a complete sentence. Repeat the individual words and then the sentences.
4. Note that in Activity 4 on page 85, the answer to the question word **qu'est-ce que (qu')** is always a thing. Therefore you should be able to guess the meaning of this question word. Does it mean *who* or *what?*
5. On page 86, after you have practiced your new words, cover up the words as you look at the drawing or photo of each classroom item. See how many you remember. If you don't remember many, you'll have to practice the words some more.

HINT Always pay careful attention to both the pronunciation and the spelling of your new words. You have now seen more than one form of certain verbs. For example: **Ils jouent. Il joue. Ils regardent. Il regarde.** Have you noticed that there is no difference in pronunciation between **regardent** and **regarde** even though they are written differently?

HINT FOR SPEAKING Whenever possible, read all the answers aloud to any activity labeled **Historiette**. Every time you do, you'll be telling a story on your own with the guidance of the activity in the text. This is an easy and useful way to get yourself speaking lots of French.

Structure

Les verbes réguliers en -er au présent
(pages 90–93)

1. Now that you know the word **on,** which almost always replaces **nous,** you will see that you really only have to pronounce two forms of a regular **-er** verb. When speaking, whether the subject of the sentence is **je, tu, il, on, elle, ils,** or **elles,** the verb sounds the same. Only the **vous** form has a different pronunciation. This makes spoken French quite easy.

1	2
je parle	
tu parles	vous regardez
il/elle/on parle	
ils/elles parlent	

2. However, when you write, remember that there are spelling changes.

    je parle
    tu parles
    il/elle/on parle
    ils/elles parlent

HINT Note that the structure activities in your book build from easy to more complex. In the beginning activities, you very often have to use only one verb form. For example, in Activity 13 on page 91, you only use the **il** form. However, in Activity 20 on page 93, you have to use all forms of the verb.

3. When doing Activity 21 on page 93, remember to use only French that you know. Refer to the list of words given here. This list will prevent you from thinking about things you cannot yet say in French.

La négation des articles indéfinis *(page 94)*
Try to condense a grammatical rule into one easy sentence that you can remember easily: **Un, une,** and **des** all become **de** after **ne... pas.**

Verbe + infinitif *(page 95)*
Note that the infinitive form of the verb used after a verb is pronounced the same as the **vous** form: **Vous travaillez.**
        J'aime travailler.
Travaillez and **travailler** are pronounced the same. When writing, remember the difference in spelling:
    Vous travaillez? Moi, j'aime travailler.
    Vous rigolez? Moi, j'aime rigoler.

Conversation
(page 96)

1. This conversation should be very easy for you. You have already learned all the French that is used in the conversation. When practicing this conversation with a classmate, feel free to make as many changes as you want, as long as they make sense.

2. In the conversation, you hear Carol say, **C'est pas vrai.** In spoken French, **ne** is often dropped from the expression **ne... pas.**

3. Note also that Cedric says **Si, c'est vrai.** When someone tells you **no** in French and you want to contradict, you say **si** rather than **oui.**

Lecture culturelle
Une journée avec Jacqueline *(pages 98–99)*

1. Look at the photos on pages 98–99. These photos let you know the reading is about:
    a. shopping for clothes
    b. going to school
    c. making a meal

2. Skim the reading selection and look for the important information such as:
    * Who's the story about?
    * Where does she live and go to school?
    * What are her school hours?

3. Factual recall is an important reading skill. First, find the facts in the reading and then commit them to memory. Activity B tells you what factual information to look for.

VOCABULAIRE *(page 108)*

As you complete the chapter, look at the reference vocabulary list. If there are several words you don't remember, go back to the **Mots 1** and **Mots 2** sections and review. If there are only one or two, you can choose to look them up in the dictionaries beginning on page H72 at the end of this book.

CHAPITRE 4

Vocabulaire

Mots 1 & 2 *(pages 112–120)*

1. In **Mots 1**, remember to listen to the words and repeat orally before reading them. Many names for family members are cognates. Be careful to repeat them correctly.

HINT If you're the type of learner who has to write something before you can remember, copy the words in the **Mots** section once or twice. Use the following learning sequence: *listen, repeat, read, write.*

2. Activity 2 on page 114 helps you review several important question words. The answer in parentheses tells you the meaning of the question word for that sentence. Look at the following question words and answers:

Quand?	aujourd'hui
Qu'est-ce que?	une fête, des cadeaux
Qui?	ses cousins, ses cousines

Decide which question words mean *who, what,* and *when.*

3. Activity 4 on page 115 helps you with productive skills. Remember that when you speak or write about yourself, you must always use the masculine form if you are a male and the feminine form if you are a female.

4. After you have learned the new words in **Mots 2,** look at each illustration, cover up the sentences, and say as much as you can about the illustration. If you can describe the illustration, you know your vocabulary. If you cannot describe it, you have to study some more.

HINT Read or say aloud all the answers to the **Historiette** activities to give you practice in telling coherent stories in French.

Structure

Le verbe **avoir** *(pages 120–122)*

So far, you have learned one irregular verb in French, the verb **être.** All forms of **être** are different. You will now learn your second irregular verb, **avoir.** All forms of **avoir** are also different.

1. Familiarize yourself with the forms of **avoir** as you go over the explanation in class.
2. Do the activities diligently. They give you the opportunity to use and learn the new verb forms without having to memorize them one by one.
3. Do the activities orally and in writing.
4. After doing the activities, reread the grammar explanation. See if you can give the forms of **avoir** on your own without reading them.

REVIEW You know that **un, une,** and **des** all change to **de** after **ne... pas.** The activities on pages 120–122 will help you review this point as you talk about your own home and family.

Conversation

(page 128)

Pay careful attention when you listen to the conversation on the CD-ROM or when other students are repeating it in class. The more you hear spoken French, the easier it will be for you to understand.

Lecture culturelle
Où habitent les Français? *(page 130–131)*

1. Read the title. When you finish this reading, what will you be able to tell?
   a. where France is
   b. who the French are
   c. where the French people live
2. As you read each paragraph, draw a mental picture of what you're reading. To help you draw your mental picture, look at the photographs, too.

C'est à vous
(pages 136–137)

In Activity 5 on page 137, you are going to write about your house or a house of your dreams.
1. Picture the house.
2. In French, think of or write a list of words you can use to identify parts of the house.
3. In French, think about or write a list of words you can use to describe a house or rooms of a house.
4. Organize your story. Divide the house into parts, such as living area, sleeping area, first floor, second floor. You may even want to make a drawing of your house. Write a few sentences about each area.
5. Put the sentences in a logical order.
6. Add a few sentences to describe the area around your house.

CHAPITRE 5

Vocabulaire

Mots 1 & 2 *(pages 154–161)*

1. It can be fun to study with a classmate. You can do the following.
   ✤ Ask one another questions in French about the illustrations.
   ✤ Have a contest. See who can give more French words describing the illustrations in a three-minute period.
   ✤ Tell your friend which of the items you would order if you were at a café.

2. Activity 1 on page 156 helps you reinforce the meaning of the important question words:

où	au café
qui	Chantal, le serveur
qu'est-ce que	une table libre, une boisson
quand	après les cours

3. Act out Activity 4 on page 157 with a classmate. The more you practice speaking French together, the better you'll be able to communicate.

Structure
Le verbe aller *(pages 162–164)*
You will now learn your third irregular verb. Make an association with another irregular verb you have already learned. Repeat the following out loud.

   je vais ➞ j'ai
   tu vas   ➞ tu as
   il va   ➞ il a
   ils vont ➞ ils ont

The forms of **aller** almost sound like the forms of **avoir** with a **v** sound.

HINT The more you practice speaking French, the better. When doing your homework, go over all the activities aloud. Don't just do your French homework silently.

Aller + *infinitif* *(page 165)*

1. The concept of an infinitive after a verb is not new to you. You already know how to express what you like to do:
   J'aime manger.
   J'aime aller au restaurant.
2. Now, using the same type of construction, you will be able to tell what you are going to do.
   J'aime manger et je vais manger quelque chose.
   J'aime aller au restaurant et je vais aller au restaurant vendredi.

Conversation

(page 170)

Listen carefully to the conversation. You can listen to your teacher or use the CD-ROM. Listen more than once. Each time listen for a different bit of information.

* Where are Claire and Loïc?
* What do they order?
* Why is there a possible disagreement?

Lecture culturelle

Au restaurant? Vraiment? *(pages 172–173)*

1. Making comparisons while reading is an important reading comprehension skill. In this reading, you learned about a cultural difference that's quite interesting. What is it? You may want to share this information with family or friends who don't know any French.
2. Finding the main idea is another important reading comprehension skill. As you read, look for the main idea in the second paragraph. What is it? What is the main idea in the third paragraph?

C'est à vous

(pages 178–179)

In Activity 4 on page 179, you're going to write about a restaurant in French.

1. Get a mental picture of the restaurant.
2. Write words you know in French to describe a restaurant and restaurant activities.
3. List items that people may order.
4. Put these words into sentences. Your first paragraph will describe the restaurant. Your second paragraph will tell what your "characters" order. Decide who pays to finish your article.

CHAPITRE 6

Vocabulaire

Mots 1 & 2 *(pages 186–193)*

1. Try to use your French as often as possible. When you see a food item at home or in a store that is labeled in French, say the French word to yourself. You'll learn to identify many more food items as you continue with your study of French.
2. As you complete the activities, answer each question orally before you write the answers for homework. Try reading your written responses aloud for Activities 2 and 3 on page 188. Activity 2 reviews the questions words **qui, qu'est-ce que, quand, où**.
3. On your own, review the foods you have learned by putting them with an appropriate package or container. For example:

    un paquet de fromage
    un paquet de six tranches de jambon
    un pot de confiture
    un paquet de légumes surgelés

HINTS Note that Activity 10 on page 193 points out that in spoken French, you can omit the **ne** in the expression **ne… pas**.

Be sure you understand the meaning of **pourquoi** and **parce que** when you finish this activity.

Structure

Le verbe **faire** *au présent* *(pages 194–195)*

1. Look at the forms of the verb **faire**. Repeat them aloud, then copy them.
2. When you complete homework activities, go back to the verb chart. Cover the verb forms and see if you can say the forms without looking at them.

Le partitif et l'article défini *(pages 196–197)*

1. Always try to make what you are learning as simple as possible. If you're talking about

something in general, you use **le, la, les.** If you're talking about "some" or "any," you use **du, de la,** or **des.**

2. When doing Activities 18 and 19 on page 197, pay particular attention to the contrast between the general sense and the partitive. You want to buy some (partitive) of the things you like (in general).

Le partitif au négatif (pages 199–201)
This concept of **de** is not new. Just remember **du, de la, de l',** and **des** all change to **de** after **ne… pas.** It's really simple, but you have to keep reminding yourself.

HINT Pay close attention as you and your classmates participate in each of these activities. The more you hear **j'ai du** (or **de la, des**) versus **je n'ai pas de,** the easier it will be for you to use the partitive.

HINTS FOR SPEAKING AND WRITING
Listen carefully for the difference in pronunciation between **bonne, bon,** and **gentille, gentil** as explained on page 201. Repeat the words carefully. Repeat the model sentences aloud, then copy them. Pay particular attention to the doubling of the consonant.

Les verbes pouvoir et vouloir
(pages 201–203)
Pay attention to the similarity between the forms of **pouvoir** and **vouloir.**

REVIEW Using the infinitive after a helping verb is not new. Remember:
> **J'aime dîner au restaurant.**
> **Je vais dîner au restaurant.**

Conversation
(page 204)
1. Intonation is the melody of a language. Intonation is produced by the rise and fall of the voice. Each language has its own intonation patterns. English intonation is very

different from French intonation. Pay special attention to the rise and fall of the speakers' voices as you listen to the conversations on the audiocassette or CD or CD-ROM.

2. Try to imitate the native speakers' intonation as accurately as possible. If you do, you'll sound much more French. Don't be inhibited. Pretend you are acting while you imitate the intonation.

Lecture culturelle
Les courses (pages 206–207)
You may not know the meaning of a certain word you come across in a reading selection. However, you can often guess the meaning of the word by the way it is used in the context of the sentence. A new word in this reading is **les commerçants.** Guess what it means by the context of these sentences:

> **Les Français aiment bien aller chez les petits commerçants du quartier—l'épicier, le boucher, le boulanger, etc.**

The fact that the word **commerçants** is followed by the words **l'épicier, le boucher, le boulanger** helps you figure out the meaning of **commerçants.** What do you think the word **commerçants** means in this context?
   a. office workers
   b. shopkeepers
   c. commercials

CHAPITRE 7

Vocabulaire

Mots 1 & 2 (pages 220–227)

1. Look at illustrations in **Mots 1** and repeat each word aloud.
2. Write each word for additional reinforcement.
3. When you have finished studying the vocabulary, determine how much you remember. Say to yourself or aloud all the items you know for boy's clothing, girl's clothing, and unisex clothing. When you get

dressed in the morning for school, notice how many words you know in French for those items you are wearing.

4. Before you write the answers to the vocabulary activities, work with a friend. Go over each exercise together orally. Then, each of you can write your answers. If you wish, you can check each other's work.

5. After studying the vocabulary in **Mots 2,** make a list of the things that you would most probably want to say in French to a salesperson when shopping for clothes.

REVIEW These vocabulary activities contain many adjectives, or descriptive words. Remember that many adjectives have an **e** when used with a feminine noun. They drop the **e** when used with a masculine noun.

La jupe est	verte. grise. petite. grande. bleue jolie.	Le blouson est	vert. gris. petit. grand. bleu. joli.

Structure
Le verbe mettre *(pages 228–229)*
1. Remember that you hear and pronounce the **t** in the plural forms of **mettre.** You do not hear or pronounce the **t** in the singular forms.
2. Do the **Attention** activity on page 229 aloud at least twice. As you do, pay very careful attention to pronunciation as well as spelling.

Le comparatif des adjectifs *(pages 230–231)*
1. Remember to make the association that **plus** (**+**) is more; **moins** (**–**) is less, and **aussi** (**=**) is the same. All three words are followed by **que.**
2. As you do these activities, pay particular attention to each adjective.

Les verbes voir *et* croire *(pages 232–233)*
1. Note that many forms of **voir** and **croire** are pronounced the same.

je crois	tu crois	il croit	ils croient
je vois	tu vois	il voit	ils voient

Conversation
(page 234)
This conversation should be very easy for you. You have already learned all the French that is used in the conversation. When practicing this conversation with a classmate, feel free to make as many changes as you want, as long as they make sense.

Lecture culturelle
On fait les courses où, a Paris?
(pages 236–237)
1. Look at the photos on pages 236–237. These photos let you know what the reading is about.
2. Look at the titles. They will give you an idea of what you'll be reading about.
3. Quickly scan the reading to get a general idea of what it's all about.
4. Activity A on page 237 will help you practice factual recall. To recall certain facts, it is often necessary to go back over the reading selection and look for details.
5. Drawing conclusions from a reading selection is another important reading comprehension skill. Based on what you read, draw a personal conclusion. Where would you shop in Paris? Why?

VOCABULAIRE *(page 246)*
As you complete the chapter, look at the reference vocabulary list. If there are quite a few words you don't know, go back to the **Mots 1** and **Mots 2** sections and review.

Verb Charts

VERBS RÉGULIERS			
INFINITIF	parler *to speak*	finir *to finish*	répondre *to answer*
PRÉSENT	je parle tu parles il parle nous parlons vous parlez ils parlent	je finis tu finis il finit nous finissons vous finissez ils finissent	je réponds tu réponds il répond nous répondons vous répondez ils répondent

VERBES AVEC CHANGEMENTS D'ORTHOGRAPHE			
INFINITIF	acheter *to buy*	appeler *to call*	commencer *to begin*
PRÉSENT	j'achète tu achètes il achète nous achetons vous achetez ils achètent	j'appelle tu appelles il appelle nous appelons vous appelez ils appellent	je commence tu commences il commence nous commençons vous commencez ils commencent
INFINITIF	manger *to eat*	payer *to pay*	préférer *to prefer*
PRÉSENT	je mange tu manges il mange nous mangeons vous mangez ils mangent	je paie tu paies il paie nous payons vous payez ils paient	je préfère tu préfères il préfère nous préférons vous préférez ils préfèrent

VERBES IRRÉGULIERS

INFINITIF	aller *to go*	avoir *to have*	croire *to believe*
PRÉSENT	je vais tu vas il va nous allons vous allez ils vont	j'ai tu as il a nous avons vous avez ils ont	je crois tu crois il croit nous croyons vous croyez ils croient

INFINITIF	être *to be*	faire *to do, to make*	mettre *to put*
PRÉSENT	je suis tu es il est nous sommes vous êtes ils sont	je fais tu fais il fait nous faisons vous faites ils font	je mets tu mets il met nous mettons vous mettez ils mettent

INFINITIF	pouvoir *to be able to*	prendre[1] *to take*
PRÉSENT	je peux tu peux il peut nous pouvons vous pouvez ils peuvent	je prends tu prends il prend nous prenons vous prenez ils prennent

INFINITIF	voir *to see*	vouloir *to want*
PRÉSENT	je vois tu vois il voit nous voyons vous voyez ils voient	je veux tu veux il veut nous voulons vous voulez ils veulent

---

[1] *Verbes similaires:* **apprendre, comprendre**

This French-English Dictionary *contains all productive and receptive vocabulary from the text. The numbers following each productive entry indicate the chapter and vocabulary section in which the word is introduced. For example,* **2.2** *means that the word first appeared in* **Chapitre 2, Mots 2. BV** *refers to the introductory* **Bienvenue** *lessons.* **L** *refers to the optional literary readings. If there is no number or letter following an entry, this means that the word or expression is there for receptive purposes only.*

A

à at, in, to, **3.1**
   À bientôt! See you soon!, **BV**
   À demain. See you tomorrow., **BV**
   à mon (ton, son, etc.) avis in my (your, his, etc.) opinion, **7.2**
   à pied on foot, **4.2**
   à point medium-rare (meat), **5.2**
   À tout à l'heure. See you later., **BV**
accessible accessible
l' **accessoire** (*m.*) accessory
accompagner to accompany, to go with
l' **achat** (*m.*) purchase
   faire des achats to shop
acheter to buy, **3.2**
l' **addition** (*f.*) check, bill (*restaurant*), **5.2**
additionner to add
l' **adolescent(e)** adolescent, teenager
   adorable adorable, **4.1**
   adorer to love
l' **adresse** (*f.*) address
l' **adulte** (*m. et f.*) adult
l' **affiche** (*f.*) poster
   africain(e) African
l' **Afrique** (*f.*) Africa
l' **âge** (*m.*) age, **4.1**
   Tu as quel âge? How old are you?, **4.1**

l' **agneau** (*m.*) lamb, **6.1**
l' **aide** (f.) aid, help
   à l'aide de with the help of
   aimer to like, love, **3.1**
   aimer mieux to prefer, **7.2**
l' **aîné(e)** older, **L1**
l' **air** (*m.*): **avoir l'air** to look
   aisé(e) well-to-do
l' **album** (*m.*) album
l' **algèbre** (*f.*) algebra, **2.2**
l' **Algérie** (*f.*) Algeria
   algérien(ne) Algerian
l' **aliment** (*m.*) food
l' **Allemagne** (*f.*) Germany
l' **allemand** (*m.*) German (*language*), **2.2**
   aller to go, **5.1**
   aller chercher to go (and) get, **6.1**
   alors so, then, well then, **BV**
   a.m. (*time*) in the morning, **BV**
   américain(e) American, **1.1**
l' **ami(e)** friend, **1.2**
   ample large, full
   amusant(e) funny; fun, **1.1**
l' **an** (*m.*) year, **4.1**
   avoir... ans to be . . . years old, **4.1**
l' **analyse** (*f.*) analysis
   analyser to analyse
   analytique analytical
l' **anatomie** (*f.*) anatomy

l' **anglais** (*m.*) English (*language*), **2.2**
   anglais(e) English
l' **animal** (*m.*) animal
l' **année** (*f.*) year
l' **anniversaire** (*m.*) birthday, **4 1**
   annoncer to announce
l' **anorak** (*m.*) ski jacket, **7.1**
   Antilles: la mer des Antilles Caribbean Sea
l' **appartement** (*m.*) apartment, **4.2**
   appeler to call
   apprécier to appreciate
   apprendre (à) to learn (to), **5**
   après after, **3.2**
l' **après-midi** (*m.*) afternoon, **3.2**
   arabe Arab
l' **arabe** (*m.*) Arabic (*language*)
l' **arbre** (*m.*) tree
l' **argent** (*m.*) money, **6.2**
   arriver to arrive, **3.1**; to happen
l' **arrondissement** (*m.*) district (*in Paris*)
l' **article** (*m.*) article
l' **artiste** (*m. et f.*) artiste
   l'artiste peintre (*m. et f.*) painter
   artistique artistic
l' **ascenseur** (*m.*) elevator, **4.2**
   asiatique Asian
   assez fairly, quite; enough, **1.1**

l' **assiette** (*f.*) plate, **5.2**

l' **attention** (*f.*) attention
Attention! Careful!
Watch out!, **4.2**

au at the, to the, **5**
au revoir good-bye, **BV**
au-dessous: la taille au-dessous the next smaller
size, **7.2**
au-dessus: la taille au-dessus the next larger
size, **7.2**
aujourd'hui today, **BV**
auprès de with

aussi also, too, **1.1;** as (*in comparisons*), **7**

l' **auteur** (*m.*) author
(*m. and f.*)
autour de around, **4.2**

autre other, **L1**
d'autres some other,
2.2
l'un… l'autre one . . . the
other
autre chose something
else
Autre chose? Anything
else? (*shopping*), **6.2**

avant before

avec with, **3.2**
Avec ça? What else?
(*shopping*), **6.1**

l' **avenir** (*m.*) future, **L2**

l' **avenue** (*f.*) avenue

l' **avis** (*m.*) opinion, **7.2**
à mon avis in my
opinion, **7.2**

avoir to have, **4.1**
avoir l'air to look
avoir… ans to be . . .
years old, **4.1**
avoir de la chance to be
lucky, to be in luck
avoir faim to be hungry,
5.1
avoir une faim de loup
to be very hungry
avoir lieu to take place
avoir peur to be afraid,
L1
avoir soif to be thirsty,
5.1

le **baccalauréat** French high
school exam

la **bactérie** bacterium
bactérien(ne) bacterial

la **baguette** loaf of French
bread, **6.1**
bain: la salle de bains
bathroom, **4.2**

le **balcon** balcony, **4.2**

la **banane** banana, **6.2**

la **banlieue** suburbs

la **base** base; basis
à base de based on

la **basket** sneaker, running
shoe, **7.1**

le **basket(-ball)** basketball
bavarder to chat
beau (bel), belle beautiful,
handsome, **4.2**

beaucoup a lot, **3.1**
beaucoup de a lot of,
many, **3.2**

le **beau-père** stepfather, **4.1**

le **bébé** baby
beige (*inv.*) beige, **7.2**
belge Belgian

la **Belgique** Belgium

la **belle-mère** stepmother,
4.1
ben (*fam.*) well
ben oui yeah

le **beurre** butter, **6.1**

la **bicyclette** bicycle
bien fine, well, **BV**
bien cuit(e) well-done
(*meat*), **5.2**
bien élevé(e) well-behaved; well-mannered
bien sûr of course
eh bien well
bientôt soon
À bientôt! See you soon!
BV

le/la **bienvenu(e)** welcome

la **biologie** biology, **2.2**
biologique biological

le/la **biologiste** biologist
blanc, blanche white,
7.2
bleu(e) blue, **7.2**
bleu marine (*inv.*) navy
blue, **7.2**

le **bloc-notes** notepad, **3.2**
blond(e) blond, **1.1**

le **blouson** (waist-length)
jacket, **7.1**

le **blue jean** (pair of) jeans

le **bœuf** beef, **6.1**
bohème bohemian
boire to drink
quelque chose à boire
something to drink

le **bois** wood

la **boisson** beverage, drink,
5.1

la **boîte de conserve** can of
food, **6.2**
boiteux, boiteuse lame

le **bol** bowl
bon(ne) correct; good,
6.2
Bon! Okay!, Right!, **6.1**
bon marché (*inv.*)
inexpensive
bonjour hello, **BV**

la **botanique** botany

le **boubou** boubou (long,
flowing garment)

le **boucher, la bouchère**
butcher

la **boucherie** butcher shop,
6.1

la **bougie** candle, **4.1**

la **boulangerie-pâtisserie**
bakery, **6.1**

la **bouteille** bottle, **6.2**

la **boutique** shop, boutique,
7.1

la **Bretagne** Brittany
breton(ne) Breton, from
Brittany

le/la **Breton(ne)** Breton (*person*)

la **brousse** bush (wilderness)
brun(e) dark-haired,
brunette, **1.1**

le **bungalow** bungalow

le **bus** bus, **5.2**

C

ça that, **BV**
  Ça fait… euros. It's
    (That's) . . . euros., **6.2**
  Ça va. Fine., Okay., **BV**
  Ça va? How's it going?,
    How are you? *(inform.)*,
    BV; How does it look?,
    7.2
le **cabaret** cabaret
la **cabine d'essayage** fitting
  room
le **cadeau** gift, present, **4.1**
le **cadet, la cadette** younger,
  L1
le **café** café **BV**; coffee, **5.1**
la **cafétéria** cafeteria
le **cahier** notebook, **3.2**
la **caisse** cash register,
  checkout counter, **3.2**
le **calcul** calculus, **2.2**
  le calcul différentiel
    differential calculus
  le calcul intégral integral
    calculus
la **calculatrice** calculator, **3.2**
le **calligramme** picture-
  poem
  calme quiet, calm
le **camembert** Camembert
  cheese
  canadien(ne) Canadian, **6**
la **cantine** school dining hall,
  3.1
  capable able
la **capitale** capital
la **caractéristique**
  characteristic
  **Caraïbes: la mer des
    Caraïbes** Caribbean Sea
la **carotte** carrot, **6.2**
la **carte** menu, **5.1**; map
la **casquette** cap, baseball
  cap, **7.1**
  casse-pieds pain in the
    neck *(fam.)*
la **cassette** cassette, tape **3.1**
le **catalogue** catalog
la **catégorie** category

le **CD** CD, **3.1**
le **CD-ROM** CD-ROM
  ce (cet) *(m.)* this, that
  ce soir tonight
  célèbre famous
la **cellule** cell
  celte Celtic
  celtique Celtic
  cent hundred, **2.2**
  pour cent percent
le **centilitre** centiliter
le **centre** center, middle
  le centre commercial
    shopping center, mall,
    7.1
le **centre-ville** downtown
le **cercle** circle
les **céréales** *(f. pl.)* cereal,
  grains
  certains some
  c'est it is, it's, **BV**
  C'est à vous. It's your
    turn.
  C'est combien? How
    much is it?, **3.2**
  C'est quel jour? What
    day is it? **BV**
  C'est tout. That's all., **6.1**
  c'est-à-dire that is
  chacun(e) each (one), **5.2**
la **chaîne** chain; TV channel
la **chaise** chair
la **chambre à coucher**
  bedroom, **4.2**
le **champ** field, **L1**
  champêtre pastoral
la **chance** luck
  avoir de la chance to be
    lucky, to be in luck
la **chanson** song
la **charcuterie** deli(catessen),
  6.1
le **chariot** shopping cart, **6.2**
le **charme** charm
le **charpentier** carpenter
le **chat** cat, **4.1**
le **château** castle, mansion
la **chaussette** sock, **7.1**
la **chaussure** shoe, **7.1**
le **chemin** road; path
la **chemise** shirt, **7.1**

le **chemisier** blouse, **7.1**
  cher, chère dear;
    expensive, **7.1**
  chercher to look for, seek
  aller chercher to go
    (and) get, **6.1**
  chez at (to) the home
    (business) of, **3.2**
le **chien** dog, **4.1**
la **chimie** chemistry, **2.2**
le/la **chimiste** chemist
  chinois(e) Chinese
la **chose** thing
  ciao good-bye *(inform.)*,
    BV
le **cirque** circus
  citer to cite, mention
le **citron pressé** lemonade,
  5.1
le/la **civilisé(e)** civilized person
  clair(e) light *(color)*
la **classe** class, **2.1**
  la salle de classe
    classroom, **2.1**
le **classeur** loose-leaf binder,
  3.2
le **clavier** keyboard
le/la **client(e)** customer
le **clown** clown
le **coca** cola, **5.1**
le **code** code, **4.2**
le **coin: du coin**
  neighborhood *(adj.)*
la **collection** collection
le **collège** junior high,
  middle school, **1.2**
le/la **collégien(ne)** middle
  school/junior high
  student
  combien (de) how much,
    how many, **3.2**
  C'est combien? How
    much is it (that)?, **3.2**
  commander to order, **5.1**
  comme like, as; for; since
  comme ci, comme ça so-
    so
  commencer to begin
  comment how, what, **1.1**
  Comment ça? How is
    that?

le/la **commerçant(e)**
shopkeeper
commun: en commun in
common
la **comparaison** comparison
comparer to compare
le/la **compatriote** compatriot
la **compétition** contest
le **complet** suit *(man's)*, **7.1**
complet, complète full,
complete
le **pain complet** whole-
wheat bread
complètement completely,
totally
compléter to complete
le **compositeur,** la
compositrice composer
comprendre to
understand, **5**
compris(e) included, **5.2**
Le service est compris.
The tip is included., **5.2**
compter to count
le **concept** concept
le **concert** concert
le **concert-bal** concert and
ball
la **confiture** jam, **6.2**
confortable comfortable
connecter to connect
connu(e) well-known
la **conserve: la boîte de
conserve** can of food, **6.2**
la **consommation** drink,
beverage, **5.1**
content(e) happy, glad
le **continent** continent
continuer to continue
la **conversation** conversation
converser to converse
le **copain** friend, pal *(m.)*, **2.1**
la **copine** friend, pal *(f.)*, **2.1**
la **cornemuse** bagpipes
le **corps** body
la **correpondance**
correspondence
la **Côte d'Azur** French
Riviera
la **Côte d'Ivoire** Ivory Coast
le **côté** side

**coucher: la chambre à
coucher** bedroom, **4.2**
la **couleur** color, **7.2**
la **cour** courtyard, **3.2**; court
courageux, courageuse
courageous, brave
le **cours** course, class, **2.1**
**en cours de (français,
etc.)** in (French, etc.)
class
les **courses** *(f. pl.):* **faire des
courses** to go shopping,
7.2
faire les courses to go
grocery shopping, **6.1**
court(e) short, **7.1**
le **couscous** couscous
le/la **cousin(e)** cousin, **4.1**
le **couteau** knife, **5.2**
coûter to cost, **3.2**
le **couturier** designer *(of
clothes)*
le **couvert** table setting, **5.2**
le **crabe** crab, **6.1**
la **cravate** tie, **7.1**
le **crayon** pencil, **3.2**
créer to create
le **crème** coffee with cream
(in a café), **5.1**
la **crémerie** dairy store, **6.1**
le **créole** Creole *(language)*
la **crêpe** crepe, pancake, **BV**
crevé(e) exhausted
la **crevette** shrimp, **6.1**
croire to believe, think,
7.2
le **croissant** croissant,
crescent roll, **5.1**
le **croque-monsieur** grilled
ham and cheese
sandwich, **5.1**
la **cuillère** spoon, **5.2**
la **cuisine** kitchen, **4.2**;
cuisine *(food)*
faire la cuisine to
cook, **6**
cuit(e): bien cuit(e) well-
done *(meat)*, **5.2**
cultiver to cultivate
la **culture** culture
culturel(le) cultural

D

d'accord: être d'accord to
agree, **2.1**
dans in, **1.2**
danser to dance
la **date** date
d'autres some other, **2.2**
de from, **1.1**; of, belonging
to, **1.2**; about
de la, de l' some, any, **6**
De quelle couleur est… ?
What color is . . . ?, **7.2**
le **début** beginning
le **décalitre** dekaliter
décider (de) to decide (to)
découvrir to discover
décrire to describe
la **déformation** alteration
déjà already, **BV**
déjeuner to eat lunch, **3.1**
le **déjeuner** lunch, **5.2**
le **petit déjeuner**
breakfast, **5.2**
délicieux, délicieuse
delicious
demain tomorrow, **BV**
À demain. See you
tomorrow., **BV**
demander to ask (for), **3.2**
demi(e): et demie half
past *(time)*, **BV**
le **demi-frère** half brother,
4.1
la **demi-sœur** half sister, **4.1**
le **département d'outre-mer**
French overseas
department
désagréable disagreeable,
unpleasant
désespéré(e) desparate
désirer to want
le **dessin** art, **2.2**
la **destinée** destiny
détester to hate, **3.1**
deuxième second, **4.2**
deviner to guess
la **devinette** riddle
le **devoir** assignment

faire ses devoirs to do homework, **6**
dévoué(e) devoted
d'habitude usually
le **dialecte** dialect
différent(e) different
difficile difficult, **2.1**
diffuser to spread, propagate
le **dîner** dinner, **5.2**
dîner to eat dinner, **5.2**
le **diplôme** diploma
la **direction** direction
discuter to discuss
le **disque** record
la **disquette** diskette
distinguer to distinguish, tell apart
divers(e) various
divisé(e) divided
diviser to divide
la **djellaba** djellaba (long, loose garment)
le **document** document
le **doigt** finger
le **dollar** dollar, **3.2**
le **dolmen** dolmen
le **domaine** domain, field
donc so, therefore
les **données** (f. pl.) data
donner to give, **4.1**
donner une fête to throw a party, **4.1**
donner sur to face, overlook, **4.2**
dormir to sleep
douloureux, douloureuse painful
le **doute** doubt
la **douzaine** dozen, **6.2**
du coin neighborhood (adj.)
dynamique dynamic, **1.2**

l' **eau** (f.) water, **6.2**
l'eau minérale mineral water, **6.2**

l' **échange** (m.) exchange
en échange de in exchange for
échanger to exchange
l' **école** (f.) school, **1.2**
l'école primaire elementary school
l'école secondaire junior high, high school, **1.2**
l' **économie** (f.) economics, **2.2**
écouter to listen (to), **3.1**
l' **écran** (m.) screen
écrire to write
l' **écrivain** (m.) writer (m. and f.), **L2**
égoïste egotistical, **1.2**
l' **élément** (m.) element
l' **élève** (m. et f.) student, **1.2**
élevé(e): bien élevé(e) well-behaved
l' **e-mail** (m.) e-mail
l' **emploi** (m.) **du temps** schedule
emprisonné(e) imprisoned
en in, **3.2**; by, **5.2**
en général in general
en solde on sale, **7.1**
en ville in town, in the city
en voiture by car, **5.2**
l' **énergie** (f.) energy
énergique energetic, **1.2**
l' **enfance** (f.) childhood
l' **enfant** (m. et f.) child, **4.1**
enfin finally; anyhow
l' **ensemble** (m.) outfit; whole, entirety
ensemble together, **5.1**
enthousiaste enthusiastic, **1.2**
entier, entière entire, whole
entre between, among, **3.2**
l' **entrée** (f.) entrance, **4.2**; admission
l' **entreprise** (f.) firm
entrer to enter, **7.1**
environ about

envoyer to send
l' **épicerie** (f.) grocery store, **6.1**
les **épinards** (m. pl.) spinach, **6.2**
l' **époque** (f.) period, times
l' **escalier** (m.) staircase, **4.2**
l' **espagnol** (m.) Spanish (language), **2.2**
l' **esprit** (m.) spirit
essayer to try on, **7.2**
et and, **BV**
établir to establish
l' **étage** (m.) floor (of a building), **4.2**
les **États-Unis** (m. pl.) United States
étranger, étrangère foreign
être to be, **1.1**
l' **étudiant(e)** (university) student
l' **étude** (f.) study
étudier to study, **3.1**
l' **euro** (m.) euro, **6.2**
l' **Europe** (f.) Europe
européen(ne) European
l' **examen** (m.) test, exam, **3.1**
excellent(e) excellent
excepté(e) except
l' **exception** (f.) exception
exceptionnel(le) exceptional
exécuter to execute, carry out
l' **exemple** (m.) example
par exemple for example
l' **exercice** (m.) exercise
exister to exist, to be
l' **explication** (f.) explanation
l' **express** (m.) espresso, black coffee, **5.1**
expulser to expel, banish
l' **extérieur** (m.) exterior, outside
à l'extérieur outside
extraordinaire extraordinary

la **fable** fable
facile easy, **2.1**
la **façon** way, manner
faible weak, **L1**
faim: avoir faim to be hungry, **5.1**
faire to do, make, **6.1**
faire du (+ nombre) to take size (+ number), **7.2**
faire des achats to shop
faire des courses to go shopping, **7.2**
faire les courses to do the grocery shopping, **6.1**
faire la cuisine to cook, **6**
faire ses devoirs to do homework, **6**
faire des études to study
faire du français (des maths, etc.) to study French (math, etc.), **6**
faire du jogging to jog
faire un pique-nique to have a picnic, **6**
Vous faites quelle pointure? What size shoe do you take?, **7.2**
Vous faites quelle taille? What size do you take/wear?, **7.2**
la **famille** family, **4.1**
le nom de famille last name
fantastique fantastic
le **fast-food** fast-food restaurant
fatigué(e) tired
la **faute** fault, mistake
faux, fausse false
favori(te) favorite, **7.2**
la **femme** woman, **7.1**; wife, **4.1**
fermé(e) closed
la **fête** party, **4.1**
donner une fête to throw a party, **4.1**

feuille: la feuille de papier sheet of paper, **3.2**
le **feutre** felt-tip pen, **3.2**
le **fichier** file (*computer*)
la **fille** girl, **1.1**; daughter, **4.1**
le **film** film, movie
le **fils** son, **4.1**
la **fleur** flower, **4.2**
fleuri(e) in bloom, **L2**
fleurir to bloom
le **fleuve** river
la **fois** time (*in a series*)
à la fois at the same time
deux fois twice
fonder to found
le **football américain** football
la **forme** form, shape
former to form; to train
fort(e) strong, **2.2**
fort(e) en maths good in math, **2.2**
la **fourchette** fork, **5.2**
la **fourniture** supply
les fournitures scolaires school supplies, **3.2**
la **fracture** fracture (of bone)
la **fraise** strawberry, **6.2**
le **français** French (*language*), **2.2**
français(e) French, **1.1**
francophone French-speaking
fréquenter to frequent, patronize
le **frère** brother, **1.2**
le **frigidaire** refrigerator
les **frites** (*f. pl.*) French fries, **5.1**
le **fromage** cheese, **5.1**
la **frontière** border
frugal(e) light, simple
le **fruit** fruit, **6.2**
le **futur** future, **L2**

gagner to earn
le **garage** garage, **4.2**

le **garçon** boy, **1.1**
garder to guard, watch
le **gâteau** cake, **4.1**
général: en général in general
généralement generally
les **gens** (*m. pl.*) people
gentil(le) nice (*person*), **6.2**
la **géographie** geography, **2.2**
la **géométrie** geometry, **2.2**
la **glace** ice cream, **5.1**
la **gomme** eraser, **3.2**
le **gourmet** gourmet
grâce à thanks to
la **grammaire** grammar
le **gramme** gram, **6.2**
grand(e) tall, big, **1.1**; great
le grand magasin department store, **7.1**
de grand standing luxury (*adj.*)
la grande surface large department store; large supermarket
grandir to grow (up) (*children*)
la **grand-mère** grandmother, **4.1**
le **grand-père** grandfather, **4.1**
les **grands-parents** (*m. pl.*) grandparents, **4.1**
la **griffe** label
la **grippe** flu
gris(e) gray, **7.2**
le **groupe** group
la **guerre** war
guillotiné(e) guillotined
le/la **guitariste** guitarist
la **gymnastique** gymnastics, **2.2**

habillé(e) dressy, **7.1**
habiter to live (*in a city, house, etc.*), **3.1**
haïtien(ne) Haitian

le **hamburger** hamburger
le **hameau** hamlet
handicapé(e) handicapped
le **hardware** *(computer)* hardware
les **haricots** *(m. pl.)* **verts** green beans, **6.2**
la **harpe** harp
l' **hectomètre** *(m.)* hectometer
l' **heure** *(f.)* time *(of day)*, **BV;** hour, **3.2**
   à quelle heure? at what time?, **2**
   À tout à l'heure. See you later., **BV**
   Il est quelle heure? What time is it?, **BV**
l' **histoire** *(f.)* history, **2.2**
l' **H.L.M.** low-income housing
l' **homme** *(m.)* man, **7.1**
horrible horrible
le **hot-dog** hot dog, **5.1**
l' **huile** *(f.)* oil, **6.1**
humain(e) human
hyper: J'ai hyper faim. I'm super hungry.
l' **hypermarché** *(m.)* large department store/supermarket

idéal(e) ideal
l' **idée** *(f.)* idea
il y a there is, there are
l' **île** *(f.)* island
immense immense
l' **immeuble** *(m.)* apartment building, **4.2**
important(e) important
impossible impossible
l' **imprimante** *(f.)* printer
indiquer to indicate, show
indiscret, indiscrète indiscreet
individuel(le) private
industriel(le) industrial

inférieur(e) lower
infini(e) infinite
l' **influence** *(f.)* influence
l' **information** *(f.)* information
   les informations *(f. pl.)* news *(TV)*
l' **informatique** *(f.)* computer science, **2.2**
insister to insist
inspirer to inspire
les **instructions** *(f. pl.)* instructions
intellectuel(le) intellectual
intelligent(e) intelligent, **1.1**
intéressant(e) interesting, **1.1**
intéresser to interest
l' **intérêt** *(m.)* interest
l' **interview** *(f.)* interview
inviter to invite, **4.1;** to pay for someone's meal, **5.2**
l' **italien** *(m.)* Italian *(language)*, **2.2**
italien(ne) Italian, **9**
l' **Ivoirien(ne)** Ivorian *(inhabitant of Côte d'Ivoire)*

jaloux, jalouse jealous
le **jambon** ham, **5.1**
janvier *(m.)* January, **BV**
le **jardin** garden, **4.2**
jaune yellow, **7.2**
je I, **1.2**
   Je t'en prie. You're welcome. *(fam.)*, **BV**
   je voudrais I would like, **5.1**
   Je vous en prie. You're welcome. *(form.)*, **BV**
le **jean** jeans, **7.1**
le **jeu** game
jeune young
les **jeunes** *(m. pl.)* young people
le **jogging: faire du jogging** to jog

joli(e) pretty, **4.2**
jouer to play, **3.2**
le **jour** day, **BV**
   tous les jours every day
la **journée** day, **3.1**
   Belle journée! What a nice day!, **4.2**
le **jumeau, la jumelle** twin, **L1**
la **jupe** skirt, **7.1**
le **jus** juice, **5.1**
le **jus de pomme** apple juice, **5.1**
le **jus d'orange** orange juice, **5.1**
   juste just, **2.1**
   juste à sa taille fitting (him/her) just right
   juste là right there

le **kilo(gramme)** kilogram, **6.2**

là there
le **laboratoire** laboratory
laisser to leave *(something behind)*, **5.2**
   laisser un pourboire to leave a tip, **5.2**
le **lait** milk, **6.1**
la **langue** language, **2.2**
la langue maternelle mother tongue
   large loose, wide, **7.2**
le **latin** Latin, **2.2**
la **leçon** lesson
la **lecture** reading
la **légende** legend
le **légume** vegetable, **6.2**
lever to raise, **3.1**
   lever la main to raise one's hand, **3.1**
la **liaison** liaison, linking
libre free, **5.1**
   avoir lieu to take place

la **ligne** line
la **limite** limit
la **limonade** lemon-lime drink, **BV**
le **liquide** liquid
le **litre** liter, **6.2**
la **littérature** literature, **2.2**
la **livre** pound, **6.2**
le **livre** book, **3.2**
le **logement** housing
le **logiciel** computer program
loin far (away)
loin de far from, **4.2**
long(ue) long, **7.1**
le **look** style
le **lycée** high school, **2.1**
le/la **lycéen(ne)** high school student

Madame (Mme) Mrs., Ms., **BV**
Mademoiselle (Mlle) Miss, Ms., **BV**
le **magasin** store, **3.2**
le grand magasin department store, **7.1**
le **magazine** magazine
le **Maghreb** Maghreb
la **main** hand, **3.1**
maintenant now, **2.2**
mais but, **2.1**
la **maison** house, **3.1**
la maison d'édition publishing house
la **maisonnette** cottage
la **majorité** majority
mal badly
Pas mal. Not bad., **BV**
malade sick, **L1**
malheureux, malheureuse unhappy
la **maman** mom
la **manche** sleeve, **7.1**
à manches longues (courtes) long-(short-) sleeved, **7.1**
manger to eat, **5.1**

la **salle à manger** dining room, **4.2**
le **manteau** coat, **7.1**
le/la **marchand(e) (de fruits et légumes)** (produce) seller, merchant, **6.2**
la **marchandise** merchandise
le **marché** market, **6.2**
bon marché inexpensive
le marché aux puces flea market
le **mari** husband, 4.1
le **mariage** marriage; wedding
le **Maroc** Morocco
marocain(e) Moroccan
marron *(inv.)* brown, **7.2**
martiniquais(e) from or of Martinique
les **mathématiques** *(f. pl.)* mathematics, **2.2**
les **maths** *(f. pl.)* math, **2.2**
la **matière** subject *(school)*, **2.2;** matter
le **matin** morning, **BV**
du matin A.M. *(time)*, **BV**
mauvais(e) bad; wrong, **2.2**
le **médecin** doctor *(m. and f.)*
la **médina** medina *(old Arab section of North African town)*
le **melon** melon, **6.2**
même *(adj.)* same, **2.1;** *(adv.)* even
tout de même all the same, **5.2**
la **mer** sea
la mer des Antilles Caribbean Sea
la mer des Caraïbes Caribbean Sea
la mer Méditerranée Mediterranean Sea
merci thank you, thanks, **BV**
la **mère** mother, **4.1**
le **message** message
la **mesure** measurement; measure
mesurer to measure

le **mètre** meter
le **métro** subway, **4.2**
la station de métro subway station, **4.2**
mettre to put (on), **7.1;** to turn on *(appliance)*, **7**
mettre la table to set the table, **7**
le **microbe** microbe, germ
microbien(ne) microbial
le **microprocesseur** microprocessor
le **microscope** microscope
midi *(m.)* noon, **BV**
mieux better, **7.2**
aimer mieux to prefer, **7.2**
mille (one) thousand, **3.2**
le **milligramme** milligram
minuit *(m.)* midnight, **BV**
la **minute** minute
la **mode: à la mode** in style
le **modem** modem
moderne modern
modeste modest; reasonably priced
moins less, **7.1;** minus
le **mois** month, **BV**
le **moment** moment, time
le **monde** world
tout le monde everyone, everybody, **1.2**
le **moniteur** *(computer)* monitor
Monsieur *(m.)* Mr., sir, **BV**
le **mont** mount, mountain
la **montagne** mountain
monter to go up, **4.2**
montrer to show
le **mot** word
la **moule** mussel
la **moutarde** mustard, **6.2**
le **mouvement** movement
multicolore multicolored
multiplier to multiply
le **musée** museum
le/la **musicien(ne)** musician
la **musique** music, **2.2**
le **mythe** myth

la **nappe** tablecloth, **5.2**

nationalité (*f.*) nationality

nature plain (*adj.*), **5.1**

naturel(le) natural

naviguer sur Internet to surf the Net

ne: ne... pas not, **1.2**

  ne... plus no longer, no more, **6.1**

né(e): elle est née she was born

nécessaire necessary

la **négritude** black pride

n'est-ce pas? isn't it?, doesn't it (he, she, etc.)?, **2.2**

le **neveu** nephew, **4.1**

la **nièce** niece, **4.1**

noble noble

noir(e) black, **7.2**

le **nom** name; noun

  le nom de famille last name

le **nombre** number

non no

le **nord** north

  nord-africain(e) North African

la **note** note; grade

nourrir to feed

la **nourriture** food, nutrition

nouveau (nouvel), nouvelle new, **4.2**

la **Nouvelle-Angleterre** New England

nul(le) (*fam.*) bad

le **numéro** number

  le numéro de téléphone telephone number

ô oh

l' **objet** (*m.*) object

obligatoire mandatory

obliger to oblige, force

observer to observe

occidental(e) western

occupé(e) occupied, taken, **5.1**; busy

l' **océan** (*m.*) ocean

l' **œuf** (*m.*) egg, **6.1**

l' **œuvre** (*f.*) work (*of art or literature*)

officiel(le) official

l' **oignon** (*m.*) onion, **5.1**

l' **oiseau** (*m.*) bird

l' **omelette** (*f.*) omelette, **5.1**

  l'omelette aux fines herbes omelette with herbs, **5.1**

  l'omelette nature plain omelette, **5.1**

on we, they, people, **3.2**

l' **oncle** (*m.*) uncle, **4.1**

l' **opéra** (*m.*) opera

l' **orange** (*f.*) orange, **6.2**

orange (*inv.*) orange (*color*), **7.2**

l' **oranger** (*m.*) orange tree, **L2**

ordinaire ordinary

l' **ordinateur** (*m.*) computer, **BV**

l' **organisme** (*m.*) organism

oriental(e) eastern

origine: d'origine américaine (française, etc.) from the U.S. (France, etc.)

orner to decorate

ôter to take off (*clothing*)

ou or, **1.1**

où where, **1.1**

  d'où from where, **1.1**

oublier to forget

oui yes, **BV**

ouvert(e) open

le **pain** bread, **6.1**

  le pain complet whole-wheat bread

  la tartine de pain beurré slice of bread and butter

pair: au pair au pair

la **paire** pair, **7.1**

le **palais** palace

le **pantalon** pants, **7.1**

la **papeterie** stationery store, **3.2**

le **papier** paper, **3.2**

  la feuille de papier sheet of paper, **3.2**

le **paquet** package, **6.2**

par by, through

  par exemple for example

  par semaine a (per) week, **3.2**

le **parc** park

parce que because

par-dessus over (*prep.*)

pardon excuse me, pardon me

les **parents** (*m. pl.*) parents, **4.1**

le **parfum** flavor

parisien(ne) Parisian

le **parking** parking lot

parler to speak, talk, **3.1**

  parler au téléphone to talk on the phone, **3.2**

les **paroles** (*f. pl.*) words, lyrics

la **partie** part

partout everywhere

pas not, **2.1**

  pas du tout not at all, **3.1**

  Pas mal. Not bad., **BV**

passer to spend (*time*), **3.1**

  passer un examen to take an exam, **3.1**

patient(e) patient, **1.1**

pauvre poor, **L1**

le **pavillon** small house, bungalow

payer to pay, **3.2**

le **pays** country

le/la **paysan(ne)** peasant, **L1**

le/la **peintre** painter, artist

la **peinture** painting

pendant during, for (*time*), **3.2**

le **père** father, **4.1**

la **période** period
la **périphérie** outskirts
permanent(e) permanent
la **personnalité** personality
la **personne** person
personnel(le) personal
petit(e) short, small, **1.1**
  le petit déjeuner
  breakfast, **5.2**
  les petits pois (*m.*) peas,
  6.2
la **petite-fille**
  granddaughter, **4.1**
le **petit-fils** grandson, **4.1**
les **petits-enfants** (*m. pl.*)
  grandchildren, **4.1**
peu: un peu a little, **2.1**
  en très peu de temps in
  a short time
  très peu seldom, **5.2**
peur: avoir peur to be
  afraid, **L1**
le **phénomène** phenomenon
la **photo** photograph
le/la **physicien(ne)** physicist
la **physique** physics, **2.2**
la **pièce** room, **4.2**; play
  la pièce de théâtre play
pied: à pied on foot, **4.2**
le **pique-nique** picnic
  faire un pique-nique to
  have a picnic, **6**
pittoresque picturesque
la **pizza** pizza, **BV**
la **place** place; square
la **plante** plant
le **plat** dish (food)
  pleurer to cry, **L1**
  plissé(e) pleated, **7.1**
la **plupart (des)** most (of)
  plus plus; more, **7.1**
    ne... plus no longer, no
    more, **6.1**
  poème poem
la **poésie** poetry
le **poète** poet (*m. and f.*)
le **poids** weight
  point: à point medium-
  rare (*meat*), **5.2**
la **pointure** size (*shoes*), **7.2**

**Vous faites quelle
  pointure?** What (shoe)
  size do you take?, **7.2**
la **poire** pear, **6.2**
le **poisson** fish, **6.1**
la **poissonnerie** fish store,
  6.1
le **poivre** pepper, **6.1**
la **politesse** courtesy,
  politeness, **BV**
le **polo** polo shirt, **7.1**
la **pomme** apple, **6.2**
  la tarte aux pommes
  apple tart, **6.1**
la **pomme de terre** potato, **6.2**
  populaire popular, **1.2**
le **porc** pork, **6.1**
le **port** port, harbor
  porter to wear, **7.1**
le/la **portraitiste** portraitist
  portugais(e) Portuguese
  poser une question to ask
  a question, **3.1**
la **position** position
  posséder to possess, own
le **pot** jar, **6.2**
le **poulet** chicken, **6.1**
  pour for, **2.1**; in order to
    pour cent percent
le **pourboire** tip (*restaurant*),
  5.2
  pourquoi why, **6.2**
    pourquoi pas? why not?
  pouvoir to be able to, can,
  6.1
  préféré(e) favorite
  préférer to prefer, **6**
le **préfixe** prefix
  premier, première first,
  4.2
  prendre to have (*to eat or
  drink*), **5.1**; to take, **5.2**; to
  buy
    prendre le petit déjeuner
    to eat breakfast, **5.2**
    prendre le métro to take
    the subway, **5.2**
  préparer to prepare
  près de near, **4.2**
  prie: Je vous en prie.
  You're welcome., **BV**

primaire: l'école (*f.*)
  primaire elementary
  school
principal(e) main,
  principal
le **prix** price, cost, **7.1**
le **problème** problem
  prochain(e) next
le **produit** product
le/la **prof** teacher (*inform.*), **2.1**
le **professeur** teacher (*m. and
  f.*), **2.1**
  professionnel(le)
  professional
la **programmation**
  programming
le **programme** program
  promotion: en promotion
  on special, on sale
les **provisions** (*f. pl.*) food
la **publicité** advertisement
  publier to publish
les **puces** (*f. pl.*): **le marché
  aux puces** flea market
le **pull** sweater, **7.1**

la **qualité** quality
  quand when, **4.1**
le **quart: et quart** a quarter
  past (*time*), **BV**
    moins le quart a quarter
    to (*time*), **BV**
le **quartier** neighborhood,
  district, **4.2**
  quatrième fourth
  que as; that; than (*in
  comparisons*), **7.2**
  québécois(e) from or of
  Quebec
  quel(le) which, what, **6**
  quelque: quelque chose
  something
    quelque chose de spécial
    something special
    quelque chose à manger
    something to eat, **5.1**
  quelquefois sometimes,
  5.2

la **question** question, 3.1
poser une question to ask a question, 3.1
qui who, 1.1; whom; which, that
quitter to leave (*a room, etc.*), 3.1

la **race** race
la **radio** radio, 3.2
rapide quick, fast
rapidement rapidly, quickly
le **rap** rap (music)
le **rayon** department (*in a store*), 7.1
le rayon des manteaux coat department, 7.1
la **récré** recess, 3.2
la **récréation** recess, 3.2
refléter to reflect
regarder to look at, 3.1
la **région** region
la **règle** ruler, 3.2; rule
regretter to be sorry, 6.1
la **reine** queen
religieux, religieuse religious
rencontrer to meet
rendre to give back
rendre bien service to be a big help
renommé(e) renowned
la **rentrée des classes** return to school, 3.2
rentrer to go home; to return, 3.2
le **repas** meal, 5.2
répéter to repeat
respirer to breathe
ressembler à to resemble
le **restaurant** restaurant, 5.2
la **restauration** food service
de restauration rapide fast-food
retrouver to meet, get together with
la **révolution** revolution

révolutionnaire revolutionary
la **revue** magazine, L2
le **rez-de-chaussée** ground floor, 4.2
riche rich
rigoler to joke around, 3.2
Tu rigoles! You're kidding!, 3.2
rigolo funny, 4.2
la **rivière** river
la **robe** dress, 7.1; robe
le **roman** novel
rose pink, 7.2
rouge red, 7.2
royal(e) royal
la **rue** street, 3.1
rural(e) rural
le **russe** Russian (*language*)

le **sac** bag, 6.1
le sac à dos backpack, 3.2
saignant(e) rare (*meat*), 5.2
la **salade** salad, 5.1; lettuce, 6.2
sale dirty
la **salle** room
la salle à manger dining room, 4.2
la salle de bains bathroom, 4.2
la salle de classe classroom, 2.1
la salle de séjour living room, 4.2
Salut. Hi.; Bye. **BV**
la **salutation** greeting
les **sandales** (*f. pl.*) sandals, 7.1
le **sandwich** sandwich, **BV**
sans without
la **sardine** sardine
la **sauce** sauce
la **saucisse de Francfort** hot dog, **BV**
le **saucisson** salami, 6.1

sauvegarder to safeguard, to save
sauver to save
le **savant** scientist
les **sciences** (*f. pl.*) science, 2.1
les sciences naturelles natural sciences, 2.1
les sciences sociales social studies, 2.1
scientifique scientific
scolaire school (*adj.*), 3.2
la **sculpture** sculpture
second(e) second
secondaire: l'école (*f.*) **secondaire** junior high, high school, 1.2
seconde: en seconde in second class
secret, secrète secret
le **séjour** stay
la salle de séjour living room, 4.2
le **sel** salt, 6.1
la **semaine** week, 3.2; allowance
la semaine prochaine next week
par semaine a (per) week, 3.2
semblable similar, L1
le/la **Sénégalais(e)** Senegalese (*person*)
séparer to separate
sérieux, sérieuse serious, 7
serré(e) tight, 7.2
le **serveur, la serveuse** waiter, waitress, 5.1
le **service** service, 5.2
Le service est compris. The tip is included., 5.2
la **serviette** napkin, 5.2
seul(e) alone, 5.2; single; only (*adj.*)
tout(e) seul(e) all alone, by himself/herself, 5.2
seulement only (*adv.*)
le **shopping** shopping, 7.2
le **short** shorts, 7.1
si if; yes (*after neg. question*), 7.2; so (*adv.*)

le **sifsari** type of veil worn by North African women

la **signification** meaning, significance

signifier to mean

simple simple

le **site** Web site

situé(e) located

sociable sociable, outgoing, **1.2**

la **sœur** sister, **1.2**

le **software** software

soi oneself, himself, herself

soif: avoir soif to be thirsty, **5.1**

le **soir** evening, **BV**

　ce soir tonight

　du soir in the evening, P.M. (*time*), **BV**

　le soir in the evening, **5.2**

les **soldes** (*m. pl.*) sale (*in a store*), **7.1**

la **solidarité** solidarity

solide solid

solitaire lonely

la **solution** solution

sombre dark

la **sorte** sort, kind, type

souffrir to suffer

le **souk** North African market

la **soupe** soup, **5.1**

　la soupe à l'oignon onion soup, **5.1**

la **source** source

la **souris** mouse

sous under

soustraire to subtract

souterrain(e) underground

souvent often, **5.2**

spécial(e) special

la **spécialité** specialty

sport (*inv.*) casual (*clothes*), **7.1**

standing: de grand standing luxury

la **station** station, **4.2**; resort

　la station de métro subway station, **4.2**

la **station-service** gas station

la **statue** statue

le **steak frites** steak and French fries, **5.2**

stocker to store

la **stratégie** strategy

strict(e) strict, **2.1**

le **studio** studio (apartment)

le **stylo-bille** ballpoint pen, **3.2**

le **succès** success

le **sud** south

suivant(e) following

le **sujet** subject

super terrific, super

supérieur(e) higher

le **supermarché** supermarket, **6.2**

sur on, **4.2**

　donner sur to face, overlook, **4.2**

sûr(e) sure, certain

　bien sûr of course

surgelé(e) frozen, **6.2**

surtout especially, above all; mostly

le **survêtement** warmup suit, **7.1**

le **sweat-shirt** sweatshirt, **7.1**

sympa (*inv.*) nice (*abbrev. for* **sympathique**), **1.2**

sympathique nice (*person*), **1.2**

le **système** system

　le système métrique metric system

la **table** table, **5.1**

le **tableau** painting; chart

la **taille** size (*clothes*), **7.2**

　juste à sa taille fitting (him/her) just right

　la taille au-dessous next smaller size, **7.2**

　la taille au-dessus next larger size, **7.2**

　Vous faites quelle taille? What size do you take/wear?, **7.2**

le **tailleur** suit (*woman's*), **7.1**; tailor

le **talent** talent

la **tante** aunt, **4.1**

la **tarte** pie, tart, **6.1**

　la tarte aux pommes apple tart, **6.1**

la **tartine de pain beurré** slice of bread and butter, **5.1**

la **tasse** cup, **5.2**

la **télé** TV

télécharger to download

le **téléphone** telephone, **3.2**

　le numéro de téléphone telephone number

téléphoner to call (*on the telephone*)

téléphonique telephone (*adj.*)

temporaire temporary

le **temps** time

　en très peu de temps in a short time

　l'emploi (*m.*) **du temps** schedule

la **terrasse** terrace, patio, **4.2**

　la terrasse d'un café sidewalk café, **5.1**

le **texte** text

　thaïlandais(e) Thai

le **thé** tea

le **théâtre** theater

　la pièce de théâtre play

timide shy, timid, **1.2**

tirer to take, to draw

les **toilettes** (*f. pl.*) bathroom, **4.2**

le **toit** roof

　le toit de chaume thatched roof

la **tomate** tomato, **6.2**

tomber to fall

　tomber malade to get sick, **L1**

toujours always, **4.2**; still

la **tour** tower

　la tour Eiffel Eiffel Tower

le **tour: à votre tour** it's your turn

tous, toutes (*adj.*) all, every, **2.1**
  tous (toutes) les deux both
tout (*pron.*) all, everything
  C'est tout. That's all., **6.1**
  pas du tout not at all, **3.1**
tout(e) (*adj.*) the whole, the entire; all; any
  tout le monde everyone, everybody, **1.2**
tout (*adv.*) very, completely, all, **4.2**
  tout(e) seul(e) all alone, all by himself/herself, **5.2**
  À tout à l'heure. See you later., **BV**
  tout de même all the same, **5.2**
  tout près de very near, **4.2**
la **tradition** tradition
traditionnel(le) traditional
traiter to treat
la **tranche** slice, **6.2**
transporter to transport
le **travail** work
travailler to work, **3.1**
très very, **BV**
la **trigonométrie** trigonometry, **2.2**
triste sad, **L1**
troisième third, **4.2**
trop too (*excessive*), **2.1**
tropical(e) tropical
trouver to find, **5.1;** to think (*opinion*), **7.2**
le **t-shirt** T-shirt, **7.1**
la **tunique** tunic
la **Tunisie** Tunisia
tunisien(ne) Tunisian
le **type** type
typique typical

l' **un(e)... l'autre** one . . . the other
unique single, only one
l' **unité** (*f.*) unit
l' **université** (*f.*) university
utiliser to use

les **vacances** (*f. pl.*) vacation
le **val** valley
la **valeur** value
la **vanille: à la vanille** vanilla (*adj.*), **5.1**
varié(e) varied
le **vendeur,** la **vendeuse** salesperson, **7.1**
le **verre** glass, **5.2**
vert(e) green, **5.1**
la **veste** (sport) jacket, **7.1**
les **vêtements** (*m. pl.*) clothes, **7.1**
la **viande** meat, **6.1**
la **vidéo** video, **3.1**
la **vie** life
  vieille old (*f.*), **4.2**
vietnamien(ne) Vietnamese, **6**
vieux (vieil) old (*m.*), **4.2**
la **villa** house
le **village** village, small town
la **ville** city, town
  en ville in town, in the city
le **vinaigre** vinegar, **6.1**
violent(e) violent; rough
le **violon** violin
viral(e) viral
le **virus** virus
visionner to view

visiter to visit (a place)
vite fast (*adv.*)
la **vitrine** (store) window, **7.1**
vivant(e) living
voici here is, here are, **4.1**
voilà there is, there are; here is, here are (*emphatic*), **1.2**
le **voile** veil
voir to see, **7.1**
le/la **voisin(e)** neighbor, **4.2**
la **voiture** car, **4.2**
  en voiture by car, **5.2**
la **voix** voice
  voudrais: je voudrais I would like, **5.1**
vouloir to want, **6.1**
vrai(e) true, real, **2.2**
vraiment really, **1.1**
la **vue** view, **4.2**

le **week-end** weekend

le **yaourt** yogurt, **6.1**
les **yeux** (*m. pl; sing.* œil) eyes, **L1**

la **zoologie** zoology
Zut! Darn!, **BV**

This English-French Dictionary *contains all productive vocabulary from the text. The numbers following each entry indicate the chapter and vocabulary section in which the word is introduced. For example,* **2.2** *means that the word first appeared in* **Chapitre 2, Mots 2. BV** *refers to the introductory Bienvenue lessons.* **L** *refers to the optional literary readings.*

A

a un, une, **1.1**
  a lot beaucoup, **3.1**
able capable
  to be able to pouvoir, **6.1**
about *(on the subject of)* de; *(approximately)* environ
above all surtout
accessible accessible
accessory l'accessoire *(m.)*
to **accompany** accompagner
to **add** additionner
adolescent l'adolescent(e)
adorable adorable, **4.1**
address l'adresse *(f.)*
adult l'adulte *(m. et f.)*
advertisement la publicité
afraid: to be afraid avoir peur, **L1**
Africa l'Afrique *(f.)*
African africain(e)
after après, **3.2**
afternoon l'après-midi *(m.)*, **3.2**
  five o'clock in the afternoon cinq heures de l'après-midi, **BV**
age l'âge *(m.)*, **4.1**
to **agree** être d'accord, **2.1**
aid l'aide *(f.)*
album l'album *(m.)*
algebra l'algèbre *(f.)*, **2.2**
Algeria l'Algérie *(f.)*
algerian algérien(ne)
all tout(e), tous, toutes, **2.1**
  all alone tout(e) seul(e), **5.2**
  all the same tout de même, **5.2**
  not at all pas du tout
  That's all. C'est tout., **6.1**

alone seul(e), **5.2**
  all alone tout(e) seul(e), **5.2**
already déjà, **BV**
also aussi, **1.1**
always toujours, **4.2**
a.m. du matin, **BV**
American *(adj.)* américain(e), **1.1**
among entre, **3.2**
to **analyse** analyser
analysis l'analyse *(f.)*
analytical analytique
and et, **BV**
animal l'animal *(m.)*
to **announce** annoncer
  Anything else? Avec ça?, **6.1**; Autre chose?, **6.2**
apartment l'appartement *(m.)*, **4.2**
apartment building l'immeuble *(m.)*, **4.2**
apple la pomme, **6.2**
  apple tart la tarte aux pommes, **6.1**
to **appreciate** apprécier
April avril *(m.)*, **BV**
Arab arabe
Arabic *(language)* l'arabe *(m.)*
arithmetic le calcul, **2.2**
around autour de, **4.2**
to **arrive** arriver, **3.1**
art le dessin *(m.)*, **2.2**
article l'article *(m.)*
artist l'artiste *(m. et f.)*; le/la peintre *(painter)*
artistic artistique
Asian asiatique
as aussi *(in comparisons)*, **7**; comme
  as . . . as aussi… que, **7**

the same . . . as le (la, les) même(s)… que
to **ask (for)** demander, **3.2**
  to ask a question poser une question, **3.1**
at à, **3.1**; chez, **3.2**
  at the home (business) of chez, **3.2**
attention l'attention *(f.)*
August août, *(m.)*, **BV**
aunt la tante, **4.1**
author l'auteur *(m.)*
avenue l'avenue *(f.)*

B

baby le bébé
backpack le sac à dos, **3.2**
bacterial bactérien(ne)
bacterium la bactérie
bad mauvais(e), **2.2**; nul(le) *(fam.)*
  Not bad. Pas mal., **BV**
badly mal
bag le sac, **6.1**
bagpipes la cornemuse
bakery la boulangerie-pâtisserie, **6.1**
balcony le balcon, **4.2**
ballpoint pen le stylo-bille, **3.2**
banana la banane, **6.2**
base la base
baseball cap la casquette, **7.1**
based on à base de
basis la base
basketball le basket(-ball)
bathroom la salle de bains, les toilettes *(f. pl.)*, **4.2**
to **be** être, **1.1**

to be able to pouvoir, **6.1**
to be afraid avoir peur, **L1**
to be hungry avoir faim, **5.1**
to be in luck avoir de la chance
to be lucky avoir de la chance
to be sorry regretter, **6.1**
to be thirsty avoir soif, **5.1**
to be . . . years old avoir… ans, **4.1**
bean: green beans les haricots verts *(m. pl.)*, **6.2**
beautiful beau (bel), belle, **4.2**
because parce que
bedroom la chambre à coucher, **4.2**
beef le bœuf, **6.1**
before avant, **7.1**
to begin commencer
beginning le début
beige beige *(inv.)*, **7.2**
Belgian belge
Belgium la Belgique
to believe croire, **7.2**
better *(adv.)* mieux, **7.2**
between entre, **3.2**
beverage la boisson; la consommation, **5.1**
bicycle la bicyclette
big grand(e), **1.1**
biological biologique
biologist le/la biologiste
biology la biologie, **2.2**
bird l'oiseau *(m.)*
birthday l'anniversaire *(m.)*, **4.1**
black noir(e), **7.2**
black pride la négritude
blond blond(e), **1.1**
bloom: in bloom fleuri(e), **L2**
to bloom fleurir
blouse le chemisier, **7.1**
blue bleu(e), **7.2**
navy blue bleu marine *(inv.)*, **7.2**

body le corps
bohemian bohème
book le livre, **3.2**
border la frontière
botany la botanique
both tous (toutes) les deux
bottle la bouteille, **6.2**
boutique la boutique, **7.1**
bowl le bol
boy le garçon, **1.1**
brave courageux, courageuse
bread le pain, **6.1**
loaf of French bread la baguette, **6.1**
slice of bread and butter la tartine de pain beurré
whole-wheat bread le pain complet
breakfast le petit déjeuner, **5.2**
to eat breakfast prendre le petit déjeuner, **5.2**
to breathe respirer
Breton breton(ne)
Brittany la Bretagne
brother le frère, **1.2**
brown brun(e), marron *(inv.)*, **7.2**
brunette brun(e), **1.1**
bungalow le bungalow
bus le bus
bush *(wilderness)* la brousse
busy occupé(e)
but mais, **2.1**
butcher le boucher, la bouchère
butcher shop la boucherie, **6.1**
butter le beurre, **6.1**
to buy acheter, **3.2**
by par
Bye. Salut., **BV**

cabaret le cabaret
café le café, **BV**
cafeteria la cafétéria
cake le gâteau, **4.1**

calculator la calculatrice, **3.2**
calculus: differential calculus le calcul différentiel
integral calculus le calcul intégral
to call appeler; *(on the telephone)* téléphoner
calm calme
Camembert cheese le camembert
can pouvoir, **6.1**
can of food la boîte de conserve, **6.2**
Canadian *(adj.)* canadien(ne), **6**
candle la bougie, **4.1**
cap la casquette, **7.1**
capital la capitale
car la voiture, **4.2**
by car en voiture, **5.2**
Careful! Attention!, **4.2**
Caribbean Sea la mer des Caraïbes, la mer des Antilles
carpenter le charpentier
carrot la carotte, **6.2**
to carry out exécuter
cash register la caisse, **3.2**
cassette la cassette, **3.1**
castle le château
casual *(clothes)* sport *(adj. inv.)*, **7.1**
cat le chat, **4.1**
catalogue le catalogue
category la catégorie
CD le CD, **3.1**
CD-ROM le CD-ROM
cell la cellule
Celtic celte, celtique
centiliter le centilitre
cereal les céréales *(f. pl.)*
chain la chaîne
to change changer (de)
channel *(TV)* la chaîne
characteristic la caractéristique
charm le charme
chart le tableau
to chat bavarder
check *(in restaurant)* l'addition *(f.)*, **5.2**

checkout counter la
  caisse, **3.2**
cheese le fromage, **5.1**
chemist le/la chimiste
chemistry la chimie, **2.2**
chic chic *(inv.)*
chicken le poulet, **6.1**
child l'enfant *(m. et f.)*, **4.1**
childhood l'enfance *(f.)*
Chinese chinois(e)
chocolate le chocolat; *(adj.)*
  au chocolat, **5.1**
circle le cercle
circus le cirque
to cite citer
city la ville
  in the city en ville
civilized civilisé(e)
class *(people)* la classe, **2.1**;
  (course) le cours, **2.1**
  in (French, etc.) class en
  cours de (français, etc.)
classroom la salle de
  classe, **2.1**
closed fermé(e)
clothes les vêtements
  (m. pl.), **7.1**
clown le clown
coat le manteau, **7.1**
  code le code, **4.2**
coffee le café, **5.1**
  black coffee l'express
  (m.), **5.1**
  coffee with cream le
  crème, **5.1**
cola le coca, **5.1**
collection la collection
color la couleur, **7.2**
  What color is . . . ? De
  quelle couleur est… ?,
  7.2
comfortable confortable
to compare comparer
compatriot le/la
  compatriote
complete complet,
  complète
to complete compléter
completely complètement
composer le compositeur,
  la compositrice
computer l'ordinateur *(m.)*
  computer science
  l'informatique *(f.)*, **2.2**

concept le concept
concert le concert
to connect connecter
contest la compétition
continent le continent
to continue continuer
conversation la
  conversation
to converse converser
to cook faire la cuisine, **6**
  correct bon(ne), **6.2**
correspondence la
  correspondance
cost le prix, **7.1**
to cost coûter, **3.2**
cottage la maisonnette
to count compter
country le pays
courageous courageux,
  courageuse
course le cours, **2.1**
  of course bien sûr
court la cour
courtesy la politesse, **BV**
courtyard la cour, **3.2**
couscous le couscous
cousin le/la cousin(e), **4.1**
crab le crabe, **6.1**
cream: coffee with cream
  le crème, **5.1**
to create créer
  Creole *(language)* le créole
crepe la crêpe, **BV**
croissant le croissant, **5.1**
to cry pleurer, **L1**
to cultivate cultiver
  cultural culturel(le)
  culture la culture
  cup la tasse, **5.2**
  customer le/la client(e)

dairy store la crémerie, **6.1**
to dance danser
  dark sombre
  dark-haired brun(e), **1.1**
  Darn! Zut!, **BV**
  data les données *(f. pl.)*
  date la date

What is today's date?
  Quelle est la date
  aujourd'hui?, **BV**
daughter la fille, **4.1**
day le jour, **BV;** la journée,
  3.1
  every day tous les jours
  What a nice day! Belle
  journée!, **4.2**
  What day is it today?
  C'est quel jour
  aujourd'hui?, **BV**
dear cher, chère
decaliter le décalitre
December décembre *(m.)*,
  BV
to decide (to) décider de
decimal *(adj.)* décimal(e)
to decorate orner
delicatessen la
  charcuterie, **6.1**
delicious délicieux,
  délicieuse
department (in a store) le
  rayon, **7.1**
  coat department le rayon
  des manteaux, **7.1**
  department store le
  grand magasin, **7.1**
  large department store
  la grande surface
descendant le/la
  descendant(e)
to describe décrire
  designer *(clothes)* le
  couturier
desperate désespéré(e)
dessert le dessert
destiny la destinée
devoted dévoué(e)
dialect le dialecte
different différent(e)
difficult difficile, **2.1**
dining hall *(school)* la
  cantine, **3.1**
dining room la salle à
  manger, **4.2**
dinner le dîner, **5.2**
  to eat dinner dîner, **5.2**
diploma le diplome
direction la direction
dirty sale
disagreeable désagréable
to discover découvrir

to **discuss** discuter
dish (*food*) le plat
diskette la disquette
to **distinguish** distinguer
district le quartier, **4.2**; (*Paris*) l'arrondissement (*m.*)
to **divide** diviser
to **do** faire, **6.1**
  to do the grocery shopping faire les courses, **6.1**
doctor le médecin (*m. et f.*)
document le document
dog le chien, **4.1**
dollar le dollar, **3.2**
domain le domaine
doubt le doute
to **download** télécharger
downtown le centre-ville
dozen la douzaine, **6.2**
dress la robe, **7.1**
dressy habillé(e), **7.1**
to **drink** boire
  something to drink quelque chose à boire
drink la boisson; la consommation, **5.1**
druid le druide
during pendant, **3.2**
dynamic dynamique, **1.2**

each (*adj.*) chaque
each (one) chacun(e), **5.2**
to **earn** gagner
eastern oriental(e)
easy facile, **2.1**
to **eat** manger, **5.1**
  to eat breakfast prendre le petit déjeuner, **5.2**
  to eat lunch déjeuner, **3.1**
economics l'économie (*f.*), **2.2**
egg l'œuf (*m.*), **6.1**
egotistical égoïste, **1.2**
elder l'aîné(e), **L1**
electric électrique
electronic électronique
element l'élément (*m.*)

elevator l'ascenseur (*m.*), **4.2**
else: something else autre chose
  Anything else? Avec ça?, **6.1**; Autre chose?, **6.2**
e-mail l'e-mail (*m.*)
energetic énergique, **1.2**
energy l'énergie (*f.*)
English anglais(e)
  English (*language*) l'anglais (*m.*), **2.2**
enough assez, **1.1**
to **enter** entrer, **7.1**
enthusiastic enthousiaste, **1.2**
entire entier, entière
entrance l'entrée (*f.*), **4.2**
equation l'équation (*f.*)
equivalent l'équivalent (*m.*)
eraser la gomme, **3.2**
especially surtout
espresso l'express (*m.*), **5.1**
to **establish** établir
euro l'euro (*m.*)
Europe l'Europe (*f.*)
European (*adj.*) européen(ne)
evening le soir, **BV**
  in the evening le soir, **5.2**
  in the evening (P.M.) du soir, **BV**
every tous, toutes, **2.1**; chaque
everybody tout le monde, **1.2**
everyone tout le monde, **1.2**
everything tout
everywhere partout
exam l'examen (*m.*), **3.1**
  to take an exam passer un examen, **3.1**
example: for example par exemple
excellent excellent(e)
except excepté(e)
exception l'exception (*f.*)
exceptional exceptionnel(le)
exchange l'échange (*m.*)

  in exchange for en échange de
to **exchange** échanger
excuse me pardon
to **execute** exécuter
exercise l'exercice (*m.*)
exhausted crevé(e)
to **exist** exister
to **expel** expulser
expensive cher, chère, **7.1**
exterior l'extérieur (*m.*)
extraordinary extraordinaire
eyes les yeux (*m. pl., sing.* œil), **L1**

fable la fable
to **face** donner sur, **4.2**
fairly assez, **1.1**
false faux, fausse
family la famille, **4.1**
famous célèbre
fantastic fantastique
far (away) loin
  far from loin de, **4.2**
fast (*adj.*) rapide; (*adv.*) vite
fast-food (*adj.*) de restauration rapide
  fast-food restaurant le fast-food
father le père, **4.1**
fault la faute
favorite favori(te); préféré(e)
February février (*m.*), **BV**
to **feed** nourrir
felt-tip pen le feutre, **3.2**
field le champ, **L1**; le domaine
file (*computer*) le fichier
film le film
finally enfin
to **find** trouver, **5.1**
fine ça va, bien, **BV**
finger le doigt
firm l'entreprise (*f.*)
first premier, première (*adj.*), **4.2**
fish le poisson, **6.1**

fish store la poissonnerie, **6.1**

fitting room la cabine d'essayage

flavor le parfum

flea market le marché aux puces

floor (*of a building*) l'étage (*m.*), **4.2**

  ground floor le rez-de-chaussée, **4.2**

flower la fleur, **4.2**

flu la grippe

following suivant(e)

food la nourriture; l'aliment (*m.*); les provisions (*f. pl.*)

  food service la restauration

foot: on foot à pied, **4.2**

football le football américain

for pour; (*time*) pendant, **3.2**

  for example par exemple

foreign étranger, étrangère

to **forget** oublier

fork la fourchette, **5.2**

form la forme

to **form** former

to **found** fonder

fourth quatrième

fracture la fracture

free libre, **5.1**

French français(e) (*adj.*), **1.1**; (*language*) le français, **2.2**

  French fries les frites (*f. pl.*), **5.1**

French-speaking francophone

to **frequent** fréquenter

Friday vendredi (*m.*), **BV**

friend l'ami(e), **1.2**; (*pal*) le copain, la copine, **2.1**

from de, **1.1**

frozen surgelé(e), **6.2**

fruit le fruit, **6.2**

fun amusant(e), **1.1**

funny amusant(e), **1.1**; rigolo, **4.2**

future l'avenir (*m.*), le futur, **L2**

game le jeu

garage le garage, **4.2**

garden le jardin, **4.2**

gas station la station-service

general: in general en général

generally généralement

geography la géographie, **2.2**

geometry la géométrie, **2.2**

germ le microbe

German (*language*) l'allemand (*m.*), **2.2**

Germany l'Allemagne (*f.*)

get: to get sick tomber malade, **L1**

  to go (and) get aller chercher, **6.1**

gift le cadeau, **4.1**

girl la fille, **1.1**

to **give** donner, **4.1**

  to give back rendre

glad content(e)

glass le verre, **5.2**

to **go** aller, **5.1**

  to go (and) get aller chercher, **6.1**

  to go home rentrer, **3.2**

  to go up monter, **4.2**

  to go with accompagner

good bon(ne), **6.2**

  good in math fort(e) en maths, **2.2**

good-bye au revoir; ciao (*inform.*), **BV**

gourmet le gourmet

grade la note

grains les céréales (*f. pl.*)

gram le gramme, **6.2**

grammar la grammaire

granddaughter la petite-fille, **4.1**

grandfather le grand-père, **4.1**

grandmother la grand-mère, **4.1**

grandparents les grands-parents (*m. pl.*), **4.1**

grandson le petit-fils, **4.1**

gray gris(e), **7.2**

great grand(e)

green vert(e), **5.1**

  green beans les haricots (*m. pl.*) verts, **6.2**

greeting la salutation

grilled ham and cheese sandwich le croque-monsieur, **5.1**

grocery store l'épicerie (*f.*), **6.1**

ground floor le rez-de-chaussée, **4.2**

group le groupe

to **grow (up)** grandir

to **guard** garder

to **guess** deviner

guillotined guillotiné(e)

guitarist le/la guitariste

gymnastics la gymnastique, **2.2**

Haitian haïtien(ne)

half: half brother le demi-frère, **4.1**

  half past (time) et demie, **BV**

  half sister la demi-sœur, **4.1**

ham le jambon, **5.1**

hamburger le hamburger

hamlet le hameau

hand la main, **3.1**

handicapé(e) handicapped

handsome beau (bel), **4.2**

happy content(e)

  Happy surfing! Bon surf!

harbor le port

hardware (*computer*) le hardware

harp la harpe

to **hate** détester, **3.1**

to **have** avoir, **4.1**; (*to eat or drink*) prendre, **5.1**

  Have a nice day! Belle journée!, **4.2**

  to have a picnic faire un pique-nique, **6**

he il, **1.1**
hello bonjour, **BV**
help l'aide (f.)
  to be a big help rendre bien service
  with the help of à l'aide de
here is, here are voici, **4.1**; (emphatic) voilà, **1.2**
hi salut, **BV**
high school le lycée, **2.1**
higher supérieur
his sa, son, ses, **4**
history l'histoire (f.), **2.2**
home: at (to) the home of chez, **3.2**
  to go home rentrer, **3.2**
homework (assignment) le devoir
  to do homework faire ses devoirs, **6**
horrible horrible
hot: hot chocolate le chocolat
  hot dog la saucisse de Francfort, **BV**
house la maison, **3.1**; la villa
  publishing house la maison d'édition
  small house le pavillon
housing le logement
how comment, **1.1**
  How are you? Ça va? Comment vas-tu? Comment allez-vous?, **BV**
  How's it going? Ça va?, **BV**
  How is that? Comment ça?
  how many, how much combien (de), **3.2**
  How much is it? C'est combien?, **3.2**
human humain(e)
hundred cent, **2.2**
hungry: to be hungry avoir faim, **5.1**
  I'm super hungry. J'ai hyper faim.
husband le mari, **4.1**

I je, **1.2**
ice cream la glace, **5.1**
idea l'idée (f.)
ideal idéal(e)
if si
immense immense
important important(e)
impossible impossible
imprisoned emprisonné(e)
in dans, **1.2**; à, **3.1**; en, **3.2**
  in common en commun
  in general en général
  In what month? En quel mois?, **BV**
included compris(e), **5.2**
  The tip is included. Le service est compris., **5.2**
to **indicate** indiquer
indiscreet indiscret, indiscrète
industrial industriel(le)
inexpensive bon marché (inv.)
infinite infini(e)
influence l'influence (f.)
information l'information (f.)
to **insist** insister
to **inspire** inspirer
instructions les instructions (f. pl.)
intellectual intellectuel(le)
intelligent intelligent(e), **1.1**
interest l'intérêt (m.)
interesting intéressant(e), **1.1**
interview l'interview (f.)
to **invite** inviter, **4.1**
island l'île (f.)
it il, elle, ça, **1.1**
  it is, it's c'est, **BV**
Italian (adj.) italien(ne)
Italian (language) l'italien (m.), **2.2**
Ivory Coast la Côte d'Ivoire

jacket le blouson, **7.1**
  (sport) jacket la veste, **7.1**
  ski jacket l'anorak (m.), **7.1**
jam la confiture, **6.2**
January janvier (m.), **BV**
jar le pot, **6.2**
jealous jaloux, jalouse
jeans le jean, **7.1**
to **jog** faire du jogging
to **joke around** rigoler, **3.2**
juice le jus, **5.1**
  apple juice le jus de pomme, **5.1**
  orange juice le jus d'orange, **5.1**
July juillet (m.), **BV**
June juin (m.), **BV**
junior high student le/la collégien(ne)
just juste, **2.1**
  fitting (him/her) just right juste à sa taille

keyboard le clavier
to **kid: You're kidding!** Tu rigoles!, **3.2**
kilogram le kilo(gramme), **6.2**
kind la sorte
kitchen la cuisine, **4.2**
knife le couteau, **5.2**

label la griffe
laboratory le laboratoire
lamb l'agneau (m.), **6.1**
lame boiteux, boiteuse
language la langue, **2.2**
large grand(e); ample
last dernier, dernière
  last name le nom de famille

later plus tard
  See you later. À tout à l'heure., **BV**
Latin le latin, **2.2**
to **learn (to)** apprendre (à), **5**
to **leave (a room, etc.)** quitter, **3.1**
  to leave (something behind) laisser, **5.2**
  to leave a tip laisser un pourboire, **5.2**
legend la légende
lemonade le citron pressé, **5.1**
lemon-lime drink la limonade, **BV**
less moins, **7.1**
  less than moins de
  less . . . than moins… que, **7**
lesson la leçon
lettuce la salade, **6.2**
liaison la liaison
life la vie
light *(color)* clair(e)
like comme
to **like** aimer, **3.1**
  I would like je voudrais, **5.1**
  What would you like? *(café, restaurant)* Vous désirez?, **5.1**
limit la limite
line la ligne
linked en liaison
linking la liaison
liquid le liquide
to **listen (to)** écouter, **3.1**
liter le litre, **6.2**
literature la littérature, **2.2**
little: a little un peu, **2.1**
to **live** *(in a city, house, etc.)* habiter, **3.1**
living vivant(e)
  living room la salle de séjour, **4.2**
located situé(e)
lonely solitaire
long long(ue), **7.1**
longer: no longer ne… plus, **6.1**
to **look** *(seem)* avoir l'air

to **look at** regarder, **3.1**
to **look for** chercher
loose *(clothing)* large, **7.2**
loose-leaf binder le classeur, **3.2**
lot: a lot beaucoup, **3.1**
  a lot of beaucoup de, **3.2**
to **love** aimer, **3.1;** adorer
lower inférieur(e)
low-income housing l' H.L.M.
luck la chance
  to be in luck avoir de la chance
lucky: to be lucky avoir de la chance
lunch le déjeuner, **5.2**
  to eat lunch déjeuner, **3.1**
luxury *(adj.)* de grand standing
lyrics les paroles *(f. pl.)*

ma'am madame, **BV**
magazine le magazine; la revue, **L2**
Maghreb le Maghreb
main principal(e)
majority la majorité
to **make** faire, **6.1**
mall le centre commercial, **7.1**
man l'homme *(m.)*, **7.1**
mandatory obligatoire
manner la façon
many beaucoup de, **3.2**
map la carte
March mars *(m.)*, **BV**
market le marché, **6.2**
  flea market le marché aux puces
marriage le mariage
masculine masculin(e)
math les maths *(f. pl.)*, **2.2**
mathematics les mathématiques *(f. pl.)*, **2.2**
May mai *(m.)*, **BV**
meal le repas, **5.2**
to **mean** signifier
meaning la signification

to **measure** mesurer
measurement la mesure
meat la viande, **6.1**
medina la médina
Mediterranean Sea la mer Méditerranée
medium-rare *(meat)* à point, **5.2**
to **meet** rencontrer; retrouver *(get together with)*
melon le melon, **6.2**
to **mention** citer
menu la carte, **5.1**
merchandise la marchandise
merchant le/la marchand(e), **6.2**
  produce merchant le/la marchand(e) de fruits et légumes, **6.2**
message le message
meter le mètre
metric system le système métrique
microbe le microbe
microbial microbien(ne)
microprocessor le microprocesseur
microscope le microscope
middle school student le/la collégien(ne)
midnight minuit *(m.)*, **BV**
milk le lait, **6.1**
milligram le milligramme
mineral water l'eau *(f.)* minérale, **6.2**
minus moins
minute la minute
Miss (Ms.) Mademoiselle (Mlle), **BV**
mistake la faute
modem le modem
modern moderne
modest modeste
mom la maman
moment le moment
Monday lundi *(m.)*, **BV**
money l'argent *(m.)*, **6.2**
monitor *(computer)* le moniteur
month le mois, **BV**
more *(comparative)* plus, **7.1**
  no more ne… plus, **6.1**

more . . . than plus… que, **7**
morning le matin, **BV**
 in the morning le matin
 in the morning (A.M.) du matin, **BV**
Morocco le Maroc
Moroccan marocain(e)
most (of) la plupart (des)
mother la mère, **4.1**
 mother tongue la langue maternelle
mount le mont
mountain le mont
mouse la souris
movement le mouvement
Mr. Monsieur (*m.*), **BV**
Mrs. (Ms.) Madame (Mme), **BV**
multicolored multicolore
to **multiply** multiplier
museum le musée
music la musique, **2.2**
musician le/la musicien(ne)
mussel la moule
mustard la moutarde, **6.2**
my ma, mon, mes, **4**
myth le mythe

name le nom
 last name le nom de famille
 My name is . . . Je m'appelle… , **BV**
 What's your name? Tu t'appelles comment?, **BV**
napkin la serviette, **5.2**
nationality la nationalité
natural naturel(le)
natural sciences les sciences naturelles (*f. pl.*), **2.1**
nature la nature
navy blue bleu marine (*inv.*), **7.2**
near près de, **4.2**
 very near tout près, **4.2**
necessary nécessaire
neighbor le/la voisin(e), **4.2**

neighborhood le quartier, **4.2**; (*adj.*) du coin
nephew le neveu, **4.1**
new nouveau (nouvel), nouvelle, **4.2**
New England la Nouvelle-Angleterre
news (*TV*) les informations (*f. pl.*)
next prochain(e)
nice (*person*) sympa, **1.2**; aimable; sympathique; gentil(le), **6.2**
niece la nièce, **4.1**
no non
 no longer ne… plus, **6.1**
 no more ne… plus, **6.1**
noble noble
noon midi (*m.*), **BV**
north le nord
North African nord-africain(e)
not ne… pas, **1.2**; pas, **2.1**
 isn't it?, doesn't it (he, she, etc.)?, n'est-ce pas?, **2.2**
 not at all pas du tout, **3.1**
 not bad pas mal, **BV**
note la note
notebook le cahier, **3.2**
notepad le bloc-notes, **3.2**
novel le roman
November novembre (*m.*), **BV**
now maintenant, **2.2**
number le nombre; le numéro
 telephone number le numéro de téléphone

object l'objet (*m.*)
to **oblige** obliger
to **observe** observer
occupied occupé(e)
ocean l'océan (*m.*)
o'clock: It's . . . o'clock. Il est… heure(s)., **BV**
October octobre (*m.*), **BV**
of (*belonging to*) de, **1.2**
 of course bien sûr

often souvent, **5.2**
official officiel(le)
oil l'huile (*f.*), **6.1**
okay (health) Ça va.; **(agreement)** d'accord, **BV**
 Okay! Bon!, **6.1**
old vieux (vieil), vieille, **4.2**
 How old are you? Tu as quel âge? (*fam.*), **4.1**
omelette (with herbs/plain) l'omelette (*f.*) (aux fines herbes/nature), **5.1**
on sur, **4.2**
 on foot à pied, **4.2**
 on sale en solde, **7.1**
onion l'oignon (*m.*), **5.1**
only seulement
open ouvert(e)
opera l'opéra (*m.*)
opinion l'avis (*m.*), **7.2**
 in my opinion à mon avis, **7.2**
or ou, **1.1**
orange (*fruit*) l'orange (*f.*), **6.2**; (*color*) orange (*inv.*), **7.2**
 orange tree l'oranger (*m.*), **L2**
order: in order to pour
to **order** commander, **5.1**
ordinary ordinaire
organism l'organisme (*m.*)
other autre
 some other d'autres, **2.2**
our notre, nos, **4**
outgoing sociable, **1.2**
outfit l'ensemble (*m.*)
outside (*n.*) l'extérieur (*m.*) (*adv.*) à l'extérieur
outskirts la périphérie
over (*prep.*) par-dessus
to **overlook** donner sur, **4.2**
overseas (*adj.*) d'outre-mer
to **own** posséder

package le paquet, **6.2**
pain in the neck (*fam.*) casse-pieds
painful douloureux, douloureuse

painter l'artiste peintre *(m. et f.)*, le/la peintre
painting la peinture; le tableau
pair la paire, **7.1**
pal le copain, la copine, **2.1**
palace le palais
pancake la crêpe, **BV**
pants le pantalon, **7.1**
paper le papier, **3.2**
  sheet of paper la feuille de papier, **3.2**
pardon me pardon
parents les parents *(m. pl.)*, **4.1**
Parisian *(adj.)* parisien(ne)
park le parc
parking lot le parking
part la partie
party la fête, **4.1**
  to throw a party donner une fête, **4.1**
patient patient(e), **1.1**
patio la terrasse, **4.2**
to **pay** payer, **3.2**
pear la poire, **6.2**
peas les petits pois *(m. pl.)*, **6.2**
peasant le/la paysan(ne), **L1**
pen: ballpoint pen le stylo-bille, **3.2**
  felt-tip pen le feutre, **3.2**
pencil le crayon, **3.2**
people les gens *(m. pl.)*
pepper le poivre, **6.1**
percent pour cent
period l'époque *(f.)*; la période
permanent permanent(e)
person la personne
personal personnel(le)
personality la personnalité
phenomenon le phénomène
photograph la photo
physicist le/la physicien(ne)
physics la physique, **2.2**
picnic le pique-nique

to have a picnic faire un pique-nique, **6**
picturesque pittoresque
pie la tarte, **6.1**
pink rose, **7.1**
pizza la pizza, **BV**
plant la plante
plate l'assiette *(f.)*, **5.2**
to **play** jouer, **3.2**
play la pièce de théâtre
please s'il vous plaît *(form.)*, s'il te plaît *(fam.)*, **BV**
pleated plissé(e), **7.1**
plus plus
p.m. de l'après-midi; du soir, **BV**
poem le poème
poet *(m. and f.)* le poète
politeness la politesse, **BV**
polo shirt le polo, **7.1**
poor pauvre, **L1**
popular populaire, **1.2**
pork le porc, **6.1**
port le port
Portuguese portugais(e)
position la position
to **possess** posséder
poster l'affiche *(f.)*
potato la pomme de terre, **6.2**
pound la livre, **6.2**
to **prefer** aimer mieux, **7.2;** préférer, **6**
prefix le préfixe
to **prepare** préparer
present le cadeau, **4.1**
pretty joli(e), **4.2**
price le prix, **7.1**
principal principal(e)
printer l'imprimante *(f.)*
private individuel(le)
problem le problème
product le produit
professional professionel(le)
program le programme; *(computer)* le logiciel
programming la programmation
to **publish** publier
purchase achat *(m.)*
to **put (on)** mettre, **7.1**

Q

quality la qualité
quarter: quarter after *(time)* et quart, **BV**
  quarter to *(time)* moins le quart, **BV**
Quebec: from or of Quebec québécois
queen la reine
question la question, **3.1**
  to ask a question poser une question, **3.1**
quick rapide
quickly rapidement
quite assez, **1.1**

R

race *(human population)* la race
radio la radio, **3.2**
to **raise** lever
  to raise one's hand lever la main, **3.1**
rap *(music)* le rap
rapidly rapidement
rare *(meat)* saignante(e), **5.2**
reading la lecture
real vrai(e), **2.2**
really vraiment, **1.1**
recess la récré(ation), **3.2**
record le disque
red rouge, **7.1**
to **reflect** refléter
refrigerator le frigidaire
region la région
religious religieux, religieuse
renowned renommé(e)
to **repeat** répéter
to **resemble** ressembler à
restaurant le restaurant, **5.2**
return to school la rentrée des classes, **3.2**
to **return** rentrer, **3.2**
revolution la révolution
revolutionary révolutionnaire

rich riche
riddle la devinette
right there juste là
river le fleuve; rivière
Riviera *(French)* la Côte d'Azur
roof le toit
  thatched roof le toit de chaume
room *(in house)* la pièce, **4.2;** la salle
  dining room la salle à manger, **4.2**
  living room la salle de séjour, **4.2**
royal royal(e)
rule la régle
ruler la règle, **3.2**
running shoe la basket, **7.1**
rural rural(e)
Russian *(language)* le russe

sad triste, **L1**
to **safeguard** sauvegarder
salad la salade, **5.1**
salami le saucisson, **6.1**
sale: on sale en solde, **7.1;** en promotion
sales les soldes *(m. pl.),* **7.1**
salesperson le vendeur, la vendeuse, **7.1**
salt le sel, **6.1**
same même, **2.1**
  all the same tout de même, **5.2**
sandals les sandals *(f. pl.),* **7.1**
sandwich le sandwich, **BV**
  grilled ham and cheese sandwich le croque-monsieur, **5.1**
sardine la sardine
Saturday samedi *(m.),* **BV**
sauce la sauce
to **save** sauver; sauvegarder
schedule l'emploi *(m.)* du temps
school l'école *(f.),* **1.2;** *(adj.)* scolaire, **3.2**

elementary school l'école primaire
junior high/high school l'école secondaire, **1.2**
high school le lycée, **2.1**
school supplies la fourniture scolaire, **3.2**
science les sciences *(f. pl.),* **2.1**
  natural sciences les sciences naturelles, **2.1**
  social sciences les sciences sociales, **2.1**
scientific scientifique
scientist le savant
screen l'écran *(m.)*
sculpture la sculpture
sea la mer
second *(adj.)* deuxième, **4.2;** second(e)
secret *(adj.)* secret, secrète
to **see** voir, **7.1**
  See you later. À tout à l'heure., **BV**
  See you soon! À bientôt!, **BV**
  See you tomorrow. À demain., **BV**
seldom très peu
seller le/la marchand(e), **6.2**
  produce seller le/la marchand(e) de fruits et légumes, **6.2**
to **send** envoyer
separate séparer
September septembre *(m.),* **BV**
serious sérieux, sérieuse, **7**
service le service, **5.2**
to **set the table** mettre la table, **7**
shape la forme
she elle, **1.1**
sheet of paper la feuille de papier, **3.2**
shirt la chemise, **7.1**
shoe la chaussure, **7.1**
shop la boutique, **7.1**
to **shop** faire des achats
shopkeeper le/la commerçant(e)
shopping le shopping, **7.2**

to do the grocery shopping faire les courses, **6.1**
to go shopping faire des courses, **7.2**
shopping cart le chariot, **6.2**
shopping center le centre commercial, **7.1**
short petit(e), **1.1;** court(e), **7.1**
  in a short time en très peu de temps
shorts le short, **7.1**
to **show** montrer
shrimp la crevette, **6.1**
shy timide, **1.2**
sick malade, **L1**
  to get sick tomber malade, **L1**
side le côté
sidewalk café la terrasse (d'un café), **5.1**
significance la signification
similar semblable, **L1**
simple simple
single unique
sir monsieur, **BV**
sister la sœur, **1.2**
size *(clothes)* la taille; *(shoes)* la pointure, **7.2**
  the next larger size la taille au-dessus, **7.2**
  the next smaller size la taille au-dessous, **7.2**
  to take size (number) faire du (nombre), **7.2**
  What size do you take/wear? Vous faites quelle taille (pointure)?, **7.2**
ski jacket l'anorak *(m.),* **7.1**
skirt la jupe, **7.1**
to **sleep** dormir
sleeve la manche, **7.1**
  long-(short-)sleeved à manches longues (courtes), **7.1**
slice la tranche, **6.2**
  slice of bread and butter la tartine de pain beurré
small petit(e), **1.1**
sneaker la basket, **7.1**
so alors, **BV;** donc; si *(adv.)*

sociable sociable, **1.2**

social sciences les sciences sociales (*f. pl.*), **2.1**

sock la chaussette, **7.1**

software le software

solid solide

solidarity la solidarité

solution la solution

some du, de la, de l', des, **6**; (*adj.*) quelques (pl.); (*pron.*) certains

  some other d'autres, **2.2**

something quelque chose

  something else autre chose

  something special quelque chose de spécial

  something to drink quelque chose à boire

sometimes quelquefois, **5.2**

son le fils, **4.1**

song la chanson

soon bientôt

  See you soon. À bientôt., **BV**

sorry: to be sorry regretter, **6.1**

so-so comme ci, comme ça

soup la soupe, **5.1**

source la source

south le sud

Spanish espagnol(e)

Spanish (*language*) l'espagnol (*m.*), **2.2**

to **speak** parler, **3.1**

special spécial(e)

specialty la spécialité

to **spend** (*time*) passer, **3.1**

spinach les épinards (*m. pl.*), **6.2**

spirit l'esprit (*m.*)

spoon la cuillère, **5.2**

square la place

staircase l'escalier (*m.*), **4.2**

station la station, **4.2**

  gas station la station-service

  subway station la station de métro, **4.2**

stationery store la papeterie, **3.2**

statue la statue

stay le séjour

steak and French fries le steak frites, **5.2**

stepfather le beau-père, **4.1**

stepmother la belle-mère, **4.1**

still toujours

store le magasin, **3.2**

  department store le grand magasin, **7.1**

to **store** stocker

strategy la stratégie

strawberry la fraise, **6.2**

street la rue, **3.1**

strict strict(e), **2.1**

strong fort(e), **2.2**

student l'élève (*m. et f.*), **1.2**; (*university*) l'étudiant(e)

studio (*apartment*) le studio

study l'étude (*f.*)

to **study** étudier, **3.1**; faire des études

  to study French (math, etc.) faire du français (des maths, etc.), **6**

style le look

  in style à la mode

subject le sujet; (*in school*) la matière, **2.2**

to **subtract** soustraire

subway le métro, **4.2**

  subway station la station de métro, **4.2**

success le succès

to **suffer** souffrir

suit (*men's*) le complet; (*women's*) le tailleur, **7.1**

Sunday dimanche (*m.*), **BV**

super super

supermarket le supermarché, **6.2**

supply la fourniture

  school supplies la fourniture scolaire, **3.2**

sure sûr(e)

to **surf the Net** naviguer sur Internet

sweater le pull, **7.1**

sweatshirt le sweat-shirt, **7.1**

system le système

  metric system le système métrique

table la table, **5.1**

  table setting le couvert, **5.2**

tablecloth la nappe, **5.2**

to **take** prendre, **5.2**

  What size do you take? Vous faites quelle taille (pointure)?, **7.2**

  to take an exam passer un examen, **3.1**

  to take off (clothing) ôter

  to take place avoir lieu

  to take size (*number*) faire du (nombre), **7.2**

  to take the subway prendre le métro, **5.2**

taken occupé(e)

talent le talent

to **talk** parler, **3.1**

  to talk on the phone parler au téléphone, **3.2**

tall grand(e), **1.1**

tape la cassette, **7.1**

tart la tarte, **6.1**

  apple tart la tarte aux pommes, **6.1**

tea le thé

teacher le/la prof (*inform.*), **2.1**; le professeur, **2.1**

teenager l'adolescent(e)

telephone le téléphone, **3.2**; (*adj.*) téléphonique

  telephone number le numéro de téléphone

temporary temporaire

ten dix, **BV**

terrace la terrasse, **4.2**

terrific super

test l'examen (*m.*), **3.1**

text le texte

Thai thaïlandais(e)

than (*in comparisons*) que, **7.2**

thank you merci, **BV**

thanks merci, **BV**

  thanks to grâce à

that ça, **BV**
  that is c'est-à-dire
  That's all. C'est tout.,
    6.1
thatched roof le toit de
  chaume
the le, la, les, **1.1**
theater le théâtre
their leur(s), **4**
then alors, **BV**
there là; y, **5.2**
  there are il y a, **4.1**
  there is il y a, **4.1**
therefore donc
they ils, elles, **2**; on, **3.2**
thing la chose
to **think** croire, **7.2**; *(opinion)*
  trouver, **7.2**
third troisième, **4.2**
thirsty: to be thirsty avoir
  soif, **5.1**
thousand mille, **3.2**
through par
to **throw a party** donner une
  fête, **4.1**
Thursday jeudi *(m.)*, **BV**
tie la cravate, **7.1**
tight serré(e), **7.2**
time *(of day)* l'heure *(f.)*,
  BV; *(in a series)* la fois; le
  temps
  at the same time à la fois
  at what time? à quelle
    heure?, **2**
  in a short time en très
    peu de temps
  times l'époque *(f.)*
  two times two deux fois
    deux
  What time is it? Il est
    quelle heure?; Quelle
    heure est-il?, **BV**
tip (restaurant) le
  pourboire, **5.2**
  to leave a tip laisser un
    pourboire, **5.2**
  The tip is included. Le
    service est compris., **5.2**
tired fatigué(e)
to à, **3.1**; *(in order to)* pour
  It's ten to five. Il est cinq
    heures moins dix., **BV**
today aujourd'hui, **BV**

together ensemble, **5.1**
tomato la tomate, **6.2**
tomorrow demain, **BV**
  See you tomorrow. À
    demain., **BV**
tonight ce soir
too *(also)* aussi, **1.1**;
  (excessive) trop, **2.1**
totally complètement
tower la tour
  Eiffel Tower la tour
    Eiffel
town la ville, le village
  in town en ville
  small town le village
tradition la tradition
traditional traditionel(le)
to **transport** transporter
to **treat** traiter
tree l'arbre *(m.)*
trigonometry le
  trigonométrie, **2.2**
tropical tropical(e)
true vrai(e), **2.2**
to **try on** essayer, **7.2**
  T-shirt le t-shirt, **7.1**
Tuesday mardi *(m.)*, **BV**
tunic la tunique
Tunisian tunisien(ne)
to **turn on** *(appliance)*
  mettre, **7**
  TV la télé
twin le jumeau, la jumelle,
  L1
type le type, la sorte
typical typique

uncle l'oncle *(m.)*, **4.1**
under sous
underground
  souterrain(e)
to **understand** comprendre, **5**
unhappy malheureux,
  malheureuse
unit l'unité *(f.)*
United States les États-
  Unis *(m. pl.)*
university l'université *(f.)*
to **use** utiliser
usually d'habitude

vacation les vacances
  (f. pl.)
valley le val
value la valeur
vanilla *(adj.)* à la vanille,
  5.1
varied varié(e)
various divers(e)
vegetable le légume, **6.2**
veil le voile
very très, **BV**; tout
  very near tout près, **4.2**
  very well très bien, **BV**
video la vidéo, **3.1**
Vietnamese
  vietnamien(ne), **6**
view la vue
to **view** visionner
village le village
vinegar le vinaigre, **6.1**
violent violent(e)
violin le violon
viral viral(e)
virus le virus
to **visit** *(a place)* visiter
voice la voix

waiter le serveur, **5.1**
waitress la serveuse, **5.1**
to **want** désirer, vouloir
war la guerre
warmup suit le
  survêtement, **7.1**
Watch out! Attention!, **4.2**
water l'eau *(f.)*, **6.2**
way la façon
we nous, **2**; on, **3.2**
weak faible, **L1**
to **wear** porter, **7.1**
  **What size do you
    wear/take?** Vous faites
    quelle taille?, **7.2**
Web site le site
wedding le mariage
Wednesday mercredi *(m.)*,
  BV

week la semaine, **3.2**
   a (per) week par semaine, **3.2**
   next week la semaine prochaine
weekend le week-end
weight le poids
welcome le/la bienvenu(e)
   Welcome! Bienvenue!
   You're welcome. Je t'en prie. *(fam.)*, **BV**; Je vous en prie. *(form.)*, **BV**
well bien, **BV**; eh bien; ben *(fam.)*
   well then alors, **BV**
well-behaved bien élevé(e)
well-done *(meat)* bien cuit(e), **5.2**
well-known connu(e)
well-to-do aisé(e)
western occidental(e)
what qu'est-ce que, **3.2**; quel(le), **6**
   What color is . . . ? De quelle couleur est… ?, **7.2**
   What is . . . like? Comment est… ?, **1.1**
   What is it? Qu'est-ce que c'est?, **3.2**

   What is today's date? Quelle est la date aujourd'hui?, **BV**
   What's your name? Tu t'appelles comment?, **BV**
when quand, **4.1**
where où, **1.1**
   from where d'où, **1.1**
which quel(le), **6**
white blanc, blanche, **7.2**
who qui, **1.1**
whole *(adj.)* entier, entière; *(n.)* l'ensemble *(m.)*
whole-wheat bread le pain complet
whom qui
why pourquoi, **6.2**
   why not? pourquoi pas?
wide large, **7.2**
wife la femme, **4.1**
to **win** gagner
window *(store)* la vitrine, **7.1**
with avec, **3.2**; auprès de
without sans
woman la femme, **7.1**
wood le bois
word le mot
   words *(of song, etc.)* les paroles *(f. pl.)*
work le travail; *(of art or literature)* l'œuvre *(f.)*

world le monde
write écrire
writer l'écrivain *(m.)*
wrong mauvais(e), **2.2**

yeah ben oui
year l'an *(m.)*, **4.1**; l'année *(f.)*
   to be . . . years old avoir… ans, **4.1**
yellow jaune, **7.2**
yes oui, **BV**; si *(after neg. question)*, **7.2**
yogurt la yaourt, **6.1**
you tu
young jeune
   young people les jeunes *(m. pl.)*
younger le cadet, la cadette, **L1**
your ton, ta, tes; votre, vos, **4**

zoology la zoologie

Index

à contractions with definite articles, **166 (5)**

adjectives agreement with singular nouns, **28 (1)**; agreement with plural nouns, **58 (2)**; comparative of, **230 (7)**; irregular, **126 (4)**; possessive, **123 (4)**; position of, **126 (4)**; **100 (4)**; **138 (5)**

agreement adjectives with singular nouns, **28 (1)**, adjectives with plural nouns, **58 (2)**; definite and indefinite articles with singular nouns, **26 (1)**; definite and indefinite articles with plural nouns; **58 (2)**; subject and verb, **30 (1)**; **60 (2)**

aller present tense, **162 (5)**; with expressions of health, **162 (5)**; with infinitive to express near future, **165 (5)**; with **y**, **162 (5)**

apprendre present tense, **168 (5)**

articles (see **definite articles, indefinite articles,** and **partitive**)

au, aux contractions of **à** + definite articles, **166 (5)**

aussi... que 230 (7)

avoir present tense, **120 (4)**; to express age, **120 (4)**

beau 126 (4)

colors 225 (7)

comparative of adjectives 230 (7)

comprendre present tense, **168 (5)**

contractions au, aux, 166 (5); du, des, 166 (5)

croire present tense, **232 (7)**

dates days of the week, **10 (BV)**; months of the year, **10 (BV)**

de after **pas** to replace indefinite article, **120 (4)**; after **pas** to replace the partitive, **198 (6)**; contractions with definite articles, **166 (5)**; to indicate possession, **166 (5)**; with plural adjectives, **126 (4)**

definite articles gender and agreement with noun, **26 (1)**; plural, **58 (2)**; singular, **26 (1)**; vs. the partitive, **196 (6)**

des contraction of **de** + **les**, **166 (5)**; partitive **196 (6)**; plural indefinite article, **94 (3)**

du contraction of **de** + **le**, **166 (5)**; partitive **196 (6)**

elision 26 (1); 90 (3); 94 (3)

-er verbs (see **present tense**)

être present tense: plural forms, **60 (2)**; present tense: singular forms **30 (1)**

faire expressions with, **194 (6)**; present tense **194 (6)**

future expressed with **aller** + infinitive, **165 (5)**

gender of adjectives, **28 (1)**; of definite articles, **26 (1)**; of indefinite articles, **26 (1)**; of nouns, **26 (1)**

il y a 120 (4)

indefinite articles gender and agreement with noun, **26 (1)**; in negative sentences, **94 (3)**; plural, **76 (3)**; singular, **26 (1)**

indefinite pronoun on, 90 (3)

infinitives with **aller** to express near future, **165 (5)**; with other verbs, **95 (3)**

irregular verbs (see individual verb entries)

liaison 26 (1); 90 (3); 123 (4); 126 (4); 230 (7)

mettre present tense **228 (7)**

moins... que, 230 (7)

negation ne... pas, 33 (1); 165 (5); of indefinite articles, **94 (3);** of the partitive, **196 (6)**

nouveau 126 (4)

numbers cardinal, 0–69, **10 (BV); 23 (1);** 70–100, **55 (2);** 101–1000, **87 (3)**

on 90 (3)

partitive 196 (6)

plural of adjectives, **58 (2);** of adjectives like **beau, nouveau, vieux, 126 (4);** of definite articles, **58 (2);** of indefinite articles, **58 (2);** of nouns, **45 (2);** of subject pronouns, **60 (2)**

plus... que 230 (7)

possession with **de, 166 (5);** *(see also possessive adjectives)*

possessive adjectives 123 (4)

pouvoir present tense **201 (6)**

prendre present tense **168 (5)**

present tense of **-er** verbs, **90 (3);** of verbs with spelling changes, **233 (7);** *(see also individual verb entries)*

pronouns on, **90 (3);** subject pronouns: singular, **30 (1);** plural, **60 (2);** y, **165 (5)**

spelling changes, verbs with, 233 (7)

subject pronouns on, **72 (3);** plural, **46 (2);** singular, **30 (1); tu** vs. **vous, 64 (2)**

time telling time, **12 (BV)**

tu vs. vous 64 (2)

verbs followed by infinitives **95 (3)**

verbs *(see individual verb entries)*

vieux 126 (4)

voir present tense, **232 (7)**

vouloir je voudrais, **201 (6);** present tense, **201 (6)**

vous vs. tu 64 (2)

y with **aller, 165 (5)**

Credits

COVER (t to b)Koji Yamashita/Panoramic Images, Michelle Busselle/Stone, Shankar/Panoramic Images, Koji Yamashita/Panoramic Images, (students)Philippe Gontier; **iv** (l)U-AT/The Stock Market, (r)Mark Burnett; **v** (l)Larry Hamill, (r)Travelpix/FPG; **vi** (tl)Timothy Fuller, (tr)Jonny Andre/Photo 20-20, (bl)Zepher Images/Sunset; **vii** (l)John Evans, (r)Mark Antman/Scribner; **viii** Timothy Fuller; **ix** (tl)Greg Bond, videographer, South Park Productions, Inc., (tr bl)Larry Hamill; **x** (tl)Moulo/Sunset, (tr)Musée d'Orsay, Paris/Lauros-Giraudon, Paris/SuperStock, (b)PhotoDisc; **xi** Owen Franken/Stock Boston; **xii** (tr)Larry Hamill, (b)David H. Endersbee/Stone; **xiii** (tl)Timothy Fuller, (bl)Larry Hamill, (br)Jeff Kaufman/FPG; **xiv** Doug Pensinger/AllSport; **xv** (t)Paul Hardy/The Stock Market, (b)Timothy Fuller; **xvi** (tl tr)Timothy Fuller, (b)Curt Fischer; **xvii** (l)Timothy Fuller, (r)Mark Burnett; **xviii** Timothy Fuller; **xix** Massino Listri/CORBIS; **xxviii** (tr)Chris Sorenson/The Stock Market, (cl)Mark Antman/The Image Works, (bl)Mark Burnett; **xxix** (tr c)Larry Hamill, (bl)Walter Bibikow/FPG, (bc)Michele Burgess/The Stock Market, (br)Alain Even/DIAF; **xl-1** (bkgd xl/2)Curt Fischer, (xl/1)David Florenz/Option Photo, (xl/3)Photobank USA/Sunset, (xl/4)Michael Krasowitz/FPG, (1/5) Curt Fischer, (1/6)Robert Fried Photography, (1/7)Timothy Fuller, (1/8)Gio Barto/The Image Bank, (1/9)Larry Hamill; **2** Larry Hamill; **3** (tl tc bc)Larry Hamill, (tr bl)Catherine et Bernard Desjeux, (br)Timothy Fuller; **4** (l)Timothy Fuller, (r)Catherine et Bernard Desjeux; **5** Timothy Fuller; **6** Larry Hamill; **7** Mark Burnett; Larry Hamill; **9** (tl)Ilico/Wallis Phototheque, (tr cl bl br)John Evans, (cc)LCI/Wallis Phototheque, (cr)Ange/Wallis Phototheque; **11** (tl tr)Ken Karp, (bl)Jean-Daniel Sudres/DIAF, (br)U-AT/The Stock Market; **13** Mark Burnett; Larry Hamill; **15** (r)Mark Burnett; **16–17** Catherine et Bernard Desjeux; **16** (b)Bridgeman Art Library; **18** Larry Hamill; **19** Timothy Fuller; **20** (tr c br)Larry Hamill, (bl)Jill Connelly/The Image Works; **21** (tl)Pacha/CORBIS, (tr)Bettman/CORBIS, (bl)Mitchell Gerber/CORBIS, (br)Christie's Images/CORBIS; **22** (tl tr br)Larry Hamill, (bl)John Evans, (br,inset)Dale Durfee/Stone; **23** (l)John Evans, (r)file photo; **24** (tl)Curt Fischer, (tr)Robert Fried Photography, (bl)Garufi/Wallis Phototheque, (br)Telegraph Colour Library/FPG; **25** (r)RAGA-France/The Stock Market, (bl)Dannic/DIAF, (br)Goumare/Wallis Phototheque; **26** Pascal Crapet/Stone; **27** P. Wysocki/S. Frances/Hémisphères Images; **28** Wayne Rowe; **31** (t)Peter McCabe/The Image Works, (bl br)Monika Graff/The Image Works; **32** (t)Larry Hamill, (b)Claudie/Sunset, (b,inset)Wayne Rowe; **33** Owen Franken/CORBIS; **34** (t)Travelpix/FPG, (b)Larry Hamill; **35** Bruno de Hogues/Stone; **36** (l)Fernand/Sunset, (r)Robert Holmes/CORBIS; **37** (t)Chris Sorenson/The Stock Market, (b)David Simson/Stock Boston; **38** (t)C. Capel/Sunset, (t,inset)Brian A. Vikander, (b)Yvan Travert/DIAF, (b,inset)Mark Antman/The Image Works; **39** (t)Private collection/The Bridgeman Art Library, (b)Jean-Daniel Sudres/DIAF; **40–41** Fototeca Storica Nazionale/PhotoDisc; **40** (t)Camille Moirenc/DIAF, (b)Sitki Tarlan/Panoramic Images; **41** (t)Doug Armand/Stone, (b)Ric Ergenbright/CORBIS; **42** (t)Larry Hamill, (c)Peter McCabe/The Image Works, (b)Chris Duranti/Wallis Phototheque; **44** Ozu Kiki/La Phototheque/SDP; **45** J. Brun/Explorer; **46** (t)Robert Holmes/CORBIS, (b)Larry Hamill; **47** (tl bl)Greg Bond, videographer, South Park Productions, Inc., (r)Curt Fischer; **48–49** Larry Hamill, (b)Barnes Foundation, Merion PA/SuperStock; **50** Christine et Bernard Desjeux; **51** (t)Larry Hamill, (b)Timothy Fuller; **52** (t)Marge/Sunset, (b)Timothy Fuller; **53** John Evans; **54** Curt Fischer; **55** John Evans; **56 57 59** (t)Larry Hamill; **60** (l)Monika Graff/The Image Works, (c)Ken Karp; **63** (t)Robert Fried Photography, (b)Photobank/Sunset; **65** (tl)Zephyr Images/Sunset, (tc)Sierpinski/DIAF, (tr)Robert Fried Photography, (bl)Sylva Villerot/DIAF, (bc)Stuart Cohen/The Image Works, (br)Robert Fried Photography; **66** Larry Hamill; **68** (tl)Michele Burgess/The Stock Market, (tr)Larry Hamill, (b)Beryl Goldberg; **69**

(t)David Grunfeld/The Image Works, (b)SuperStock; **70** (t)Larry Hamill, (b)Curt Fischer; **71–72** (bkgd)The Studio Dog/PhotoDisc, **71** (tl)Larry Hamill, (tr)Stephane Cande/Mission/Wallis Phototheque, (b)Robert Holmes/CORBIS; **72** (l)Jean-Paul Garcin/DIAF, (r)Art Wolfe/Stone; **73** (t)Beryl Goldberg, (b)Mark Burnett; **74** Larry Hamill; **75** (t b)Larry Hamill, (b,inset)Capel/Sunset; **77** Jenny Andre/Photo 20-20; **78** (t)Larry Hamill, (b)Curt Fischer; **79** (tl b)Greg Bond, videographer, South Park Productions, Inc., (tr)Robert Holmes/CORBIS; **80–81** Bob Handelman/Stone, **80** (b)Musée du Louvre, Paris/SuperStock; **82** Larry Hamill; **83** Alain Le Bot/DIAF; **84** (t)R. Lucas/The Image Works, (b)Larry Hamill; **85** Ken Karp; **86** (alpha order, top to bottom a b)Aaron Haupt, (c f l m)Curt Fischer, (d e g h i j k)Amanita Pictures; **87** Larry Hamill; **88** (t c)Amanita Pictures, (b)Valerie Simmons; **89** Amanita Pictures; **91** (t)John Evans, (bl br)Ken Karp; **92** (t)Matthieu Colin/Hémisphères Images, (bl br)Ken Karp; **94** Beryl Goldberg; **96** (t)Larry Hamill, (b)John Evans; **98** (tr)Robert Fried Photography, (bl)John Evans, (br)Hartmut Krinitz/Hémisphères Images; **99** Larry Hamill; **100** (l)Beryl Goldberg, (tr)Guido Cozzi/Agence ANA; **101** (t)Larry Hamill, (b)Christian Roger; **102–103** (bkgd)PhotoDisc, **102** Cheryl Fenton; **103** Ed Taylor Studio/FPG; **104 105** Larry Hamill; **107** Mark Antman/Scribner; **109** (tl br)Greg Bond, videographer, South Park Productions, Inc., (r)Philip Gould/CORBIS; **110** (b)Metropolitan Museum of Art, New York/SuperStock; **112** (tl tr cl br)Larry Hamill, (b)PhotoDisc; **113** Timothy Fuller; **114** (t)Mark Burnett; **115** Giraudon/Art Resource, New York; **117** Larry Hamill; **118** Karin Ansara/Wallis Phototheque; **119** (l)Grant V. Faint/The Image Bank, (c)Stéphane Frances/Hémisphères Images, (r)Claude/Sunset; **121** (t)Michelle Chaplow, (b)Zephyr Images/Sunset; **123** Michelle Chaplow; **124** Pawel Wysocki/Hémisphères Images; **125** Daniel Thierry/DIAF; **126** Walter Bibikow/FPG; **128** Larry Hamill; **129** (r)Ken Karp; **130** (l)Pratt-Pries/DIAF, **131** (t)Weststock/Sunset, (b)Sandra Baker/Liaison Agency; **132** (t)SuperStock, (tr)Jean-Daniel Sudres/DIAF, (br)LCI/Wallis Phototheque; **134–135** (bkgd)CORBIS, **134** (t)Lauros-Giraudon/Art Resource, New York, (b)Réunion des Musées Nationaux/Art Resource, New York; **135** (t)David Noble/FPG, (c)Desvignes/Sunset, (b)Gianni Dagli Orti/CORBIS; **137** Travelpix/FPG; **139** Curt Fischer; **140** (t)Timothy Fuller, (bl)Pratt-Pries/DIAF, (br)Travelpix/FPG, **141** (tl bl)Greg Bond, videographer, South Park Productions, Inc., (tr)Dave G. Houser; **142** (t)Larry Hamill, (b)Mark Burnett; **143** Wayne Rowe; **144** (t)Timothy Fuller, (b)Larry Hamill; **145** R. Rozencwajg/DIAF; **147** Larry Hamill; **148–149** (bkgd)Michael Busselle/Stone, (148/2)Laurent Rebours, AP/Wide World Photos, (148/3)Bernard Boutrit/Photo Researchers, (148/4)Marie-José Jarry & Jean-François Tripelon/Agence Top/National Geographic Image Collection, (148/5)Steve McCurry/National Geographic Image Collection, (149/6)P. Bennett/AA Photo Library, (149/7)Martha Bates/Stock Boston; **150–151** (bkgd)Chad Ehlers/Stone, (150/9)Steve Vidler/Leo de Wys Stock Photo Agency, (150/10)Patrick Ingrand/Stone, (150/11)Patrick Zachmann/Magnum, (150/12)Christophe Ena, AP/Wide World Photos, (151/13)Craig Aurness/CORBIS, (151/14)Suzanne & Nick Geary/Stone; **152–153** (bkgd) John Lawrence/Stone; **152** (b)Erich Lessing/Art Resource; **155** (l to r,alpha c d)Timothy Fuller, (o)Aaron Haupt, (others)John Evans; **156** Timothy Fuller; **157** Gérard Gsell/DIAF; **158** Larry Hamill; **159** (t)John Evans, (c r)Aaron Haupt; **160** (t)Timothy Fuller, (b)Curt Fischer; **162** H. Gyssels/DIAF; **164** (l)Eve Morcrette/Wallis Phototheque, (c)file photo; **166** Gerard Lacz/Sunset; **167** (l)Bill Deering/FPG; **168** James Davis/International Stock; **169 170** Larry Hamill; **172** (l)Timothy Fuller, (r)Christine et Bernard Desjeux; **173** (l)Wayne Rowe; **174** (l)Bob Krist/The Stock Market, (tr)Larry Hamill, (br)Explorer/Photo Researchers; **175** (tl)Quinard/Wallis Phototheque, (tr)Robert Fried Photography; **176–177** (bkgd)Sami Sarkis/PhotoDisc; **178** (b)Larry Hamill; **179** David Simson/Stock Boston; **180** Wayne

Rowe; **182** (t)Gerard Lucz/Sunset, (others)John Evans; **183** (tl b)Greg Bond, videographer, South Park Productions, Inc., (r)Bruno De Hogues/Stone; **184–185** SuperStock; **184** (b)Musée d'Orsay, Paris/Lauros-Giraudon, Paris/SuperStock; **187** (tl bl br)Larry Hamill, (tr)Curt Fischer; **188** (t)Larry Hamill, (b)Mark Burnett; **189** (t)Curt Fischer, (b)Wayne Rowe; **190** Larry Hamill; **191** (t)Timothy Fuller, (bl)Terry Sutherland, (others)Larry Hamill; **192** PhotoDisc; **193** (l)Peter McCabe/The Image Works, (r)Monika Graff/The Image Works; **194** Larry Hamill; **195** (t)Larry Hamill, (l)Monika Graff/The Image Works, (r)Ken Karp; **197** (tl tr)Monika Graff/The Image Works, (c)J.-Ch. Gerard/DIAF, (bl)Moulo/Sunset; **199** (tl tr)Monika Graff/The Image Works, (b)Beryl Goldberg; **200** Larry Hamill, (inset)Curt Fischer; **202** (t)Michael Busselle/CORBIS, (b)Ken Karp; **204** Timothy Fuller; **205** Andrew Payti; **206** (l)George Gibbons/FPG, (r)Larry Hamill; **207** (l)Michael Busselle/Stone, (r)Christophe Duranti/Wallis Phototheque; **208** (l)Alain Le Bot/DIAF, (r)Laurent Giraudou/Hémisphères Images; **209** (tr)Chad Ehlers/International Stock, (l)Andrew Payti, (br)Robert Fried Photography; **210–211** (bkgd)PhotoLink/PhotoDisc, **210** (tl)Charlie Abad/SDP, (tr)Lee Snider/The Image Works, (br)Mark Antman/The Image Works; **211** (t)Mark Antman/The Image Works, (b)Spot/SDP; **212** Todd Gipstein/CORBIS; **213** M. Huet/Hoa Qui; **215** Larry Hamill; **216** (t)Moulo/Sunset, (bl)Terry Sutherland, (bc br)Larry Hamill; **217** (tl bl)Greg Bond, videographer, South Park Productions, Inc., (tr)Gilles Serrano/Liaison Agency; **218–219** Mark Gibson/Photo 20-20, **218** (b)Werner Forman Archive/Museum fur Volkerkunde, Berlin/Art Resource, New York; **220** John Evans; **221 222** (tl b)Larry Hamill, (tr)Timothy Fuller; **223** Iconos/DIAF; **224** Larry Hamill; **225** (t)John Evans, (b)Timothy Fuller; **226** (t)Larry Hamill, (b)Japack/Sunset; **228** Beryl Goldberg; **231** Larry Hamill; **232** Chris/Sunset; **234** Larry Hamill; **235** Michael Dwyer/Stock Boston; **236** (t)Robert Holmes/CORBIS, (b)Tim Gibson/Envision; **237** (t)Curt Fischer, (b)Owen Franken/Stock Boston; **238** (t)H. Rogers/TRIP, (tl)Gossler/Schuster/Explorer, (bl)Jose Nicolas/Hémisphères Images; **239** Japack/Sunset; **240–241** (bkgd)Geoff Butler, **240** (l)FPG, (r)Archivo Iconografico, S.A./CORBIS; **241** Bettmann/CORBIS; **242** Beryl Goldberg; **243** Sylva Villerot/DIAF; **245** Wayne Rowe; **246** (t)Larry Hamill, (b)John Evans; **247** (tl bl)Greg Bond, videographer, South Park Productions, Inc., (tr)Shinichi Kanno/FPG; **248** (t)Larry Hamill, (b)Tim Gibson/Envision; **250** (t)Bertrand Rieger/Hémisphères Images, (b)Steven Needham/Envision; **252** Larry Hamill; **253** Timothy Fuller; **254–255** (bkgd)Steven Rothfeld/Stone, (254/2)M & E Bernheim/Woodfin Camp & Associates, (254/3)Bruno De Hogues/Stone, (254/4)Photri/Microstock, (254/5)Nik Wheeler/CORBIS, (255/6)Tim Hall/Retna, (255/7)M & E Bernheim/Woodfin Camp & Associates; **256–257** (bkgd)Kevin Schafer/CORBIS, (256/9)Bruno De Hogues/Stone, (256/10)Betty Press/Woodfin Camp & Associates, (256/11)Giacomo Pirozzi/Panos Pictures, (256/12)TempSport/CORBIS, (257/13)Carol Beckwith & Angela Fisher; (257/14)Caroline Penn/Panos Pictures; Tibor Bognar/The Stock Market, **502–503** Massimo Listri/CORBIS; **505** Jean-Daniel Sudres/DIAF; **506** Archiv/Photo Researchers, Inc; **507** Scala/Art Resource, New York; **508** Christie's Images; **510** Bridgeman Art Library; **511** (t)H. Reinhard/Sunset, (b)Elizabeth Barakah Hodges/SuperStock; **512–H1** Suzanne & Nick Geary/Stone; **H3** (tl tr)Larry Hamill, (bl)John Evans, (br)Garufi/Wallis Phototheque; **H4** (tl)Pacha/CORBIS, (tr)Bettmann/CORBIS, (bl)Mitchell Gerber/CORBIS, (br)Christie's Images/CORBIS; **H5** Larry Hamill; **H8** John Evans; **H14** EleveA (tl)Woodfin Camp & Associates, (br)Timothy Fuller, (others)EleveB (all)John Evans; **H18** EleveA (t)Terry Sutherland, (others)Larry Hamill, EleveB (tl)Timothy Fuller, (others)Larry Hamill.

In appreciation

Special thanks to the following for their cordial assistance and participation in the photo illustrations:

Aeroport Charles De Gaulle; Affinage du Val d'Yerres, Montgeron, Air Afrique, Air France, Banque de France, Café Les Deux Magots, Paris, Cafeteria Flunch Evry, Centre Commercial des Halles, Paris, Club Hyppique, Varennes Jarcy, Colleg de Montois, Donnemarie-Dontilly, College Pasteur de Brunoy, Cora Boussy Saint Antoine, Crep' Yerres, Creperie au Mystere de Carnac, Montgeron, Cuisines AJ, Yerres, Docteur Ponnoussamy, Electro Star, Bonneuil, Espace Photo, Vigneux, Fermelec de L'essonne, Galeries Lafayette, Hippopotamus, Horizon F.M., International School of Paris, Kosque du Palais Royal, Paris, Laboratoire d'Analyses Medicales des Godeaux, Le Restaurant Mona Lisa, Lycee Janson de Sailly, Lycee Louis-le-Grand, Maison de la Presse Montgeron, Maison de la Presse S.G.E.C., Evry, Marche des Champs Elysees, Musée d'Orsay, Paris, Musée du Louvre, Paris, Nicolas Dupont-Aignan/Depute Maire de Yerres, Pharmacie des Godeaux, Yerres, Pharmacie Laurence Dony, Yerres, Piscine de Brunoy, RATP, Relais-H Gare de Lyon, Restaurant Chez Paul, Restaurant le Clos Saint Jacques, Paris, Restaurant Procope, SAMU de Paris, SNCF-TGV, Yerres Ecole National de Musique et de Danse.

Glencoe would like to acknowledge the artists and agencies who participated in illustrating this program: Domenick D'Andrea; Fanny Mellet Berry represented by Anita Grien; Len Ebert; Carlos Lacamara; Jane McCreary; Ortelius Design; Carol Strebel; Shannon Stirnweis; Joseph Hammond, Susan Jaekel and DJ Simison represented by Ann Remen-Willis.